THE BANKRUPTCY KIT

SECOND EDITION

John Ventura

Dearborn
Financial Publishing, Inc.

Dedication

To Mary Ellen
I'll love you forever, and no other.

This publication is designed to provide accurate and authoritative information in regard to the subject matter covered. It is sold with the understanding that the publisher is not engaged in rendering legal, accounting or other professional service. If legal advice or other expert assistance is required, the services of a competent professional person should be sought.

Managing Editor: Jack Kiburz
Senior Associate Editor: Karen A. Christensen
Interior Design: Lucy Jenkins
Cover Design: S. Laird Jenkins Corporation

© 1991 and 1996 by John Ventura

Published by Dearborn Financial Publishing, Inc.®

Printed in the United States of America

96 97 98   10 9 8 7 6 5 4 3 2 1

Library of Congress Cataloging-in-Publication Data

Ventura, John.
    The bankruptcy kit / John Ventura. — 2nd ed.
      p.   cm.
    Includes index.
    ISBN 0-7931-1518-3
    1. Bankruptcy—United States—Popular works. I. Title.
KF1524.6.V46 1996
346.73′078—dc20
[347.30678]
                                      95-34623
                                         CIP

Foreword

The emotional stress that accompanies serious financial problems makes it terribly difficult to separate fact from hearsay, sort through available alternatives and make an informed decision. John Ventura has provided the facts in plain language to help his readers understand what bankruptcy is and what it is not. He clears away many misconceptions about bankruptcy and helps the reader know what to expect from attorneys and the courts. Knowledge is the first step toward financial recovery, and many readers will learn for the first time that there are alternatives to bankruptcy. For some, one of those alternatives may provide a better choice.

Lonnie Williams, Director
Consumer Credit Counseling Service
Austin, Texas

Also by John Ventura

The Credit Repair Kit

Fresh Start

The Small Business Survival Kit

Contents

Chapter 11 Understanding Taxes and Bankruptcy   83

Chapter 12 Divorce and Bankruptcy   91

Chapter 13 Conclusion: Making a Fresh Start   97

Appendix A Chapter 7 Bankruptcy Forms   101

Appendix B Chapter 13 Bankruptcy Forms   123

Appendix C Federal Bankruptcy Exemptions   145

Appendix D State Bankruptcy Exemptions   148

Preface

In my 17 years of work as a bankruptcy attorney, countless financially troubled consumers and business owners have come to my office full of anxiety, depression and fear about the prospect of filing for bankruptcy. In nearly every case, I found that if I took the time to explain the bankruptcy process to them and to describe the roles of lawyers, the court and other players in the process, they usually left my office feeling a lot better.

In 1990, with bankruptcies at record levels and even greater numbers predicted for the coming years, I decided to write a book about bankruptcy for consumers and small business people. Avoiding legal mumbo jumbo, I intended this book to provide readers with much of the same information I give my clients, guiding them through the bankruptcy process and telling them what their lawyers should be doing for them. The result was the first edition of *The Bankruptcy Kit*.

Since the publication of that first edition, 3,587,530 new bankruptcies have been filed in the United States, and the U.S. Bankruptcy Court predicts that there will be 845,000 more in 1995 alone. Obviously, there is an even greater need than ever before for the information and advice in *The Bankruptcy Kit*, particularly since the 1994 passage of the Bankruptcy Reform Act. This new legislation made many changes to the bankruptcy code that will affect consumers and small business people in important ways. Therefore, to ensure that *The Bankruptcy Kit* continues to be a valuable resource for those contemplating bankruptcy as well as for those who have already filed, I have written a new edition of my book. The second edition of *The Bankruptcy Kit* not only explains these new changes in the law but also includes two new chapters: one covers divorce and the other covers taxes.

I know that filing for bankruptcy is never easy, but sometimes it's the best decision. I hope that the information and advice in *The Bankruptcy Kit* will help make that important decision an easier one for people in serious financial trouble. And I hope that knowing what to expect in bankruptcy will ease their anxiety and fear.

WARNING

The information in this book reflects the state of the law at the time of publication. Please note that laws change, and the reader is therefore urged to seek legal counsel on any important issue.

John Ventura
June 1995

"I would like to amend this bill, if it were legal to do, by putting in a provision making it a capital offense for any of you retailers to seduce these people into installment purchasing beyond their means."
—Congressman Hobbs, in hearings before the Subcommittee on the Judiciary on H.R. 8046, 75th Congress, First Session, page 13, 1937.

"It's too damned easy to file bankruptcy. These people just don't suffer enough."
—Comment overheard at a meeting of the Seattle Consumer Credit Association, 1981.

CHAPTER ONE

What Is Bankruptcy?

The Bankruptcy Reform Act of 1994

On October 22, 1994, the president signed into law the Bankruptcy Reform Act of 1994. The act represents the most sweeping revisions in bankruptcy law since the Bankruptcy Code was enacted in 1978. The revisions will have a major impact on anyone considering bankruptcy as a solution to their financial problems. Some benefit consumers; others harm them. This new edition of *The Bankruptcy Kit* will discuss all of the changes in the Bankruptcy Code that are important for debtors to understand; however, some of the most significant, beneficial changes are:

- The total debt limits for a Chapter 13 bankruptcy have been increased to $750,000 for secured debt and $250,000 for unsecured debt. Previously, the limits were much lower—$350,000 and $100,000, respectively. Chapter 13 is a type of bankruptcy that allows debtors to pay off their debt by making lower monthly payments to creditors. (This and other types of bankruptcy are defined in Chapter 2 of this book.) The higher limits mean that more consumers will be eligible to file Chapter 13 bankruptcy.

- The federal exemptions that describe the kind of property and the value of the property that a debtor in bankruptcy may keep have been doubled. This means consumers will be able to keep more of their property when they file. In addition, inflation indexing every three years has been mandated to help ensure that the value of the exemptions keeps pace with inflation. (See Appendix C for a more complete description of the federal exemptions available to debtors.)

- Property liens due to judgments will be easier to avoid.

- There will be no interest on mortgage arrearages in Chapter 13; however, this applies only to mortgages entered into after October 22, 1994.

- Consumers will have up to five years to pay off their mortgage if the note comes due on their home, they owe a large balance and they can't pay it.

- Debtors who convert from a Chapter 13 adjustment of debt plan to a Chapter 7 liquidation bankruptcy will be able to keep the property they acquired during Chapter 13.

This book also will describe the provisions of the new law that further restrict the rights of debtors in bankruptcy. For example, the law now says that if you borrow money to pay taxes, the loan will not be wiped out through bankruptcy. In other words, you will still be obligated to pay the loan once your bankruptcy is over. Also, there is now greater protection for former spouses who are owed child support, maintenance and alimony.

What Is Bankruptcy?

Bankruptcy is a constitutional right of protection against creditors. It allows people or businesses to make a fresh start after experiencing financial difficulties so severe that creditors' demands can no longer be reasonably satisfied. Filing for bankruptcy protection solves financial problems either by wiping out debt or by reorganizing debt so that it can be paid within the budget of the debtor. In exchange for this fresh start, the debtor may be refused credit for up to ten years and may lose assets as well.

You may know that filing bankruptcy will help you, but you struggle with the decision to take action. If you are like most people, you have spent a lifetime trying to do the right thing. You have sacrificed in order to meet your obligations. Sometimes you pay creditors when you really cannot afford to do so. You may ignore medical needs or perhaps sacrifice the comfort and well-being of your loved ones to satisfy an obligation.

But there may come a time when, no matter how much you sacrifice, there just is not enough money to meet your obligations. Your creditors are not happy because you cannot pay them the way they expect to be paid. You are not happy because, as hard as you try and as much as you sacrifice, you are not able to solve your financial problems. If anything, they get worse. Bankruptcy begins to look like the solution to your problems.

If you have filed bankruptcy, you need to fully understand what your attorney is supposed to do for you at each stage of the bankruptcy process. If you have not filed bankruptcy but are considering it, you need to know what protection the law affords you, what you will be required to give up for that protection and how to proceed.

No one sets out in the direction of a financial crisis. Once you reach that point, however, you should make an informed decision concerning your options, so that you emerge in the best possible position to rescue your financial life.

 WARNING

It is your attorney's job to make sure that you understand all legal terms used. The attorney should not assume that you have had the benefit of a legal education, and you should ask that terms be explained if you do not understand them.

How To Locate a Good Bankruptcy Attorney

What qualities are you looking for in a bankruptcy attorney? First of all, you must feel comfortable with the attorney. This usually means the attorney's skills are commensurate with your needs and that he or she is sensitive to your situation. You also want to feel confident that the fees charged are reasonable. Finding such a person can be difficult.

Here are a few suggestions to help you get started:

- *Look in the yellow pages of your phone directory and find out if attorneys are certified as specialists in bankruptcy in your area.* Some states allow board certification in bankruptcy. This means that these attorneys have worked in the bankruptcy area of the law for a number of years, have personally handled a substantial number of cases and have passed a test to prove their knowledge of the law.

Contact board-certified attorneys in your area to find out what they charge and whether you feel comfortable with them.

- *Contact lawyers who advertise.* These people sometimes price their services more reasonably than other attorneys. You may find some attorneys who also are board certified that advertise; this is a winning combination.

- *Contact an attorney you know and ask for a referral to a bankruptcy attorney.* Good attorneys have reputations among their colleagues, and you may be directed to the best available practitioner in your area.

- *Call the bankruptcy court in your area and obtain the names and phone numbers of the local bankruptcy trustees.* These people work in the bankruptcy system every day and know which attorneys do the best work. They will usually recommend several attorneys from which you can choose.

- *Contact the American Bankruptcy Board of Certification* (44 Canal Center Plaza, Suite 404, Alexandria, VA 22314, 703-739-0800). This national organization certifies consumer bankruptcy attorneys all across the United States.

 WARNING

Go to see several attorneys to judge whether they understand your problems and can express clear solutions, and also to compare prices.

What Your Attorney Should Warn You About Before Filing Bankruptcy

Your attorney should warn you against some improper actions you may be inclined to take before filing bankruptcy. How effective these warnings are will depend upon how early you consult an attorney.

When you are considering bankruptcy, you should at minimum be told the following five things:

1. *Do not do anything that will cause you to give up a necessity or give a creditor undue power over you.* For example, do not voluntarily give up a car if you need it. If you do not voluntarily relinquish something you own, the creditor is required to obtain a court order to make you do so or to try to repossess it.

2. *Do not give creditors postdated checks.* If the checks bounce, you may face criminal charges. The protection of the bankruptcy court does not extend to criminal matters. Stop payment immediately on any postdated checks you have written. Try to avoid panic. Remember that bill collectors use fear and intimidation to try to make you pay. If you succumb to threats and abuse, you may lose things you could have used for a longer period of time.

3. *Do not transfer property to friends or relatives in the belief you are protecting the asset.* This is a waste of time if you are going to file bankruptcy, and doing so might be considered a fraudulent act. You will be asked specifically on the schedules you swear to if you have transferred property. (See Appendixes A and B for copies of bankruptcy forms.) If the answer is "yes," the transfer can be voided by the trustee. The trustee usually looks at all transfers of property that have occurred within one year of filing the bankruptcy. The trustee is the person appointed by the court to make sure the debtor abides by the bankruptcy rules.

4. *Do not charge up your credit cards or obtain cash advances immediately before filing for bankruptcy.* The law states that if you incur more than "$1,000 worth of debt on luxury goods or services" from a single creditor "within 60 days" of filing bankruptcy, the debt will not be wiped out by the bankruptcy, and you will have to pay the creditor. This also applies if you obtain a cash advance of "more than $1,000 within 60 days of filing bankruptcy." Note that the rules apply to luxury goods or services. Occasionally you may have no choice but to charge medical services or medicine. In that case, do what you need to do. This is not a luxury item or service; it will probably be a dischargeable debt, a debt that will be wiped out by your bankruptcy.

5. *Do not pay a favorite unsecured creditor to the exclusion of others within 90 days of filing bankruptcy in the hope that the creditor will treat you better after bankruptcy.* Preferential treatment of one creditor over others can be voided by the trustee in bankruptcy and the money can be recovered from the favored creditor.

> ## WARNING
>
> If you have made any transfers of property, do not make any changes until you have talked to an attorney.

Alternatives to Bankruptcy

Any competent bankruptcy attorney will tell you that bankruptcy, no matter what kind, is a remedy of last resort. Turn to it only after you have exhausted other means of helping yourself. During your initial visit, the attorney should determine whether or not you have tried all other avenues and should suggest alternatives.

How To Avoid Bankruptcy

The following are the most common ways to avoid bankruptcy (short of winning the lottery):

Spend less. You should begin with your budget. If you can find ways to reduce your expenses, you will have more money to pay your debts. This is not possible for many people. There may be only enough money coming in now for bare necessities. You may be struggling simply to pay for housing, food and utilities.

Earn more. Are you producing all the income you can? If your situation is not too serious, a second job for a while could solve the problem. And if you have teenagers, put them to work. Let older children know you are experiencing difficult times and enlist their help. This can pay a dividend in family closeness in addition to improving your cash situation.

Give up something. Are you buying something on time that you could voluntarily part with, making it easier to keep everything else? A big part of your problem may be the monthly payments on a second car or a music system or a vacation condo. If you don't need it, drop it. Do not, however, give up necessities.

This can be the hardest choice to make in a credit card society. You have worked for your possessions, even if the bills aren't fully paid. Giving up anything may make you feel like a failure, but be reasonable with yourself. Give up what you cannot afford now and make do with what you have. Then, when times improve, buy what you want. Although self-denial is no longer a popular concept in this country, it makes sense when you are short on resources.

Make a deal. Have you tried to convince your creditors to allow you to pay bills at lower rates? Have you consulted a financial counselor to help you? A little old-fashioned horse-trading can sometimes yield excellent results.

First, try contacting each of your creditors yourself. If your financial problems are temporary, you may get enough of a break from some of your creditors to see you through the hard times. If you cannot successfully deal with them yourself, go to a financial counselor for help. Also, contact your local Consumer Credit Counseling Service office, a creditor-supported national nonprofit organization that assists people with financial problems. They will contact creditors and negotiate lower payments.

Do nothing. This may be difficult. Doing nothing may be effective only if you do not have assets that creditors can take from you. If you do not have anything, then you may be able to endure the harassment of creditors until you are making more money. The difficulty here is that you must put up with the strong collection tactics of creditors and, of course, you can consider your credit ruined.

Should You Consolidate Bills? Borrow from Relatives?

Definitely do *not* borrow money commercially to consolidate your loans. All you are doing is trading one kind of debt for another, and it will cost you much more money in the long run. And, do not borrow money

WARNING

If you do borrow money from a relative, make sure the loan is secured by collateral and the lien is properly perfected. This means that you do what your state requires to ensure that your relative will have a legal claim to the collateral if you default on your payments. It will give your relative a better position with other creditors if you have to file bankruptcy in the future.

from friends or relatives. They usually cannot afford to give it to you, so a loan may produce an uncomfortable situation. Save the relationship; find another way to solve your problems.

What You Keep and What You Give Up When You File Bankruptcy

In bankruptcy, the court refers to the property you are entitled to keep as *exempt property*. Exempt property is one of the most important concepts you need to understand, because it explains what property you have to give up if you file a Chapter 7 liquidation bankruptcy. It also determines the minimum amount you must pay your creditors if you choose a reorganization of debt program in the bankruptcy court. Reorganizations do not necessarily require you to surrender nonexempt property.

The idea of exemptions was derived from the belief that debtors should be permitted to retain some property with which to start over, if they have gone so far into debt that creditors demand the liquidation of property to reimburse them for money owed.

State and Federal Exemptions

Individual states have created exemption laws that allow people to keep certain property that cannot be taken by creditors to satisfy debts. Each state has its own exemption laws, and the amount of property that is exempt varies from state to state. There is also a set of federal exemptions; in some states you can choose between the federal and state exemptions when you file bankruptcy.

The following states require you to use only the state exemptions: Alabama, Alaska, Arizona, Arkansas, California, Colorado, Delaware, Florida, Georgia, Idaho, Illinois, Indiana, Iowa, Kansas, Kentucky, Louisiana, Maine, Maryland, Mississippi, Missouri, Montana, Nebraska, Nevada, New Hampshire, New York, North Carolina, North Dakota, Ohio, Oklahoma, Oregon, South Carolina, South Dakota, Tennessee, Utah, Virginia, West Virginia and Wyoming.

The federal exemptions are shown in Appendix C; brief listings of each state's exemptions are shown in Appendix D. Ask your attorney to give you a copy of the exemptions allowed in your particular state, so you can be confident that you are receiving all your exemptions.

Exception to Exemption Laws

The only exception to the exemption laws occurs when there is a purchase-money security interest in your property. This means you financed the property when you purchased it. Even if the property is exempt, you must pay that secured creditor or you could lose the property.

Your attorney should explain to you which assets are exempt and which ones are not.

How To Keep Nonexempt Property

If you have property that you could lose by filing a Chapter 7 liquidation bankruptcy, your attorney should explain the following:

- In a Chapter 7 you can purchase your nonexempt property from the trustee. The trustee could allow you to purchase your own assets back if you offer a fair price.

- If the nonexempt property has minimum value, the bankruptcy trustee may decide the cost of liquidating the asset would offset any profit received. In that case, the trustee could abandon the property and you would get to keep it.

- If you cannot come up with a lump sum to repurchase your nonexempt property and the trustee will not abandon it, your lawyer should suggest you file a Chapter 13 reorganization. In Chapter 13 you can keep your nonexempt property. However, in your reorganization plan you must pay at least the value of your nonexempt property to your unsecured creditors.

For example, if you have a nonexempt tract of land worth $6,000, you will have to pay a minimum of $6,000 to your unsecured creditors over the term of your reorganization plan. Under the maximum 60-month plan, that would be $100 a month.

 WARNING

If you are confused about anything, especially how bankruptcy affects your personal situation, ask questions until you understand. Attorneys are human. They may assume you know what they are talking about and fail to explain it completely.

CHAPTER TWO

The Different Types of Bankruptcy

There are four basic types of bankruptcy; these are usually referred to by the number of the section of the U.S. Bankruptcy Code in which the rules and requirements for each are set out. Your attorney should explain each type to you and help you choose the one that suits your needs. The four are as follows:

1. Chapter 13—a court-supervised reorganization of debts, reducing a debtor's monthly payment over a specified period of time

2. Chapter 7—a liquidation of debt, wiping out all debt (except certain excluded debt) but exposing the debtor to loss of property

3. Chapter 11—reorganization used by businesses and, sometimes, by individuals who do not qualify for a Chapter 13. Since this book is primarily for individuals and small business owners who are not incorporated, Chapter 11 will not be explained here.

4. Chapter 12—reorganization for family farmers. It is a specialized type of reorganization in bankruptcy and will not be explained here.

Chapter 13—Adjustment of Debts of an Individual with a Regular Income

A Chapter 13 bankruptcy gives you the chance to reduce the amount you pay on debts, allowing you to keep property you otherwise might not be able to afford while protecting you from your creditors. A Chapter 13 should always be the first kind of bankruptcy to consider.

Do You Qualify for Chapter 13?

Only individuals can seek protection under a Chapter 13 bankruptcy, although small businesses can use a Chapter 13 to reorganize if they are sole proprietorships. Chapter 13 bankruptcy is available to individuals and sole proprietorships that do not owe more than $250,000 in unsecured debt or more than $750,000 in secured debt. These upper limits were increased to this level in 1994 to make Chapter 13 reorganizations more available to consumers and small business people. As a result, many debtors who in the past would have had to liquidate assets using Chapter 7 bankruptcy now have the option of staying in business by reorganizing their debts. Corporations and partnerships do not qualify for this type of reorganization. Your attorney should help you understand secured debts—debts on which you pledged property as security. When you buy a car, a house or furniture, the debt is usually secured by the items you buy. Most other debts are unsecured. Credit card bills, doctor bills and signature loans are usually unsecured debts. (A secured debt and an unsecured debt are both defined in the Glossary.)

Chapter 13 Procedure in Brief

Next, the attorney should explain that Chapter 13 requires you to pay your debts over three to five years. You must begin paying on the plan 30 days after you file the petition with the court. There is a move in most districts to deduct payments to the trustee from your paycheck and send it directly to the court. However, if you do not like this arrangement, the court will sometimes allow you to pay the trustee directly. Of course, if you are in business for yourself, you would pay directly.

Ordinarily you would make one monthly payment to a trustee who would then distribute the money to your creditors, but a Chapter 13 plan can propose alternatives, in case you have special needs. For instance, if you are a seasonal worker, you can arrange to pay less during the slow months and more during the months when you earn more money.

Luxury Items Are in Jeopardy

An attorney who finds that you own luxury items, such as a lake lot, extra cars or a boat, should warn you that you may not be able to get your plan confirmed if you keep them. Some judges believe that it is unfair to creditors, where they receive less than 100 percent return on their debt, to permit the debtor to pay for a luxury item. The judge may decide not to confirm a plan on the basis that the plan is not filed in "good faith."

The concept of "good faith" is somewhat vague in the law. When a judge decides that the debtor is not eligible for the benefits of a Chapter 13 and cannot deny the plan for any other reason, the judge may deny the plan using the "good faith" test.

WARNING

Part of the attorney's fees for filing Chapter 13 can be paid out through the plan. Discuss this with your attorney.

Chapter 13 for Small, Individually Owned Businesses

If you own a small business, your lawyer should explain how a Chapter 13 adjustment of debt program could help you.

Chapter 13 versus Chapter 11 for Small Businesses

Prior to 1979, if a person who ran a small or middle-sized business experienced financial difficulty, few alternatives were available. If new sources of operating funds could not be found or private arrangements with creditors could not be made, either the business had to be shut down (usually bankrupted) or reorganized through Chapter 11 in the bankruptcy court. Because Chapter 11 was expensive, burdensome and complicated, only strong companies could reorganize successfully.

However, in 1979, Chapter 13 was created, providing many small business owners as well as consumers with a new alternative. If your business qualifies, Chapter 13 offers the same benefits that are available to the individual debtor. Chapter 13 means an inexpensive, simplified, court-supervised reorganization of debt. But, as with individuals, the small or middle-sized business must meet certain conditions.

Qualifying for Chapter 13—Small Business

The first qualification concerns ownership of the business. The business must be owned as a sole proprietorship by either an individual or a married couple. A partnership involving two persons other than a husband and wife will not qualify. A corporation, even if owned solely by one individual, will not qualify. This is a problem for many business people because when they begin a business, they are usually advised to incorporate immediately. No one considers, when a business starts, that incorporating could limit alternatives if the business is not successful. Since most business failures occur during the first three to five years of operation, it would seem prudent to wait to incorporate until the period of hazard is past.

If the business qualifies because it is owned by an individual, and is not a partnership (except for a husband and wife) or corporation, then the amount of debt owed is the next qualifying area. Just as for individuals, the business cannot owe more than $250,000 in unsecured debts or more than $750,000 in secured debts.

Benefits for Small Business

The business that qualifies receives many benefits. Most benefits are recognized when you compare them to reorganization under a Chapter 11 (the only other court-supervised reorganization process available to businesses other than small farms). The most important benefit is reduced costs. A Chapter 13 is much cheaper to effect than a Chapter 11.

 WARNING

If you are considering Chapter 13 to reorganize a small business, be sure that your suppliers will continue to do business with you or that you have other sources. If you cannot obtain supplies, inventory or product, you are out of business.

Chapter 7—Straight Liquidation Bankruptcy

In Chapter 7 bankruptcy, most debts are wiped out and you never have to pay them. Once you discharge your debts in a Chapter 7 bankruptcy, you cannot file for a Chapter 7 bankruptcy again for another six years.

In Chapter 7 bankruptcy, you provide the court a list of all your debts and a list of everything you own. You also answer questions about your past financial dealings. You then claim as exempt the property you are allowed by law. This property you may keep. The trustee has the right to liquidate any property that cannot be claimed as exempt and then apply the cash to your debts.

The only restriction on keeping exempt property is that you still must pay purchase-money liens, the liens placed on property you buy. For example, if you plan to keep your car or house, you are still required to make the regular contractual payments to the creditor.

Some Debts Survive Bankruptcy

Certain types of debts are not discharged in a Chapter 7 bankruptcy and you have to pay them. The following are nondischargeable debts:

- Debts not listed on your petition.

- Debts incurred through fraud. You borrowed money and gave false information on a financial statement to the lending institution.

- Alimony and child support payments.

- Debts incurred when you willfully or maliciously injured someone.

- Noncompensatory (punitive) fines. Restitution ordered by a judge in a criminal case as well as traffic fines are examples.

- Certain educational loans.

- Debts remaining from a prior bankruptcy.

- Most types of taxes.

- Consumer debts owed to a single creditor aggregating more than $1,000 for luxury goods or services, incurred within 60 days of filing the petition for bankruptcy.

- Cash advances aggregating more than $1,000 that are extensions of consumer credit under an open-ended credit plan, obtained within 60 days before filing the petition. These exceptions to discharge are intended to prevent people from charging up their credit cards just before they file bankruptcy.

- Debts that arise from damages you caused as a result of operating a motor vehicle while legally intoxicated.

Positive and Negative Aspects of Bankruptcy

After explaining the different kinds of bankruptcy, your attorney should discuss the positive and negative aspects of each so you can make the right choice. Figure 2.1 compares some of the positive and negative aspects of Chapter 13 and Chapter 7 bankruptcy.

Special Considerations Regarding Taxes

When the federal Bankruptcy Code was amended in 1994, changes were made regarding how a loan to pay taxes is treated in bankruptcy. In the past, many debtors took out bank loans to pay off back taxes or paid off their debt using a credit card. They payed off their taxes this way because interest and penalties then stopped accruing and because the loan or credit card debt would be wiped out through bankruptcy. Now, however, these loans or credit card debts will be treated as nondischargeable debts. In other words, they will remain once a debtor is out of bankruptcy.

FIGURE 2.1

Advantages and Disadvantages of Filing Chapter 13 and Chapter 7

Positive Aspects of Chapter 13

- *Payments can be reduced; you can modify the rights of most secured creditors.*

- *Power of the automatic stay keeps creditors off your back.*

- *Allows you to keep all of your property, including nonexempt property.* Remember, however, that judges are wary of letting you keep what they consider to be luxury items on which you still owe unless you are paying 100 percent of your debts.

- *Wipes out more debts than a Chapter 7.*

- *Gives you up to five years to pay money you may owe the IRS or another taxing authority.*

- *If you are behind on your mortgage payments, gives you three to five years to make up the payments you may have missed.*

- *Some percentage of your unsecured debts may be forgiven,* although you are expected to pay as much as you can afford.

- *Allows you to pay unsecured creditors only what you can afford to pay them over the three to five years of your bankruptcy.* However, you cannot pay less than what a creditor would have received if you had filed a straight liquidation bankruptcy, your property were liquidated and the proceeds used to pay creditors.

Negative Aspects of Chapter 13

- *Hurts your credit,* if it was good when you filed. Typically not the actual case due to financial stresses prior to bankruptcy.

- *Long periods of involvement with the court even though your obligation is just to keep up payments.* Chapter 13 is best if you have secured debts, like a house, a car and furniture. If you are having trouble paying for these items, a Chapter 13 could lower the payments enough so that you may be able to keep them. If you are behind on paying your bills, you may also be behind on making your house payments. A Chapter 13 is an especially effective way to keep your house if you are about to lose it. Usually your house is most important to you.

(continued)

FIGURE 2.1 (continued)

Positive Aspects of Chapter 7

- *Immediately upon filing your petition with the court, an automatic stay is invoked and creditors must cease their collection actions against you.* This means they cannot call or write you, or repossess or foreclose on your property. In addition, the automatic stay will stop any lawsuits that may have been filed against you. This immediate action of the court will relieve the pressure on you and your family.

- *With some exceptions, most of your debts are wiped out.*

- *The process is completed relatively quickly. It usually takes about 120 days.*

Negative Aspects of Chapter 7

- *Filing Chapter 7 damages your credit rating, if you had good credit.* A Chapter 7 bankruptcy can be reported for ten years on your credit records. This may not be as discouraging as it sounds; most people who consider bankruptcy already have damaged credit, so a bankruptcy is unlikely to harm it further.

- *Chapter 7 does not discharge all debts.*

- *Rights of secured creditors cannot be modified.* Your only options when you want to keep an asset that is collateral for a debt are to:

  1. make contractual payments promptly;

  2. reaffirm the debt with different terms and possibly make up missed payments (the creditor does not have to reaffirm the debt if the contract is in default);

  3. redeem the property by paying its value in a lump sum; or

  4. give up the asset to satisfy the debt.

- *You could lose some of your property if it were designated nonexempt.* Chapter 7 is a good option for debtors who owe so much that, given their income, they have no hope of paying off what they owe by filing a Chapter 13 bankruptcy. It is also a good option for debtors who do not own a lot of property since they will lose much of their nonexempt property through the Chapter 7 liquidation process.

CHAPTER THREE

The Procedures of Bankruptcy

During your first meetings, your attorney should explain the procedures of bankruptcy. These are outlined below in concise form for the two bankruptcy types—Chapter 7 and Chapter 13—addressed in this book.

Chapter 7—Straight Liquidation Bankruptcy

Let's look at the ten chronological steps in a typical Chapter 7 case.

1. *You fill out forms that reveal your assets and debts.* You also complete forms that ask questions about your financial affairs. Complete and accurate answers are important and could determine how smoothly your case goes.

2. *You meet several times with your attorney or your attorney's legal assistants, who discuss your situation and provide information about your case.* With your attorney's help, you decide whether to file a Chapter 7 straight liquidation bankruptcy or a

Chapter 13 reorganization of debt. At these preliminary meetings, you should receive answers to all your questions.

3. *Your attorney prepares the required schedules to be filed in your case, with special attention to the exemptions, so you do not lose anything you are entitled to keep.*

4. *Your attorney files the necessary papers with the court to invoke the automatic stay of collection actions against you, giving you protection from your creditors.* As soon as this is done, your attorney should give notice to your creditors. Whether your attorney gives notice to all the creditors, or to just an important few, should be worked out with you in advance. The notices will be written and/or verbal, and they will serve the purpose of stopping creditor collection activities, including the repossession of vehicles and the foreclosure on your home.

5. *During the approximately 40 to 60 days after the filing of the petition, your attorney should be working out any difficulties with creditors.* Creditors will decide whether to wait and see what happens in your case or, if they are secured creditors, they may file a motion to try to obtain their collateral or to ask you to agree to pay for it.

6. *About six to eight weeks after the bankruptcy is filed, you and your attorney will attend a creditors' meeting, sometimes called a 341A meeting because that 341A is the United States Bankruptcy Code section that authorizes the meeting.* This will take place at the courthouse, and the trustee appointed to your case will preside over it. Any of your creditors may attend.

    At this meeting, the trustee wants to discover whether you have any nonexempt property that can be sold so that the proceeds can be used to pay on your debts. The trustee will also try to find out if, before you filed bankruptcy, you transferred any property that you should not have transferred or paid any debts you should not have paid. For example, did you transfer an asset to a relative before filing or did you pay a favorite creditor or a relative to whom you owed money right before you filed? Your attorney should prepare you for questions about these things before the meeting.

    Your creditors can also ask you questions at this meeting. If they are secured creditors, they will want to know if you wish to keep the collateral and pay for it. They will usually tell you how they want you to pay if you decide to keep the collateral. If they are unsecured creditors, they will want to know if you are going to pay them anything.

Also at this meeting, the trustee will make sure that you fully understand the implications of filing for Chapter 7. Specifically, the trustee wants to find out if you are aware of the potential implications of filing for bankruptcy, including its potential effect on your credit history, your ability to file a petition under another chapter of the Bankruptcy Code, the effects of receiving a discharge of your bankruptcy, and the effects of reaffirming a debt. These are all things that your attorney should explain to you. There are no wrong answers to these questions; your answers to them will not affect your bankruptcy.

7. *If any of your creditors files an adversary proceeding against you in the bankruptcy court (trying to obtain their collateral or complaining about you in some other way), you probably will have to attend the hearing to defend yourself.*

8. *You will need to submit to an examination of your financial affairs.* Although this usually consists of the trustee reviewing the documents filed in your behalf and asking you questions about your financial affairs at the creditors' meeting, this could also require that you provide the trustee with documents concerning your past financial dealings. The trustee also has the right to inspect your assets, for example, any real estate you may own. You must cooperate with the trustee during the investigation of your financial affairs. If you don't, you may be denied a discharge of your debt.

9. *In the 60 days after the creditors' meeting, your creditors can object to the discharge of their debt.* They must provide a reason to do this. Your attorney should explain what debts can survive a bankruptcy. They are listed in Chapter 2 of this book, in the section "Some Debts Survive Bankruptcy."

10. *You may have to attend a discharge hearing. This hearing ends the process and takes place approximately 60 to 120 days after the creditors' meeting.* At the hearing, the judge will officially discharge the debts you owed, except for those that cannot be discharged or the ones you wish to reaffirm. In some districts you may need only to attend the discharge hearing if you have a debt to reaffirm. However, under the present law, an attorney can file an affidavit that says the consequences of a reaffirmation have been explained to you. In this case, you will not have to attend the hearing.

Chapter 13—Adjustment of Debts for Individuals

Now let's look at the 11 chronological steps that usually make up a Chapter 13 adjustment of debt program.

1. *Just as in Chapter 7 bankruptcy, you fill out forms that reveal your assets and debts.* Again, completeness and accuracy are important.

2. *You meet with your attorney to discuss the plan you are going to propose to the court.* The different types of debts that can be treated in a Chapter 13 should be explained to you.

3. *Your attorney prepares the necessary schedules to be filed in your case.* Your plan of reorganization will be prepared at this time. In preparing it, your attorney will try to lower your payments to creditors as far as possible and, at the same time, ensure that you keep all the assets you want to keep. Be sure you understand the plan that is being proposed in your behalf and what your obligations are under it.

4. *Your attorney files the petition to stop all creditors' activity against you.* After your attorney files the necessary papers with the court, the court notifies your creditors that they should cease their collection actions. Your attorney should also notify them.

5. *Thirty days after the filing of your petition and proposed plan of reorganization, you must begin paying the trustee according to your plan.* Most trustees in the United States insist that payments be deducted automatically from your paycheck. Some trustees may allow you to pay directly.

6. *Prior to your creditors' meeting, your attorney negotiates with your creditors to avoid objections to your plan of reorganization.*

7. *At the creditors' meeting, approximately 40 to 60 days after the filing of your petition, your attorney will try to complete any negotiations with any creditors objecting to your reorganization plan.* Creditors who want to can attend this meeting to find out how they are going to be treated in your plan. Usually, just secured creditors attend this meeting, but it is not uncommon for no creditors to attend.

    The trustee will conduct the meeting and ask questions to determine if your plan is feasible. Then, the trustee will either recommend confirmation of your plan or suggest changes that must be made before he or she will recommend the plan to the judge.

8. *Your secured creditors will decide whether to file a motion with the court to obtain their collateral or to file an objection to your plan.* Either they think they are not being treated correctly, or they are willing to accept the payment you are offering.

9. *After the creditors' meeting, there will be a confirmation hearing before the bankruptcy judge.* Some districts conduct this hearing on the same day as the creditors' meeting; others hold it three to four weeks later. If there are no objections, the judge will confirm the plan. If there is an objection, the judge will hear it and then decide whether or not to confirm your plan. If the plan is not confirmed, the court will usually give you time to change your plan and propose it at a later date.

10. *After the plan is confirmed, you will continue to send your payments to the trustee according to the terms of your plan for a specific period of time, usually from three to five years.* These payments will include money for your creditors and possibly trustee fees as well. While your plan is in effect, if you have problems making your payments, you can modify your plan to change the way you are paying or you can convert your case to a Chapter 7 liquidation bankruptcy.

11. *When you have completed your plan, the court will give you a discharge.* Any unsecured debts that have not been paid in full by this time will be wiped out.

 WARNING

Before attending any hearing at the courthouse, ask your attorney exactly what to expect. Also ask how you should dress. Jewelry may not be appropriate.

The Cost of Filing Bankruptcy

"How much will it cost?" If you are considering bankruptcy, this is often your first concern. Costs vary around the United States. You must pay both your attorney's fee and the court's filing fee.

Flat Rate for Attorneys

Most bankruptcies are not complicated cases for experienced bankruptcy attorneys. Therefore, some attorneys quote a flat rate for rendering their bankruptcy services, knowing in advance what services will be expected. Flat fees on ordinary cases range from $300 to $1,500, plus the filing fee. The filing fee is $160, except for a Chapter 11 reorganization, which is $800 plus $.50 for each creditor. Since bankruptcy is a federal law, the filing fees are the same everywhere in the United States.

Some attorneys want to be paid their entire fee before any work is done because of the fundamental nature of bankruptcy actions. Some will allow a down payment and let you pay out the balance later. However, you will rarely get more than four months to pay the balance, the length of time a bankruptcy usually takes to be processed through the courts. Generally, the lawyers who advertise have the lowest flat-fee prices. Usually they are good enough to get you through the bankruptcy process; some in fact are better than average or are even specialists in this area of law. However, if your case is at all complicated, find out how much bankruptcy experience the lawyer has.

Hourly Rate for Attorneys

Some attorneys charge an hourly rate and bill you for the time they spend working on your case. Hourly rates range from $50 an hour to $200 an hour, depending on the area of the country where you live and the lawyer's expertise and experience. On average, the billable hours do not add up to much more than the flat-fee rates, but they can.

Generally, the lawyer expects you to pay a *retainer* of $200 to $700 before work begins. This is an initial fee to cover the immediate costs of prosecuting your case. Sometimes the retainer is very large, especially in Chapter 11 reorganizations. In Chapter 11 cases, after you pay the initial retainer, the attorney must make application to the court to be paid again, a time-consuming process. You are usually billed monthly as the work is done.

In an uncomplicated case, most of the work is completed in the first 30 to 60 days of the bankruptcy process. Things slow down after that.

Fees Reviewed by Court

The bankruptcy court surveys what your attorney charges. This is the only area of the law that requires fee monitoring by the court. All attorneys in bankruptcy must file a disclosure statement in every case, setting out their fee arrangements and the source of the funds. If the court decides that an attorney charges too much, the court can require a refund of all or part of the fee.

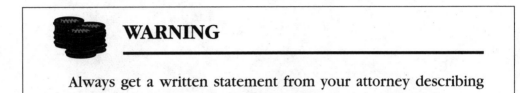

WARNING

Always get a written statement from your attorney describing fees for work to be performed and other anticipated work.

Filing Fees That You Pay the Court

Below are the filing fees that you must pay to the court according to the type of bankruptcy you are filing:

- Chapter 7, liquidation bankruptcy: $160

- Chapter 13, adjustment of debts for individuals: $160

- Chapter 11, reorganization: $800

- Chapter 12, adjustment of debts for farmers: $200

CHAPTER FOUR

Filing a Chapter 7 Bankruptcy

Gathering Information on Debts and Assets

A lawyer will prepare and file your schedules, making sure all information is provided to the court and all your exemptions are correctly claimed. If you have hired an attorney to file a Chapter 7 liquidation bankruptcy, you want the attorney to make sure you will be able to keep everything you are entitled to keep and that all debts that can be discharged are discharged.

You will begin by providing all the required information for presentation to the court. This is essentially a list of all your debts and assets. Most bankruptcy attorneys will give you worksheets to complete.

After you complete the worksheets, the attorney will transfer the information from your worksheets onto the required forms that later will be filed with the court. Together, you and your attorney should review all your debts and assets information so that matters will be resolved favorably on your behalf.

What To Watch for in Listing Debts

In reviewing your list of debts, the attorney should tell you that any debt not listed or listed with an improper address will not be discharged. You should list not only the obvious debts but also the names of everyone who *might* have a claim, such as ex-business partners, former customers or anyone who has not yet raised a claim against you but might do so.

Listing a possible claim may wipe it out; that would mean that you would not have to worry about it anymore.

Once all your debts are listed in the schedules, you should review them to make sure they are listed properly.

Priority Claims, Secured Claims and Unsecured Claims

As the attorney lists the debts in the schedules, the debts should be divided into proper categories. The three main categories are *priority claims*, *secured claims* and *unsecured claims.*

- In listing your *priority debts,* your attorney should look closely at any taxes you owe. In most cases they are not dischargeable, but the taxing authority cannot collect from you while you are in bankruptcy. However, as soon as you are discharged, the taxing authority can resume collecting from you. The attorney should check to see if any of your federal income taxes *can* be discharged. Under certain circumstances this is possible, for instance, if the income taxes were due more than three years before the filing of the bankruptcy petition.

- In listing all your *secured debts,* it is important that your attorney describe the collateral completely and state their most accurate values in the schedules. Most debtors overestimate the value of their assets, and this is not advisable. The attorney's experience should help you develop accurate values. Remember, the court is not looking for what you would have to spend to replace the asset. Instead, the court wants the present fair market value: what you would get if you had to sell it immediately.

  Proper valuation is important because the larger the equity you have in assets, the more likely you will be to use up your exemptions and be required to relinquish an asset to the trustee. Your attorney should inform you that if you plan to keep any asset that is collateral on a loan, such as your house, car or furniture, you must continue to make payments. You should be informed that if there is something you wish to give up, like a second car or real estate, you can return it in bankruptcy and the balance due the creditor will be discharged.

FIGURE 4.1

Examples of Secured, Unsecured and Priority Debts

Secured debt is debt that has been collateralized. Examples of this type of debt include: real estate, vehicles, furniture and equipment.

Unsecured debt is debt that is not collateralized. It includes credit card debt, some small bank loans and loans from friends or family.

Priority debts are debts that must be paid before all other debts in a bankruptcy, assuming there are sufficient funds from the sale of non-exempt property to pay them. These types of debt can include taxes and bankruptcy-related administrative expenses. However, in reality, in most Chapter 7 bankruptcies, it is rare that there is any money to pay creditors even if they are a priority. In addition, some priority debt cannot be wiped out by a Chapter 7 discharge. This means that after the Chapter 7 bankruptcy is over, the debt remains as an obligation of the debtor, and the creditor who is owed the money can still try to collect. Examples of this type of debt include student loans that became due less than seven years before a bankruptcy was filed and payroll taxes that were withheld by a business but never paid to the IRS.

Your attorney should also make clear that if you are behind on your payments on anything you want to keep, like your house or car, in a Chapter 7 bankruptcy you cannot force the creditor to work out payment arrangements that allow you to catch up. Creditors can demand that you become current before they allow you to reaffirm the debt with them. Most creditors will make some arrangement with you; however, the creditor sets the terms.

• In itemizing the *unsecured debts* in your petition, your attorney should check to be sure you have provided complete addresses to ensure that the debts will be discharged. The date the debt was incurred is significant. If the debt was incurred just before the filing of the bankruptcy, the attorney should discuss with you the possibility that the debt may not be discharged. Remember that some charges and cash advances cannot be discharged if they were made just before the filing of the bankruptcy.

Listing Assets and Claiming Exemptions

After the attorney has listed all your debts and your assets, he or she must elect the exemptions you are entitled to receive. This is most important in a Chapter 7 because it determines what you will be able to keep. You should be informed of any property that is not exempt because property that must be surrendered to the trustee may be important to you. If it is property you do not wish to lose, you should know that you can buy it from the trustee yourself. Usually your attorney will negotiate this for you. If you cannot afford to buy an asset from the trustee, your attorney should talk to you about filing a Chapter 13 reorganization, instead of a Chapter 7 liquidation bankruptcy, because in a Chapter 13 you can keep nonexempt property.

WARNING

If you have a tax refund coming, try not to file bankruptcy until you have received and spent it so there is no chance you will lose it.

Reviewing the Statement of Financial Affairs

After your assets are listed, the last document that you must complete is a statement of financial affairs. Completion of the statement of financial affairs is required for both Chapter 7 and Chapter 13 bankruptcies.

Trap for the Unwary

The questions in the statement of financial affairs are intended to discover inappropriate financial transactions and to locate additional assets. Your attorney will review your answers to all of the questions and will discuss with you any potential problems, based on the answers you gave.

Why Certain Questions Are Asked

It is important to know why some questions are asked and what answers will cause problems with the trustee. The following are the most important to consider:

Questions 1 and 2 ask what amount of income you have received from your trade or profession and from other sources during each of the two calendar years immediately preceding the filing of the original petition.

The trustee will look at past income to see how it compares to present debts and property. If you have made a lot of money but do not show many debts or assets, the trustee may wonder what happened to the money. Could you have bought assets that you have not listed?

Question 3 asks what payments in whole or in part you have made during the 90 days immediately preceding the filing of the original petition.

The trustee will determine whether any payments were made to prefer one creditor over another. If so, the trustee may try to have the money returned and distributed more evenly to all your creditors.

Question 4 asks if you were a party to any suit pending at the time of the filing of the original petition.

If you received money from a lawsuit, the trustee will want to know whether it can be exempted. If not, the trustee could settle the suit in your behalf and use the money to pay your creditors.

Question 6 asks if you have made any assignment of your property for the benefit of your creditors, or any general settlement with your creditors, within 120 days immediately preceding the filing of the original petition.

The trustee may think that an assignment of property or the payment to creditors to settle claims before the bankruptcy was filed, showed preference to those creditors over others, and the trustee will try to recover the money or property.

Question 7 asks if you have made any gifts to relatives or others during the year immediately preceding the filing of the original petition.

The trustee will decide from your answer whether or not you might have given up assets so creditors would not get them. Trying to conceal assets is not allowed. The trustee will attempt to recover any such property given as gifts or otherwise transferred.

Question 11 asks that you list financial accounts, certificates of deposit and safe deposit boxes.

Trustees can use this information to find out how you spent your money during the year before you filed. Perhaps it will reveal assets purchased but not listed on your schedules. Large amounts of money may have disappeared. Or, your information may show payments to relatives or friends. All of these could signal problems. It is illegal to knowingly conceal assets from creditors. However, as a general rule, trustees seldom check records, but they can if they wish.

Your attorney will review your answers to all the questions and discuss any potential problems you might have, based on the answers you gave.

Your attorney should be aware of any property you transferred before the filing of the bankruptcy that could be considered improper by the trustee. Any transfers of property to friends or family within one year of the filing of your bankruptcy are suspect. If the trustee thinks the transfer was an attempt to get rid of assets so as not to lose them to your creditors, the transfer could be reversed. The law regards such transfers as fraudulent.

Your attorney should also be looking for evidence of preference, where you might have treated one of your creditors better than others before you filed bankruptcy. Any payments to creditors before the filing of the bankruptcy are scrutinized by the trustee to determine if one creditor was preferred over the others. For example, you might have paid your next-door neighbor the money you owed him, but paid no one else with that last $1,000 in your bank account before you filed bankruptcy.

If you answered any questions in the statement of financial affairs that would be questioned by the trustee, your attorney should, in advance, discuss the consequences with you. The attorney should also caution you not to hide information. If you have done something you were not supposed to do, be sure you describe the event in the schedules. Otherwise, if the trustee finds out about it, you may be accused of committing fraud; then you may face criminal charges. It obviously would be better to lose property than go to jail.

WARNING

Incomplete schedules may not only cause you problems with a trustee, but correcting them later will usually cost you more in attorney's fees.

Notifying Your Creditors When You File Chapter 7 Bankruptcy

You have come to the part of the bankruptcy process that will give you the most immediate relief. When your attorney has prepared the schedules for your bankruptcy, the next step will be to file them with the court. At that time, the court gives the attorney your case number.

Stopping Creditor Harassment by Automatic Stay

Something very powerful happens at this point. The court invokes what is known as the *automatic stay.* The automatic stay immediately stops creditors from trying to collect what you owe them. Once they know you have filed with the court, they may not call, write, sue or take anything away from you. The key here is that they must *know* about the bankruptcy.

The bankruptcy court will eventually notify all the creditors, but that could take some time. In some districts, it could be a month before the court sends out a notice. Your attorney should be aware of any creditors giving you an especially hard time and notify them that you have filed; the automatic stay prevents further creditor collection. It is especially important that all your secured creditors be notified immediately, either by letter or by phone (preferably both), because they are the most dangerous to a debtor since they may repossess and foreclose on property. Your attorney should also contact any other problem creditors. This will be one of the most important services the attorney performs for you, because it will give you peace of mind and will prevent your creditors from taking from you something that may be very difficult to retrieve.

If your attorney fails to contact your creditors, there is nothing wrong with your doing it. If you get bills in the mail, just write on them that you have filed bankruptcy, give your case number and the name, address and phone number of your attorney and send them back to the creditors.

Changes in the Automatic Stay

The Bankruptcy Reform Act of 1994 made some changes in the law regarding the automatic stay. Due to those changes, the automatic stay will not stop a taxing authority from putting you through a tax audit, giving you notice of a tax deficiency, demanding that you file tax returns or from assessing an uncontested tax liability. If you have a business, the revised law gives your trade creditors ten extra days to reclaim property after your bankruptcy begins.

Also due to changes in the law, the automatic stay will not stop any legal actions to establish that a debtor is the father of a child, nor will it stop any legal actions to establish or modify alimony, maintenance or support (child or spousal) obligations. This new exception to the automatic stay is in addition to the exception that already existed permitting legal actions to collect alimony, maintenance or support from property that is not property of the estate.

An exception to the automatic stay was also granted to property taxing authorities allowing them to create and perfect a statutory lien for taxes that come due after the filing of the bankruptcy. Therefore, under the new law, if a debtor wants to sell property after a bankruptcy has been filed, the debtor must pay the taxes. Prior to the revisions in the law, if the taxing authority was unable to legally attach a lien to the debtor's collateral, then the debtor could sell the property, not pay the taxes, and the unpaid taxes would be treated as an unsecured claim.

Violating the Automatic Stay

What happens if a creditor continues to harass you in trying to collect the debt? Tell your lawyer. There might be only a misunderstanding, and the attorney may need to notify the creditor again. If the collection activity is intentional and it does not look as if the creditor is going to stop, then your attorney should file an application with the bankruptcy court asking that the creditor be held in civil contempt. If it can be proven that the creditor intentionally violated the automatic stay, the court can award you damages, make the creditor pay your attorney's fee and give you any other relief it thinks is fair. Your attorney should not permit a creditor to bother you once the case has been filed.

Another interesting change brought about by The Bankruptcy Reform Act of 1994 relates to government agencies who violate the automatic stay. The change says that the government no longer has sovereign immunity in this regard. This means that if the government, through one of its agencies, the Internal Revenue Service for instance, violates the automatic stay, the debtor can make the government pay for damages.

 WARNING

Do not tell a secured creditor you are going to file bankruptcy. Some creditors will try to repossess the collateral before you file. Let the news come from your attorney after you file.

CHAPTER FIVE

The Automatic Stay

How the Automatic Stay Protects You

What is the automatic stay and how does it protect you? No matter what type of bankruptcy you file, once your petition has been filed, the automatic stay will be invoked to stop creditors' actions against you. The automatic stay is the most dramatic and immediate relief involved in all types of bankruptcy. You will have the protection of the automatic stay as long as you are in an active bankruptcy. If your case is closed or dismissed or if you receive a discharge of your debts, the protection of the automatic stay ends.

Usually the motivation for filing bankruptcy arises out of a creditor's particularly aggressive collection activity. For example, the debtor may face the loss of some asset through repossession; or a creditor's harassment at work threatens the debtor's job. The automatic stay gives harried debtors immediate relief from these pressures. Because of the automatic stay's basic importance to the bankruptcy process, let's take a closer look at how it can work for you.

The automatic stay becomes effective the moment you file your petition with the court. Creditors must be notified immediately to give you the swiftest relief, and because the courts frequently do not immediately send out notices, your lawyer or you may do so. The stay's protection extends to most areas of collection. With some exceptions, it means that lawsuits against you are stopped and your creditors cannot enforce judgments against you, even if they have filed lawsuits against you and won. It also means that a creditor cannot obtain possession of any of your property, so there can be no repossessions of cars or furniture and no foreclosure on your home. The automatic stay also prevents creditors from putting a lien on any of your property after the stay is invoked. The only exception to this relates to property taxing authorities.

In addition, the stay stops collection activity by taxing authorities: the Internal Revenue Service cannot garnish your wages or even continue a proceeding in the United States Tax Court.

The law states that creditors cannot do any "act to collect, or assess, or recover a claim against the debtor that arose before the commencement of the case." [11 U.S.C. Sec. 362 (a) (6)].

What the Automatic Stay Can and Cannot Do

The automatic stay will not stop any criminal action against you. This exception most commonly is invoked when a person has written an insufficient-funds check. Since writing a "hot" check is a criminal offense, the automatic stay will not prevent the creditor from filing charges against you. In some districts, if the debtor brings the charge before the bankruptcy court, the bankruptcy judge may look at the motive of the person filing the hot check charge. If he or she determines that the sole motive of the creditor in bringing the hot check charge is to collect the debt, the judge may rule that the creditor cannot pursue the hot check charge. However, if the district attorney wants to bring criminal charges against the debtor for a hot check, the judge cannot stop that action. To be safe, if you have a hot check problem, the best thing to do is find the funds to pay.

Automatic Stay and Your Ex-Spouse

The automatic stay cannot stop an ex-spouse from collecting alimony, maintenance and support payments from property that is not property of the bankruptcy estate. In a Chapter 13, all of a debtor's property is considered property of the estate. In a Chapter 7, nonexempt property is considered the property of the estate. Exactly which assets are not part of a debtor's bankruptcy estate will depend on the contents of the debtor's reorganization plan and on the laws in the debtor's state. However, the automatic stay can stop the efforts of a former spouse to enforce a debtor's obligations under a division of property agreement. This is an agreement that spells out how a couple's property will be divided between them; it is part of their divorce agreement. In Chapter 13, the debtor's wages are property of the estate, at least until the debtor's reorganization plan is confirmed. Therefore, the automatic stay would protect the debtor's wages from collection efforts involving alimony, maintenance and support.

An ex-spouse can have a state court judge set or modify a support obligation while the debtor is in a Chapter 13, but the ex-spouse cannot collect past due alimony, maintenance or support payments. Since these obligations became due before the Chapter 13 was filed, they must be paid in full through the Chapter 13 plan. However, any alimony, maintenance or child support payments that become due to a debtor's ex-spouse after the debtor's bankruptcy was filed must be paid by the debtor as they come due. And, if the debtor does not stay current on those obligations, the ex-spouse can collect against any property that is not part of the bankruptcy estate.

WARNING

If you are the former spouse of someone who is in bankruptcy and if the debtor is not staying current on his alimony, maintenance or support obligations, consult with a bankruptcy attorney before trying to collect from the assets that are not part of the debtor's bankruptcy estate. This will ensure that you do not violate the automatic stay that is in place.

Automatic Stay and a Governmental Unit

When a governmental unit is trying to enforce its regulatory policies or trying to enforce a judgment that is not a money judgment, the automatic stay does not protect you. For example, if city authorities told you to remove an abandoned car from your property, you would have to do it.

Automatic Stay and the IRS

The automatic stay will not stop the IRS from auditing you. Even though the IRS cannot collect from you on past-due taxes, it has the right to send you a notice of tax deficiency and the right to contact you and determine if a tax deficiency exists.

The Bankruptcy Reform Act of 1994 now allows a taxing authority like the IRS to assess and issue a demand for payment on back taxes, but it does not let the authority actually collect the tax obligation from you once you have filed for protection of the bankruptcy court.

The changes in the law also now permit a local taxing authority to take a lien against property for taxes that become due after the filing of the bankruptcy despite the automatic stay.

Automatic Stay and Commodity Futures

Another exception to the automatic stay deals with commodity futures, but because it doesn't apply to most people it need not be discussed here. If you deal in commodity futures, consult your attorney to see how the automatic stay relates to you.

Relief from the Automatic Stay

In most cases, the automatic stay stops creditors from further collection activity. However, creditors have the right to ask the court to give them relief from the automatic stay. If a creditor asks for relief, preliminary and final hearings will be scheduled. If the final hearing is not concluded within 30 days of the preliminary hearing, the creditor will be granted the relief requested.

There are other specific instances in which the court will give a creditor relief. For example, if the creditor has a lien on your property, the creditor can claim that the lien is not adequately protected because it is going to be some time before you begin paying against the debt, and because meanwhile, the property is losing value. Under such a circumstance, the court will usually give the creditor the right to adequate protection. For instance, if you have financed a car, your creditor would be given the right to ask that payments be made immediately.

The creditor may even ask the court's permission to go ahead and take the property. However, the creditor must prove that you do not have any equity in the property and that you do not need the property to help you in the reorganization of your debt if you've filed for Chapter 13 bankruptcy.

In most cases, creditors do not ask for relief because it creates additional expenses for them and because the asset involved may be property that you need for your reorganization. For example, you may need your car to get to work every day. In such an instance, the court would be reluctant to grant a creditor relief.

Since creditors have the right to ask for relief from an automatic stay if they believe the appropriate conditions exist, the process of going through a Chapter 13 or Chapter 7 can be complicated.

Automatic Stay and Unexpired Leases

The automatic stay often raises three special questions that need addressing.

1. How does the automatic stay affect executory contracts and unexpired leases, such as the lease on your car, apartment or your business? Your business may be leasing business equipment or office space.

2. How does it affect the utility company to which you may owe a large bill that you cannot pay?

3. How does it affect the co-debtors who helped you by cosigning for loans?

In Chapter 13 or Chapter 7, you, through the trustee, have the right to accept or reject *executory contracts* or unexpired leases. This means that if you have a contract in which both parties still have some portion to perform and if the contract is not to your benefit, you can end the contract. For example, you may have entered into a membership contract with a health club for a year or more, and you may have agreed to make monthly payments. In bankruptcy you are allowed to break the contract so that you don't have to pay on it any more; however, when you do so, you also lose your club membership.

Another common circumstance involves *unexpired leases*. For example, you may be overdue on your rent and may even be facing eviction. This is when the automatic stay may help you in a limited way. It can allow you to remain in your apartment for a period of time while you decide whether you want to find a new apartment or stay in your current apartment with your current lease. It can also give you time to make an orderly move if you choose not to stay. If you decide that you want to stay, you can accept the lease as long as you first cure the default. How quickly you must cure the default depends upon where you live. It could mean you will have several months to make up back payments or it could mean you have only a few days. The automatic stay could benefit you in a similar way if you were leasing a car and were behind on your payments.

Automatic Stay and Utility Bills

Utility companies are a special case. On a one-time basis only, if you owe a large bill when you file bankruptcy, you can include that debt in bankruptcy so the debt will be wiped out and the utility company cannot "alter, refuse or discontinue" service to you. In other words, the automatic stay prevents the utility company from disconnecting your service if you owe the company money, provided it is notified that you have filed bankruptcy. Although this may provide short-term relief, within 20 days from the date you filed your petition, the utility company can demand that you pay it a "reasonable" deposit if you have not already paid one. The court, as a general rule, defines this deposit amount as equal to two months of average service. Thus, if you are about to have your utility service disconnected at the time you file your petition, you can use the automatic stay to stop the interruption of service. However, the relief may only be temporary because you may have to come up with deposit money for the utility company within 20 days after filing your petition.

Automatic Stay and Co-Debtors

One of the most notable changes in the law concerns co-debtors, that is, persons who have cosigned with you on a debt. Cosigners can include the father who co-signs his daughter's car loan or a spouse who co-signs a note with her husband. Before the United States Bankruptcy Code was enacted in 1979, a person who filed any type of bankruptcy usually found that a creditor would put pressure on a co-debtor, often the debtor's relative, as a means of forcing the debtor to pay. Therefore, when Chapter 13 was enacted, Congress provided special protection for co-debtors. This special protection is available only in a Chapter 13. If you file a Chapter 7 liquidation bankruptcy, the co-debtor protection does not apply.

This special co-debtor stay is available only for a consumer debt. This means that Congress intended to help the debtor whose relatives or friends cosigned on debts relating to personal needs such as a car, furniture, etc. The co-debtor stay does not apply if you borrowed money with a cosigner to start a business. If you do not propose to pay this type of debt in full in your Chapter 13 plan, the creditor can ask the court for relief from the stay to collect the difference from the co-debtor. The creditor can also ask for relief if the co-debtor actually received some benefit for cosigning. An example of this would be a cosigner who was induced to cosign by being paid.

 WARNING

Make sure you and your attorney agree about which creditors are to be notified, when they are to be notified and who will notify them.

CHAPTER SIX

The Chapter 7 Process

What Your Creditors Will Do After You File Bankruptcy

Creditors, once they learn that you have filed bankruptcy, have several options. They will decide, during the time after you file and before the first meeting of creditors, which option to choose.

Minimum Creditor Action

The first option amounts to accepting what has happened and not spending any more time and effort trying to collect from you. This usually means taking your file out of the normal collection channels, then filing a proof of claim with the court to assure them of being reimbursed should there be any funds. Most unsecured creditors and many secured creditors choose this option.

Filing a Motion To Lift Stay

Some secured creditors, especially if a large amount of money is involved, will elect another option. If you are behind on your payments, a creditor can file a motion to lift the automatic stay in order to try to recover the collateral. The creditor can recover collateral if there is proof that you have no equity in the property and that you do not need it to reorganize. In most instances, this is hard to prove because the collateral usually is a debtor's car, furniture or house. If this is true, why would the creditor go through all the trouble of filing a motion to lift stay? It is because, even if the creditor is unable to recover the property, the court will give him or her "adequate protection." That usually means the debtor will be required to start making monthly payments to that creditor immediately. In deciding whether to file a motion to lift the automatic stay, the creditor will balance the cost involved against the chances of recovering the collateral; if the collateral cannot be recovered, the cost involved is weighed against what the creditor is likely to receive as adequate protection. In typical consumer cases, the system is set up to discourage the creditor from filing a motion to lift the automatic stay, but it does happen.

The Bankruptcy Reform Act of 1994 made some changes in the law regulating the protection you receive under the automatic stay. One change says that the final hearing on a motion to lift stay must be concluded within 30 days of the preliminary hearing. This means that, in most cases, the judge will decide much sooner than in the past whether or not you get to keep your property and under what conditions. This will not affect most cases involving individuals because those cases are generally concluded by the time a preliminary hearing is held, usually within 30 days of the creditor filing a motion to lift stay.

Other changes say that automatic stay does not apply to taxing authorities who want to assess a tax, audit you or demand that you file tax returns. This means that if your property taxes come due after you file for bankruptcy, the automatic stay will not prevent the taxing authority from placing a statutory lien on your property.

What You Need To Do Before the Creditors' Meeting

Soon after your Chapter 7 petition is filed and your creditors have been given notice, your attorney should begin contacting your secured creditors to let them know your intentions concerning the collateral.

A debt is secured if you have an asset that has been pledged to secure the debt. If you do not pay the debt, the creditor can repossess or foreclose on that asset. The most common examples of this are the loans you make to purchase your car or house.

In a Chapter 7 bankruptcy, you must decide whether to keep the asset and continue paying the creditor, or give it up. If the asset is worth more than what is owed on it, the bankruptcy trustee checks to see if you have exempted the property. If the property is exempt, the trustee will not care whether you give it up or keep it. If the property has not been exempted and it has some value above what is owed, the trustee will attempt to sell the property and will use any remaining money, after the lien on the property is paid, to pay your creditors. If you want to buy any nonexempt property from the trustee, your attorney should contact the trustee and make an offer. If the offer is reasonable and the trustee cannot sell the property at a higher price, you will be permitted to buy it.

Reaffirmation of Debts

If the property in question is exempt and you wish to relinquish it, your attorney will contact the creditor and make arrangements for the property to be picked up; if you wish to keep the property and the trustee has no interest in it, your attorney will inform the creditor of your intention.

If your payments are current on something you wish to keep, your attorney should advise you to continue making the payments in accordance with the terms of the contract. If you are behind on payments, your attorney should contact the creditor and try to work out an arrangement for you to become current. Usually creditors will let you catch up; however, they are not required to. They can require that you immediately produce all your missed payments as a condition for letting you keep the property.

When you agree to keep property and continue to pay the debt on it, the creditor will probably want you to enter into a reaffirmation agreement. This is an agreement between the creditor and debtor in which the debtor agrees to have the debt survive the bankruptcy and not be discharged. Reaffirmations must be approved by the bankruptcy judge. If you enter into a reaffirmation agreement and later, after the bankruptcy is over, cannot make your payments, the creditor can repossess the property, sell it and make you pay the difference between what the property is sold for and what you owe on the debt. This difference is called a *deficiency*.

Reaffirmations Not Recommended

Your attorney should advise you to try to get the creditor to accept payments and allow you to keep the property, without a formal reaffirmation agreement being approved by the court. If a debt has not been reaffirmed and approved by the bankruptcy judge, the worst that can happen, if you cannot pay the debt after bankruptcy, is that the creditor could take the property. You would not be liable for a deficiency if a reaffirmation agreement had not been approved.

Your attorney should explain to you that if you enter into a reaffirmation agreement, you have 60 days to change your mind after the court approves the reaffirmation. If you do change your mind during that time, you must notify the creditor in writing that you wish to rescind the agreement.

To help debtors avoid another court appearance, the Bankruptcy Reform Act of 1994 now says that a reaffirmation hearing is not necessary if you are represented by an attorney. It also requires that the reaffirmation agreement state that the agreement is not required by the Bankruptcy Code. Be sure your attorney explains to you the legal effects and consequences of entering into a reaffirmation agreement before you do so.

Redemption of Property

You also have the right of property redemption. If you wish to redeem something, the attorney should make arrangements with the creditor. Right of redemption means that if you have exempt property that is worth less than what you owe on it and you can come up with the full amount of the value, you have the right to keep it by paying the value of the property. For example, you owe $1,000 on furniture, but the furniture is worth only $300. If you can come up with the $300, you can pay that to the creditor and keep the furniture.

Redemption is not used much because the debtor usually does not have the cash. Also, if the creditor disagrees with the debtor's assessment of the value of the property, the debtor's attorney has to file a motion to redeem the property, and a hearing is required so that the judge can decide what value must be paid before the property can be redeemed. Because this requires preparing and filing documents with the court and a hearing before a judge, attorneys usually charge extra for this. The attorney's fee must always be considered by the debtor when deciding whether to redeem property.

Additional Help from Your Attorney

Prior to the creditors' meeting your attorney will answer phone calls from creditors. Sometimes creditors are angry or confused and do not understand the bankruptcy process. Part of your attorney's service to you includes taking time to talk to your creditors in order to calm them down and to help them understand the process. Such courtesy and attention by your attorney could mean that your creditors will not cause unnecessary litigation in your case.

The Creditors' Meeting

Between 40 and 60 days after you file for bankruptcy, the court will set the first meeting of creditors. At this meeting, the Chapter 7 trustee and any of your creditors can question you about your financial affairs.

Preparing for the Hearing

Your attorney should prepare you for this meeting by going over the questions he or she expects you will be asked; if your case has any sensitive areas, the attorney usually will review the questions with you at his or her law offices prior to the hearing. However, if your attorney does not expect any tough questions, this preparation may occur at the courthouse before you go into the meeting. If you are nervous about the creditors' meeting, call your attorney and talk over your fears in advance. The attorney should be able to reassure you and give you the information you need to feel more confident.

The new changes in the Bankruptcy Code now require that the trustee question you to make sure you are aware of: "(1) the potential consequences of seeking a discharge in bankruptcy, including the effects on credit history; (2) the debtor's ability to file a petition under a different chapter of this title; (3) the effect of receiving a discharge of debts under this title; (4) the effect of reaffirming a debt, including the debtor's knowledge of the provisions of section 524 (d) of this title." [11 U.S.C. 341]

Don't worry, there is nothing to memorize. The trustee just wants to be sure you understand that although filing bankruptcy hurts your credit it wipes out debt you cannot afford to pay. The trustee also wants to be sure you cannot afford to make payments on your debts under a Chapter 13 reorganization and make sure you understand that if you reaffirm a debt, you will have 60 days to change your mind, but that if you don't change your mind, you will be fully liable for the debt again.

According to former Congressman Jack Brooks, who was involved in passing the Bankruptcy Reform Act of 1994, the purpose of all the questions is "solely informational; it is not intended to be an interrogation to which the debtor must give any specific answers or which could be used against the debtor in some later proceeding." In other words, there are no wrong answers.

What Happens at the Creditors' Meeting?

After you arrive at the courthouse and find the room where the creditors' meetings are held, locate your attorney. Other people will be waiting their turn to see the trustee. Sometimes these meetings are held in private rooms, and you may have to wait your turn outside. If you are allowed to wait your turn in the meeting room, do so. Use this time to listen to the types of questions the trustee asks other debtors. For some trustees, these meetings become habit, and they tend to ask the same questions of each debtor. Pay close attention to the responses given by other debtors and the reactions of the trustee. If you are not sure how you would answer the questions, talk to your attorney about it before your meeting begins.

When it is your turn, the trustee will call your name and you will enter and be sworn in. These meetings are usually conducted at a table where you sit with your attorney. The trustee may sit at the head of the table, or at the front of the room. Regardless of where the trustee sits, it is the trustee who conducts the meeting.

Besides anticipating some of the questions, it is important to know the motives behind the trustee's questions. That helps you understand why a creditor would come to this meeting and ask you questions.

What Questions Will the Trustee Ask You?

The trustee's questions have two motives. One purpose is to find any assets that can be liquidated, so that the money can be applied to the debts. The trustee has an incentive for doing this. Trustees are paid a percentage of any money they administer. This percentage is small, but it helps compensate the trustee for all the work required to administer a debtor's bankruptcy estate. The other reason the trustee asks questions is to determine how honest the debtor has been in disclosing all financial information. If a trustee finds that a debtor is using the bankruptcy court to defraud creditors, two things will probably happen. The debtor will be reported to the U.S. Attorney for possible criminal prosecution, and the trustee will file a complaint with the bankruptcy court, objecting to the debtor's discharge of debts.

Given those two motives, the following are a few of the most common questions a trustee will ask a debtor at the creditors' meeting:

- *Why did you have to file bankruptcy?* The trustee asks this question to find out if the reason you filed was because of a business failure;

if so, the trustee will want to make sure you have disclosed that information in your schedules. This is usually followed by a question about what happened to the assets of the business, if a business is involved. The trustee is looking for assets to liquidate.

- *Have you listed all your debts and all your assets in your schedules?* The trustee notes whether you say yes on the record under oath. If the trustee later learns that you were not telling the truth, then there is evidence for a charge of perjury. The trustee also asks this question to determine whether you forgot to put something in your petition and now wish to do so.

- *How did you come up with the values of these assets?* The trustee tries to make sure that the values you placed on your assets are realistic. If the trustee is not satisfied with your answers, he or she may want to make an independent appraisal of your assets. Did you place too low a value on your assets? If you did, the true market value might make some of your assets nonexempt, and they could be liquidated by the trustee.

- *Have you been in any accidents in the last year?* If you are entitled to receive compensation for damages and you have not listed that claim against the other party as an asset, the trustee will insist you do so. If you cannot exempt your claim, the trustee will have the opportunity to step into your shoes in the lawsuit and settle it for much less than you think it is worth. The money will then go to pay your debts.

- *Are you entitled to an income tax refund that you have not yet received?* Again, if you were entitled to a refund at the time you filed your bankruptcy and have not received it, you must list it as an asset. If you cannot exempt the refund, the trustee will take it.

- *Do you have copies of appropriate financial information?* Sometimes, before the creditors' meeting, a trustee will ask a debtor to provide additional information, such as a copy of bank statements, canceled checks and copies of income tax returns. At the creditors' meeting, the trustee may ask questions based on a review of your documents. For example, if your bank statements show you had a larger balance in your account on the day you filed bankruptcy than you stated in your schedules, you will be asked to explain the discrepancy. A discrepancy can occur, for instance, if the check you wrote for rent did not clear the bank by the time you filed, leaving a larger balance than you thought you had in your account. If the additional money cannot be exempted, the trustee will ask for it. To avoid this, make sure you know exactly what is in your account at the time you file.

If the trustee finds you wrote checks for large amounts of money close to the time of filing, you will be asked to explain them. The trustee is trying to find out if any creditor was given a preference. If this can be proven, the trustee may require that the preferred creditor turn over to the court the money you paid the creditor so it can be more fairly dispersed.

If you bought season football tickets and those tickets are not listed as an asset and exempted, you will be asked to explain. If assets you are depreciating on your income tax are not listed on your schedules, you will be asked to explain what became of the property.

- *Are you entitled to an inheritance or is there the possibility you will be entitled to an inheritance within six months of the filing of the bankruptcy?* An inheritance is an asset that has to be exempted if you plan to keep it. And if a relative dies after the bankruptcy, but before six months have passed since you originally filed, the inheritance would become part of your bankruptcy estate. You are obligated to report the inheritance to the trustee, and there must be a determination of whether or not you can exempt it. If not, it goes to the trustee to liquidate, so the money can be used to pay your debts.

These are just a few of the questions a trustee might ask. There could be others, depending on your special circumstances. Your attorney should know what questions to discuss with you beforehand by looking at your schedules.

Other Questions the Trustee Will Ask You

At the creditor's meeting, the trustee is required to ask you another series of questions to make sure that you have a full understanding of the Chapter 7 bankruptcy process and how that process may affect you. The trustee will talk with you about the potential consequences of bankruptcy, including its possible effects on your credit record. It is important for debtors to be aware of the fact that a bankruptcy will remain in their credit file for up to ten years and can make it difficult to gain new credit during those years. The trustee will also make sure you understand that you can file a bankruptcy petition under a different chapter, what happens when your debt's are discharged and what it means to reaffirm a debt.

What Questions Will Your Creditors Ask?

Creditors sometimes attend the creditors' meeting. They will attend for a variety of reasons, and they may or may not ask questions of the debtor and the debtor's attorney. The following are a few of the major reasons why creditors would attend and some of the questions they might ask.

- *An unsecured creditor may attend to find out if there is going to be any distribution of funds to pay the debt.* This is rare; in most cases there is no distribution made to unsecured creditors. These creditors will know there is no money to disburse to them because the notice of the creditors' meeting they receive will indicate this is a "No Asset Case." These creditors usually do not ask questions, and if they do, their questions are usually directed to the trustee.

- *Secured creditors may attend the creditors' meeting to find out if you are going to reaffirm debt.* If it has not already been dealt with by your attorney, this is generally the time to discuss reaffirmations with your creditors. Sometimes a secured creditor will question you about a financial statement you may have submitted to induce him or her to give you a loan. The creditor may want you to explain any differences in values you placed on assets you listed in your schedules and those same assets listed in the financial statement. You could also be asked to explain why assets are listed on the financial statement and not on your bankruptcy schedules.

Creditors ask these questions to determine whether you lied on your financial statement. If there is proof that you lied, the creditor can file a complaint against you asking that the debt be determined nondischargeable. If the creditor wins, you will still owe the debt after the bankruptcy. The creditor has 60 days after the creditors' meeting to object to the discharge of the debt.

After the creditors' meeting, your attorney can tell you about any problems in your case that were revealed at the meeting. If there are problems, your attorney should discuss their consequences and how to deal with them.

The 60-Day Period After the Creditors' Meeting

There is a 60-day wait after your creditors' meeting before you are discharged from your debts. During this period, the following should be done:

- Make sure all creditors are listed. If you have forgotten to list any creditors, this is the time to do it. If you obtain a discharge without listing all your debts, those not listed will not be discharged. Also, take the time to review your petition again to make sure your attorney listed correctly all the creditors' names and addresses you provided. It is your responsibility to bring any errors or omissions to the attention of your attorney and to get them corrected before the discharge date.

- Your creditors have only these last 60 days to file an objection to discharge a debt, if there are grounds. Once the 60 days pass, they loose the chance to do this.

- This is the time to make final arrangements with any secured creditors concerning debts you wish to reaffirm. After the 60 days pass and you obtain a discharge, the automatic stay will no longer be available to protect you, and it may be impossible to work out a solution with a creditor.

The Discharge Hearing

This is the day your bankruptcy is over and you are discharged from your debts. This is the beginning of the fresh start that bankruptcy promises.

Your attorney should explain how the discharge is handled in your district. In some districts, a discharge hearing is held. You go to the courthouse and sit in a courtroom along with many other people whose cases are set for discharge. The judge enters the courtroom, gives a short speech, signs an order officially discharging you of your debts and then wishes you well. Later you will be sent the order of discharge in the mail.

Presently, there are districts that do not hold discharge hearings. The court may be so busy that the judge will not take the time. If you live in one of these districts, you will be mailed an order signed by the judge.

Reaffirming a Debt

If you are going to reaffirm a debt, even in districts where no discharge hearing is held, the court will set a hearing date for you to come to court and appear before the judge. This is done because the judge must approve the reaffirmation. To approve the reaffirmation, the judge has to be assured that you are entering into the reaffirmation agreement of your own free will, and that you know the agreement can be rescinded within 60 days. The new Bankruptcy Code says that a hearing does not have to be held to approve a reaffirmation agreement if a debtor is represented by a lawyer. Instead of a hearing, your attorney can file an affidavit saying that you have been told about the consequences of reaffirming a debt and that reaffirmation is not required by the Bankruptcy Code. This will be enough to satisfy the court that you know your rights and therefore, a hearing won't be necessary.

When you receive your order of discharge in the mail, be sure to make several copies and keep them in a safe place. On occasion, a creditor will ignore the entire bankruptcy process, and then one day after the bankruptcy is over, send you a letter or make a phone call demanding payment. If this happens, send a copy of your discharge order to this creditor, with the information that the debt has been discharged and can no longer be collected.

You should also send a copy of your discharge order and a copy of your schedules listing your debts to the local credit-reporting agency. The agency will enter into your record that all the debts you listed are now discharged and you are no longer responsible for them. Credit bureaus say this will help if you wish to rebuild your credit.

 WARNING

If you have not received your discharge order in four weeks from the time of your discharge, ask your attorney to follow up on it.

CHAPTER
SEVEN

Preparing Your Chapter 13 Schedules and Plan

What do you want to accomplish when you file a Chapter 13? You want to reduce your payments to creditors as low as the court will allow, and you want protection from those creditors while you are making these more-affordable payments. That is what your attorney should succeed in doing for you.

How does an attorney do this? It all begins with the information you give your attorney about what you own and what you owe. Your attorney uses this information to create your plan of reorganization, so the schedules should be as complete as possible. You must list all your assets, giving each its proper value, and you must list all your debts.

Your attorney should make sure the maximum exemptions are claimed in your behalf. This is important because it will determine the minimum amount of money you will be allowed to pay into your plan to satisfy your unsecured creditors.

Another section of the schedules your attorney should scrutinize, especially important in a Chapter 13, concerns your budget and statement of income. Your attorney needs to make sure, when creating a plan for you, that a realistic payment schedule that fits your budget is proposed. It does not help if the payments proposed in the schedule are too high for you to make. In reviewing the budget you provide, your attorney should know what the court in your district considers reasonable expenditures in all the categories listed in the budget.

Figure 7.1 illustrates the categories listed on the budget page you will be asked to complete in a Chapter 13 adjustment of debt program.

Once your attorney knows what you earn and what you have to spend on necessities, your reorganization plan can be created. The court will want

FIGURE 7.1

Monthly Expenses

Rent or Home Loan Payment		$_____
Utilities:		
Electricity	$_____	
Water	$_____	
Heat	$_____	
Telephone	$_____	
Other	$_____	
Total Utilities:		$_____
Food		$_____
Clothing		$_____
Laundry & Cleaning		$_____
Newspapers, Periodicals & Books (including school books)		$_____
Doctor & Medical Expenses		$_____
Transportation (not including auto payments to be paid under the plan)		$_____
Recreation, Club & Entertainment		$_____
Insurance (not deducted from wages):		
Auto	$_____	
Life	$_____	
Other	$_____	
Total Insurance:		$_____
Taxes (not deducted from wages or included in home loan payments)		$_____
Alimony or Support Payments		$_____
Payment for Support of Additional Dependents Not Living at Your Home		$_____
Other (explain): _____		

_____

_____

_____

you to pay as much as you can afford after expenses. Your attorney should be concerned that the proposed plan is one you can comfortably afford. If you propose any amount that would be questioned by the court, your attorney should ask you to explain it.

The Chapter 13 Plan

To understand how your attorney creates a Chapter 13 plan, you need to know how different creditors are treated in a Chapter 13. All your debts are divided into three major categories: *priority, secured* and *unsecured claims.*

The debts that make up the first category are called priority claims because they will have to be paid in full over the term of the plan. Taxes are the most common examples of priority claims. They can be property taxes or income taxes or any other type of taxes. For example, if you owe $3,000 in taxes, you can pay them out over the full 60 months that the plan can run. That means your attorney would begin developing the plan by budgeting $50 a month for the taxes you owe.

With the 1994 revisions to the Bankruptcy Code, alimony, maintenance and support payments are also treated as priority claims now.

The new bankruptcy laws have added another kind of debt that has to be paid in full in a Chapter 13. It treats a criminal fine as a nondischargeable debt. For instance, if you were convicted of a crime such as writing "hot" checks and the criminal court judge said you had to pay a criminal fine of $100 besides paying restitution on the checks, the $100 as well as the restitution would have to be paid in full in the Chapter 13 plan.

The next category is secured debts. A debt is called *secured* if it has a specific asset, such as a car, furniture or house, pledged to it. This category is divided into the money owed on a homestead, the house where you live, and money owed on everything else, such as your car and furniture.

How Your Home Mortgage and Other Secured Debts Are Paid

You cannot modify the rights of a creditor who has a lien on your home. That means you will make the same payments each month that you contracted to pay when you took out the loan. However, if you were four months behind on your payments and the mortgage company was about to foreclose on the property before you filed your Chapter 13, the mortgage company would not be able to take your home, and you would be allowed to pay the past-due payments, plus interest, over the term of the plan. With the passage of the 1994 revisions to the Bankruptcy Code, you no longer have to pay interest on the amount of the mortgage that is in arrears. There are exceptions to this, however, including if your mortgage agreement requires you to do so and if a nonbankruptcy law in your state requires it. However, this exception only applies to new or refinanced loans made after October 22, 1994. All loans entered into before that date will come under the old law, and the lienholder will be entitled to interest on the arrearage paid under the plan. Usually, the amount in arrears will be paid over 36 months; if you need to pay over a longer period of time and can justify it to the judge, you will be given additional time.

Another change in the law that concerns home mortgages deals with the problem that arises when the entire mortgage is due, perhaps because the loan had a balloon payment, and the debtor cannot make that one large payment. The new law says a debtor can pay off the balloon payment over the five years under a Chapter 13 plan.

The way you pay for your car, furniture or other secured debts can be modified too. The debtor is allowed to pay the value of the collateral over the term of the plan. For example, if you owe $10,000 on your car and are making monthly payments of $350, but the car is only worth $6,000, then you may pay $6,000 in smaller monthly payments over the term of the plan. This usually results in your paying back to the secured creditor a lower amount than you originally contracted to pay.

You May Not Have To Pay 100 Percent of Your Debts

Unsecured debts are dealt with last. Your attorney determines the minimum that you can pay to your unsecured creditors by looking at the value of your nonexempt property. This is the property that you would have to give up to a trustee if you filed a Chapter 7 liquidation bankruptcy. The rule is that the unsecured creditors must receive, over the term of the plan, as much as they would have gotten if you had filed a Chapter 7 liquidation bankruptcy. If you have $1,000 worth of nonexempt property, you must pay at least $16.60 a month to your unsecured creditors over a 60-month term. That is the minimum. If you can afford to pay more, after paying your living expenses, priority claims and secured claims, the court wants you to do so.

When your attorney has completed your schedules and plan, you will be asked to read and sign them. Go over them and make sure you understand what obligations you are undertaking. If you feel concerned about anything at all in the plan, discuss those concerns with your attorney.

How To Make Payments on Your Plan

Thirty days after your attorney files your plan and schedules with the court, you will be expected to start making payments on your plan. You will make these payments to the trustee who has been appointed to your case. Your attorney will give you the name and address of the trustee.

Some districts allow you to mail the payments directly to the trustee. Others insist that the payments be taken out of your paycheck and sent to the trustee by your employer. If your district requires payments to be deducted from your paycheck, and you feel this may cause problems with your employer, tell your attorney in advance. Your attorney may be able to file a motion with the court asking that you be excused from this requirement. Your attorney should also inform you that it is against the law for your employer to discriminate against you because you have filed a Chapter 13.

What Happens After Your Plan Is Filed

After the plan and schedules are filed, your attorney should make sure your creditors are notified so that they will stop all collection activity. The attorney usually does this by sending a letter to each creditor, or he or she may call your creditors the day your petition is filed and give notice to them over the phone.

Telephone notification is necessary when there is a possibility that a creditor is about to repossess something of yours. Make sure you know which creditors are notified and whether they were notifed by mail or phone.

After notifying your creditors so that they cease their collection activity against you, your attorney will start the process of contacting the priority and secured creditors involved in the case. At this time your attorney should try to work out all disagreements with these creditors.

In addition, during the period after your bankruptcy petition has been filed, your attorney will also make sure the trustee has all the necessary documents in your case.

The Trustee's Role in a Chapter 13 Program

When you file a Chapter 13 reorganization, the court appoints a trustee to your case. The trustee's duties include administering the plan. Besides receiving the money you pay toward your debts and disbursing that money to your creditors, the trustee, as an adviser, also monitors the success of the plan.

In some districts, the trustee is involved with the Chapter 13 process from the very beginning. Some trustees assist debtors in formulating their plans. More commonly, though, debtor and attorney propose a plan, then the trustee reviews it.

First Meeting with the Trustee

In most districts, the first time you see the trustee is at the initial meeting for your case. This is known as the first meeting of creditors (see p. 58) because creditors may attend to determine how their claims are going to be treated under your plan. By the time of this first meeting of creditors, the trustee will have already begun reviewing your case. The purpose of the trustee's review is to determine whether your budget allows reasonable amounts for each category. The trustee will not recommend confirmation of your proposed plan if you have not budgeted enough money for your personal needs. In such a situation it would be unreasonable to assume you could actually afford what you intend to pay your creditors. Reviewing your case before the first meeting and questioning you at the meeting concerning your Chapter 13 fulfill the duty of the trustee to investigate your financial affairs.

Other Major Duties of the Trustee

The other major duties of the trustee that arise at the beginning of your case include presiding over the meeting of creditors, examining the claims submitted by your creditors and objecting to any improper claims. In some districts, the trustee leaves it up to the debtor and the attorney to object to improper claims, on the theory that they are in a better position to know if the claim is improper. Ask your attorney how the trustee in your district handles this important duty. If the trustee handles improper creditors' claims, you will not have to pay your attorney a fee for this extra work.

After presiding over the creditors' meeting, the next duty of the trustee is to recommend or oppose confirmation of your plan. The trustee may oppose it if he or she believes that the proposed plan is impractical, if you cannot afford to comply, or if the plan is in "bad faith" or not your best effort.

In most districts, the trustee's recommendation carries great weight with the judge, who must decide whether to grant you a Chapter 13 reorganization. Be cooperative with the trustee: First impressions do matter.

Besides the importance of a recommendation to obtain confirmation of your plan, you want to get off on the right foot with the trustee because you will deal with each other regularly during your Chapter 13 reorganization.

When you have successfully hurdled the first obstacle, obtaining the judge's approval of your proposed Chapter 13 plan of reorganization—and you are paying the trustee the monies that go toward paying your creditors—you may need financial counseling. This leads to one of the most controversial duties of the trustee. According to the statutory provisions of a Chapter 13, the trustee must advise, other than on legal matters, and assist the debtor in performance under the plan. Controversy surrounds what "advise" and "assist" mean.

Records from the districts that have had Chapter 13 cases for many years show the most successful programs are those in which the trustee does more than just disburse money. In successful districts, the trustee works closely with the debtors, providing advice about financial matters, finding programs that teach debtors how to handle their money more efficiently and doing everything possible to ensure that these people have an opportunity to learn better ways to manage their money. For instance, a trustee can provide instructions on budgeting and on how to determine whether you can afford future credit. The trustee can give pointers on the following issues: how to live within your means; how to prepare for an emergency; the importance of savings; what to consider when trying to decide on major purchases like homes and cars; the importance of continued education; learning new job skills to improve your present position; and job retraining in another skill, should you lose your job. In other words, the trustee can teach debtors the importance of being aware of the potential consequences of a financial decision and of understanding what that decision might cost them.

Trustees May Advise

Trustees vary a great deal in the degree to which they advise and assist. Some districts have mandatory debtor schools that teach skills in financial matters. In other districts, the trustee is available at regular hours to discuss, on a one-to-one basis, whatever financial questions a debtor may have. Unfortunately, in some districts, the trustee does little more than disburse money to creditors. If you are in a district where the trustee takes an active role in advising and assisting debtors, the trustee's help will be of great benefit to you. If you have hired an attorney who specializes in bankruptcy law, he or she should be able to tell you the policies of the trustee in your area.

How Trustees Are Paid

It is also important for you to know how trustees are paid for their services. Basically, the code says that up to 10 percent of what you pay toward your debts goes to administrative costs and salary for the trustee. The percentage varies according to the amount of money paid into confirmed Chapter 13 plans in a particular district. It works like this: with the help of your attorney, you propose to pay your creditors a specific amount of money; let's say $100 per month. If your district permits the trustee to take the full 10 percent for administrative costs and salary, $10 will go to the trustee, and $90 will be disbursed to your creditors.

If you cannot pay your creditors 100 percent of what you owe them, you pay only what you can afford, no matter what the trustee takes. However, if you can afford to pay 100 percent to your creditors, the trustee's fee for services performed will be added to that. Remember, the court wants you to pay as much as you can afford.

The Creditors' Meeting

Usually, the first real contact with the court system for debtors who file Chapter 13 reorganization is at the creditors' meeting. You need to understand the significance of this meeting because it is important in getting your plan confirmed by the judge. Understanding the process will, perhaps, ease your anxiety.

The court sets a certain time for the meeting, and you will receive notice far enough in advance to arrange your work schedule. The trustee presides over this meeting. Any creditors who want to can attend the meeting to discuss how their claims are being treated. The tone of this meeting is usually informal, although creditors' attorneys may be aggressive in their questioning.

Preparing for the Meeting

Before the meeting begins, your attorney will try to talk to all the creditors present with the goal of finalizing these issues: exactly what is owed, the value of collateral and the amounts in arrears on large debts, such as mortgages on your home. Your creditors may also want to know whether you have insurance on the collateral that secures their loan, since insurance is required. In addition, your attorney and the creditors may discuss potential problems in your case and attempt to reach compromises on these problems.

While your attorney tries to settle these details with the representatives of your various creditors, you will wait for your case to be called by the trustee. It may help, while you wait, to observe the creditors' meetings of other debtors that are scheduled before yours. Doing so may lessen your nervousness and prepare you for what to expect. You can do this only if the creditors' meetings are held in an open courtroom. Sometimes they are not.

When your case is called, you, your attorney and any creditors' representatives will come forward to a table where a trustee presides. The trustee will swear you in and then ask questions about the petition that has been presented to the court in your case. You will be asked to confirm that you are the person who filed this petition and to confirm that you still earn your money as you stated in the petition and that your income is the same. The trustee will ask if all the information on your schedules is true and correct.

Notify Your Attorney Before You Make Any Changes

Any changes should have been discussed with your attorney before the creditors' meeting, so a determination could be made about how the change affects this proceeding. Occasionally, in a Chapter 13 adjustment of debt program, a debtor suddenly thinks that if he tells the trustee he earns less, it will mean he will pay less. Usually the attorney has proposed a plan that will be accepted by the court; a sudden change jeopardizes the plan's chance of being confirmed. So, cooperate with your attorney and discuss any changes before you go to the creditors' meeting. Don't do anything that will take your attorney by surprise.

Here is an example of one way a sudden change can work against you. Assume that your plan provides for a minimum payment to creditors, and one of your creditors holds a note on your car. Your attorney has determined the minimum payment that would enable you to keep the car and pay something to your other creditors. Later however, if you say that your income has dropped, instead of showing that you would have to make smaller payments on your debts, it may show that you do not earn enough to pay the minimum necessary to afford to keep the car.

You must begin paying the trustee 30 days after you file your petition, before the creditors' meeting and confirmation of your plan. However, if you have not begun paying the trustee before the creditors' meeting, have your first payment ready to present at the meeting. This will make a good impression on the trustee and will demonstrate your good faith. The trustee cannot disburse these funds until after confirmation, so if for any reason your plan is not confirmed, the money must be returned to you.

After the creditors have been dealt with and the trustee has asked questions and perhaps issued some instructions, the meeting will conclude. Probably you will leave this meeting knowing when the confirmation hearing will be held, whether or not the trustee is going to recommend that your plan be confirmed and whether any creditors are going to object to the court's confirming your plan.

 WARNING

Do not surprise your attorney with new information at the time of a hearing. Discuss changes with your attorney before hearings.

CHAPTER
EIGHT

Handling Objections to Confirmation: Creditors' Rights and Duties

During the creditors' meeting, you may discover that one or several creditors object to the confirmation of your Chapter 13 plan. On what grounds can a creditor object, and what are creditors' rights and duties? Various creditors' claims are categorized by the court, and the law specifies how those claims must be treated.

Creditors' claims are divided into three categories: *secured, unsecured* and *priority claims.* Some creditors' claims may be considered both secured and unsecured. (See also the section on priority, secured and unsecured claims at the beginning of Chapter 4.)

Proof of Claims

Before these claims can be considered, the creditor must file a proof of claim with the court. If proof is not filed within certain specified times, the creditor's right to have his or her claim considered may be forfeited.

Secured creditors have 90 days after the first meeting of creditors to file their proof of claim. Failure to do so will mean that the secured creditor can be treated as an unsecured creditor and will receive less money from you under the plan. If the secured creditor does not file in time and is treated as unsecured, he or she still retains security interest in the collateral; this means you may get some immediate relief on that particular debt, but when the Chapter 13 plan ends or if you ever sell the collateral, you still will have to deal with that creditor in order to clear the title.

Unsecured creditors have 90 days after the first meeting of creditors to file their proof of claim. If a claim is not filed within this period, the unsecured creditor loses all rights to receive money from you under the Chapter 13 plan. The money that would have gone to that unsecured creditor will then pass to your other creditors, up to the point of payment in full, if your plan proposes less than 100 percent payout to your creditors. If enough creditors do not file proof of claim, you might have your Chapter 13 reorganization plan shortened and concluded before the completion of the 36-month or 60-month term.

How Claims Are Treated

If the creditor's claim is filed on time, it can be treated according to its particular classification: priority, secured or unsecured.

Priority claims must be paid in full. The most common priority claims are taxes owed, such as federal income taxes. This type of debt can be paid out in monthly installments over the length of your plan or in any other way, such as from the sale of an asset. No matter how you do it, the debt must be paid in full. Since the IRS is prevented from trying to collect from you while you are under the protection of a Chapter 13 plan, a reorganization may offer peace of mind and an affordable way to pay the IRS.

Another example of claims that must be paid in full are criminal fines. The Bankruptcy Reform Act of 1994 made these nondischargeable in Chapter 13 cases; this means that unless the fine is paid during the bankruptcy, it will remain as an obligation of the debtor after his or her reorganization plan has been completed.

Other claims that must be paid in full are claims for alimony, maintenance and support as well as student loans that became due less than seven years before the filing of the bankruptcy. So, for example, if your ex-spouse filed for bankruptcy and you were expecting alimony payments, you would still be entitled to receive them. Also, any claim for death or personal injury due to the debtor's operation of a vehicle, if such operation was unlawful because the debtor was intoxicated from using alcohol, drugs or other substances, must be paid in full.

There are several options with secured claims, and there are several different types of secured creditors. Each type is treated differently. Your three options for treating a secured debt are discussed below.

1. *The collateral may be returned to the creditor, who will then sell it.* If the creditor does not sell the property for enough to cover what you owe, the remaining balance is called a *deficiency;* that part of the debt changes status to become unsecured and is treated the same as other unsecured debts, as described in this section.

2. *The rights of a secured creditor may be modified by the debtor paying only the value of the collateral, stretched out in monthly installments over the term of the plan, with some interest added.* This is the option chosen by many debtors. It is one of the special benefits of Chapter 13: *You may pay less than you owe on the debt to keep an asset.* The most common example of this is your automobile. Say you owe $8,000 and the current value, determined usually by the *National Automobile Dealers Association Guidebook (The Blue Book),* is $6,000. You are entitled to pay the $6,000 in monthly installments over the length of the plan, with some interest, and the car will be yours. Such an arrangement can result not only in a great reduction in your monthly car payments but also a great savings in what you pay overall. You can use the option of paying just the value of the collateral for furniture, boats or any other personal property you own. However, the modification of a secured creditor's rights does not apply to the mortgage company that carries your home loan.

3. *The debtor can pay the secured creditor the remainder of the original contract amount, especially if the collateral is worth more than you owe on it.* For example, you may own a car that is worth $8,000, and you may owe $6,000 on it. In such an instance, you may want to pay the secured creditor the remainder of the original contract amount, if you can afford to, because of a special relationship you may have with that creditor. For instance, that creditor might be the credit union where you work, and you may feel that if the credit union's rights are modified, your job may be affected in some way. Although the law says that a person cannot be fired because he or she has filed for bankruptcy, there have been

instances where credit unions have found ways to get rid of a person who filed for bankruptcy.

If you want to take advantage of this option, remember that you can pay the original contract amount only if the property that secures the debt is worth more than what you owe on it.

These three options apply to most secured creditors; however, you should be aware of the two exceptions discussed below.

1. *Your home mortgage cannot be modified, although you can cure any default in your mortgage payments through your Chapter 13 plan.* For example, if you are two months behind in your house payments, you can pay off back payments in monthly installments through your Chapter 13 plan, while you continue current payments. If the entire note on your home becomes due according to the terms of the note and you can not pay it, you can file a Chapter 13 and pay the entire balance over the five years of your reorganization plan. This is due to changes in the law resulting from the Bankruptcy Reform Act of 1994.

2. *Non-purchase-money, non-possessory secured liens exist when you borrow money from a finance company, and they ask you to put up your household goods as collateral for the loan.* The money borrowed is not used to buy the furniture, so it is *non-purchase money;* you, not your creditor, keep possession of the furniture, so it is *non-possessory.* The law gives you a big break in some states if you have a secured claim like this when you file for bankruptcy. In bankruptcy you can void the lien this creditor has on your household goods, and then you can treat that claim as unsecured.

Unsecured claims are debts for which there is no security, such as debts owed to credit card companies or to doctors. Here the court can substantially reduce your payments to creditors. Unsecured creditors usually do not receive interest, so the 18 percent to 22 percent that you are now being charged on some unsecured debts is eliminated.

As long as you treat all the unsecured creditors equally in your plan, you do not necessarily have to pay the unsecured creditors 100 percent of what you owe them. The court would like you to pay 100 percent. However, if you cannot afford to, you pay only what you can.

How To Handle Objections to Your Plan

At some time before your plan is confirmed by the court, one or more creditors may object to its confirmation. The most common objections center around how your plan intends to treat a creditor's claim. If the claim is not treated as described earlier in this chapter, the creditor can object to confirmation of your plan in order to receive the proper treatment.

The objection will come in the form of a legal document entitled "Objection to Confirmation of the Debtor's Plan." It will spell out what the creditor finds objectionable about your plan. At this point, your attorney will discuss the objection with the creditor to determine if it is valid and, if so, whether a compromise can be worked out. If no agreement can be reached, a hearing is held. The creditor's objection is usually heard at the time of the confirmation hearing. The hearing on the objection consists of the creditor's explaining the objections to the court, usually through witnesses. Your attorney will present your side of the objection. You might be asked to testify, and sometimes witnesses will testify for your side. The judge, after hearing both sides, will decide who is right.

If the judge decides in your favor, your plan will be confirmed as you proposed it. If the creditor wins, the plan will be adjusted accordingly.

In most cases there are no objections. However, you need to know that the possibility exists. In some districts, the creditors are particularly litigious, and the court encourages them. If you live in such a district, the likelihood of an objection to your plan is much greater.

 WARNING

Make sure you are current on your payments to the trustee by the time of the confirmation. Starting off your plan in default could cause the court to deny your plan or dismiss your case.

CHAPTER NINE

The Confirmation Hearing

At the confirmation hearing your plan is actually presented to the judge, and a decision is made about whether you are going to get what you requested in your plan. Each district in the United States has its own way of handling the procedures of this particular hearing. You need to know exactly what the court is considering and what you can do to improve the chances of having your plan confirmed.

Each district handles the hearing procedures differently. Basically, however, after you have gone through a creditors' meeting, a time is set for the presentation of your plan to the appropriate judge. Creditors will have time before the confirmation hearing to object to your confirmation, and their objections are usually heard at this hearing. If there are no objections from your creditors, the trustee presents your plan to the court for confirmation. It is assumed that the trustee has already reviewed and approved your petition, and the judge simply accepts his recommendation and confirms your plan. Sometimes the judge asks questions about the case. Consult your attorney to find out how the court in your district handles the procedures of the confirmation hearing and whether you have to appear.

For your appearance at the hearing, dress conservatively and do not wear jewelry. Bankruptcy judges, as a rule, are conservative. They want to give the rights and privileges of Chapter 13 to deserving people. Encourage this by your appearance and demeanor.

Requirements for Confirmation

However different the procedures are in each district, all the courts, in their own particular way, consider the same issues in a Chapter 13 case when deciding whether or not to confirm it. Be sure you understand each of these issues and know what the court expects from you. Consider your situation in relation to these issues to see if there might be any problems getting your plan confirmed. The following requirements of confirmation are paraphrased to make them more understandable.

Requirement One: *The proposed reorganization plan complies with all the rules and provisions of Chapter 13.*

This requirement covers the technical aspects of Chapter 13. In other words, were the forms complete and were they filed on time? These technical problems usually do not prevent a plan from being confirmed, because they can all be cured if there is a fault. However, any problems in this area often irritate the court because they cause delay and extra work. This is one of the reasons you hire an experienced attorney to help you with your Chapter 13. It is the attorney's job to know what is required in presenting the petition to the court. The attorney should be familiar with the local rules, which vary from district to district, as well as with the rules of bankruptcy procedures. If the papers as presented to the court appear professional and provide all the information the court needs to make its decision, and if the petition is presented properly and on time, you will have won the initial good will of the court.

Requirement Two: *You have paid your filing fee.*

The fee for filing a Chapter 13 is $160. Usually this is not a problem, but there may be rare cases in which a person needs the protection of a Chapter 13 but cannot even afford the filing fee. If this is true in your case, you can apply to the court to pay the $160 in installments.

Requirement Three: *You have proposed your plan in good faith.*

Of all the requirements, "good faith" is the vaguest and has caused the most problems in the courts. Courts across the country have not uniformly decided what the term means. The issue of good faith most commonly arises when debtors propose plans that pay unsecured creditors nothing or a very low percentage of the debt owed. Some courts confirm these plans. Other courts will not confirm them, claiming that it is not good faith to propose such a low percentage to unsecured creditors. No one knows what the final answer will be on this issue.

"Good Faith"

"Good faith" is the hook on which the court will hang a denial of confirmation if the judge feels you do not deserve the benefit of bankruptcy protection. The code says that the court must confirm your plan if all of the requirements are met. However, the good faith requirement gives judges much discretion in making the final decision. For the average person filing Chapter 13 for the purpose intended, there will be little problem with good faith. The basic question to ask yourself is, "Why am I doing this?" If the answer is, "Because I want to find a way to meet my obligations in a manner I can afford," you are using the law as it was intended, and you will have little trouble with a judge deciding that you are not filing in "good faith."

Requirement Four: *You are paying the unsecured creditors at least as much as they would have received if you had filed a straight Chapter 7 bankruptcy.*

If you were to file straight bankruptcy, the court would look at all your assets and allow you to keep all the property that is considered exempt. The trustee would take all the nonexempt property and sell it, so that the proceeds could be disbursed to the unsecured creditors after all your priority claims were paid. Assume that if this were done in your case, your unsecured creditors would receive 20 percent of their claims. That means they must receive at least 20 percent of their claims under your Chapter 13. The difference is that all your assets are not sold to pay the 20 percent or 30 percent or 100 percent that the unsecured creditors must receive. You get to keep your assets in return for promising to pay, out of your future income, that amount to the unsecured creditors. Unsecured creditors do not receive any interest, so 20 percent paid over 36 months is a lot better for you than 20 percent paid at once from the sale of your assets. Of course, that is the bare minimum the creditors must receive for you to qualify for a Chapter 13; the court wants you to pay as much as you can afford.

However, most people are so heavily burdened with debt when they take advantage of Chapter 13, and their income is so low, that they can pay only minimum amounts. Sometimes debtors want to try paying their creditors over a 60-month period, which is the maximum allowed, in order to pay more to their creditors.

Requirement Five: *The secured creditors either receive their collateral or are paid the value of the collateral over the term of the plan while retaining their lien on the collateral.*

Most debtors have creditors who secured their debts with collateral. The most common example is the debt you owe when you buy a car or furniture. As explained before, this creditor is secured because of the lien they take against the property they sold to you. The lien allows them to re-possess the property if you do not make your debt payments to them. The threat of property repossession is usually what prompts people to file bankruptcy.

The court requires you, if you have a secured creditor, either to return the property, if you cannot pay for it, or pay the value of the collateral over the length of the plan. Most people do not want to give up the collateral and are in a Chapter 13 to find a way to keep the property. So, assume that you have decided to keep the property. Remember, it is your decision. The court will not force you to give up property, although it will insist that you be realistic. If you decide to keep the property, the court, before confirming your plan, will make you demonstrate that you can afford it.

Can You Afford a Chapter 13 Plan?

What exactly must you afford? You have to pay the value of the collateral. For instance, if you have a car that you are financing and you owe $10,000 on it, but the value of the vehicle is $8,000, you will pay the $8,000 over the length of the plan (usually 36 months), with appropriate interest added to compensate the creditor for receiving the money over 36 months. You can see that, in most instances, the value of the collateral is less than what you owe; being allowed to pay that over time will reduce your original payments. This is one of the ways Chapter 13 makes it possible for you to afford the property.

The issues that arise before your plan can be confirmed concern the property value and an appropriate interest rate. In most districts, these details are worked out by agreement. If you have an inexperienced attorney or try to handle your own case, the creditor's attorney may get more than the creditor is entitled to, because you do not know any better.

If a value cannot be agreed upon, a valuation hearing must be held. Both sides will have a chance to present evidence about the value of the property, and the judge will decide what value should be used.

The creditor must retain a lien on the property while being paid under the plan. The proposed plan must recite this language because, once your plan is confirmed by the court, all of your property that was brought under the jurisdiction of the bankruptcy court by the filing of your Chapter 13 will be vested back in you, the debtor. Unless there is a provision in your plan for the secured creditor to retain a lien on your property, vesting the property in you will result in the creditor losing his or her lien.

This rule about secured creditors applies to all secured creditors except those who have a security interest in the real property that is your residence. In other words, as far as your house mortgage is concerned, you cannot modify that creditor's rights except to pay the amount in arrears through the plan. So you will still make the same monthly payments for the note on your home.

The court does not look too closely into what you propose to give secured creditors, because it usually assumes that the secured creditors are looking out for their own interests and that they have required you to give them what they are entitled to under the law. However, this is one of the requirements for confirmation, so you must propose a plan that complies with this rule.

Requirement Six: *The debtor has the ability to make the payments under the plan.*

If a creditor objects to the confirmation of your plan, your ability to pay is one of the issues that will come under close scrutiny. A creditor might complain that you will not be able to pay for the property, even with reduced payments. The amount you pay under a Chapter 13 will be compared with your income and expenses. The court usually would have given this some attention also.

Above all, the court wants your Chapter 13 to succeed, so it tries to make sure your proposed plan is practical. The first consideration is your income. You may not have to prove what you earn unless a creditor objects and uses this as one of the grounds for objecting. Usually the court will believe you; however, the trustee can request some proof of your income.

The court wants to make sure that your budget is appropriate. In preparing a budget for your petition, so many variables are at play that a realistic budget could be extremely difficult to construct. After all, you are going to be under the plan for three years. Has that been considered? Have you considered the fluctuations in utility bills over a year's time? These and many other considerations will influence the court's decision that you have a practical plan.

Do You Earn Enough To Qualify?

One of the major problems in preparing your plan for confirmation comes at the juncture of comparing your budget with your income and how much you have to pay creditors to allow you to keep the property you want. If you earn $1,500 a month and your expenses are $1,400 a month and you need to pay your creditors the minimum of $200 a month to be able to keep the collateral, a major problem exists. This problem can be resolved in several ways, and to make sure your plan is confirmed, you must decide the direction to take before you get to the confirmation hearing.

If your budget cannot go any lower and you are already working two jobs and there is nothing to give up, then a Chapter 13 is not the correct remedy for you. Of course, you do not want to make this discovery at the confirmation hearing. That is why it is important to have an experienced attorney help you make realistic and appropriate decisions.

The court considers your proposed Chapter 13 plan in the light of applicable legal requirements. If there have been no objections to your plan by creditors or the objections that have been presented have been overcome and the court decides you have met all the requirements, it must confirm your plan.

When the court has confirmed your plan, what happens? You would already have made arrangements to start making your payments to the trustee. These payments should have begun within 30 days of filing Chapter 13. How the payments are to be made, and when, is usually left up to you. However, there is something you can do to get yourself off to a good start, which could be helpful in the successful completion of your plan.

Making Payments After Your Plan Is Confirmed

When you file a Chapter 13, your main responsibility is to make the payments to the trustee as you have proposed. Most people need to make this process as simple as possible so they can be free to concentrate on other matters, such as careers and families. One way to make it simple and automatic (mandatory in some districts), is to have the trustee deduct the payments from your paycheck, so you do not have to worry about them. Willingness to do this will impress your trustee and the court.

Modifications of a Chapter 13 Plan, Conversions and the Hardship Discharge

The confirmation of your plan signals a new start. Your debt payments become manageable. You are protected by the court from creditor harassment.

Most people in a Chapter 13 go on to improve their financial situations and succeed in returning to lives of normalcy. Some, however, are plagued by additional troubles. Several alternatives are available to debtors when something in their lives changes to affect their ability to pay on their plans.

Moratoriums

If you have a temporary setback, such as missing a paycheck because of illness, consult the trustee. Generally, the trustee will work with you informally to allow you to catch up on a missed payment. A creditor may complain about a missed payment but usually will not file an adversary proceeding with the court if just one payment is missed and if by some informal arrangement with the trustee you are actively catching up.

Modifications

Something may happen in your life that makes it impossible to continue paying on your plan as you agreed to: a job loss, a divorce, a long illness or even a death in the family. If you cannot continue to pay as scheduled, you must consider, first, a modification of your plan. In a modification, you ask the court to change the way you are paying on the plan. In other words, you try to get your payments lowered. The court may give you several options to accomplish this.

1. *The court may extend the time over which you are to pay.* For instance, if you are paying out your plan in 36 months, you may request that the plan be extended to 48 months or the maximum 60 months. Extending the time allows you to reduce the payments by paying secured creditors over a longer period.

2. *Plan payments may be reduced with a modification to pay your unsecured creditors less.* As long as you comply with the rule that creditors must receive as much as they would have received if you had filed a straight Chapter 7 liquidation bankruptcy, this option will be permitted. If you originally proposed paying unsecured creditors 80 percent of their claims, then you might want to propose paying them only 20 percent under your modification in order to lower your payments enough for you to afford the plan.

3. *You may agree to give up something you are paying for, in order to afford the rest.* For instance, you may be trying to pay for two vehicles. You may decide to give up one and have your plan modified to make the plan payments affordable and to give you a chance to pay for and keep your other assets.

How Modifications Work

Here's how you can file a modification. Your lawyer files a modification request with the court, and gives a notice to all your creditors. The creditors have an opportunity to object. If a creditor objects, the judge holds a hearing and listens to the creditor, who will usually complain about having his or her claim modified again. Then the judge listens as your attorney and/or you explain why you need the modification and then decides whether to allow the modification and whether or not to make you change the way you are treating the creditor who complained.

If no creditor objects and if your modified plan continues to meet all of the basic requirements of the original confirmation, the court will allow the modification. These basic requirements assume that you are contributing all of your disposable income to the plan.

Converting a Chapter 13 to Chapter 7

Sometimes you consider a modification and try every way imaginable to lower payments, but nothing can lower them enough for you to be able to keep making them. If this happens, your alternatives are to convert the case to a straight liquidation bankruptcy or to ask for a hardship discharge. Even though these alternatives follow different steps, the basic results are the same.

As discussed earlier, when you convert from a Chapter 13 to a Chapter 7 bankruptcy, you will be allowed, under a straight liquidation bankruptcy, to keep all your exempt property. All nonexempt property will be sold to satisfy your debts. All unsecured debts not satisfied by this process will be officially discharged. If any of your exempt property, such as a car, is still being paid for, you must continue to pay the creditor in order to keep the property.

How the Conversion Works

The procedures for converting a case to a liquidation bankruptcy are simple. Your attorney will file a request for conversion to a Chapter 7 bankruptcy with the court, along with any additional information the court requires. There will be no hearing. You have an absolute right to convert at any time.

Once the court converts your case to a Chapter 7 liquidation bankruptcy, a new trustee is appointed, another creditors' meeting is held and, finally, there is a discharge hearing to wipe out your debt. A new trustee will be appointed because Chapter 13 trustees do not get involved in Chapter 7 bankruptcies.

The Bankruptcy Reform Act of 1994 cleared up a problem related to the conversion of a case from a Chapter 13 to a Chapter 7. Prior to this act, bankruptcy courts differed about what they considered to be the property of the estate when such a conversion took place. Some courts argued that the property of a bankruptcy estate was the property that existed at the time the case was originally filed as a Chapter 13, meaning that any property the debtor acquired after filing was not part of the estate. Other courts asserted that the property of the estate also included any property that was accumulated after the bankruptcy was filed.

The new law says that the only property that is included in a bankruptcy estate is the property that was the debtor's property at the time the original Chapter 13 was filed and that the debtor still possesses at the time of conversion. This means that the debtor who converts to a Chapter 7 can keep more of his or her property. However, if the debtor converts in bad faith—lies to the court, does not cooperate with the trustee or does anything that would defraud a creditor—the property of the debtor's bankruptcy estate will also include all of the property that the debtor had at the time of the conversion.

The Hardship Discharge

A hardship discharge is very rare. It differs from a modification or conversion in that the requirements are as follows:

1. *The debtor's failure to comply with the Chapter 13 reorganization plan is due to circumstances that were not the debtor's fault or beyond the debtor's control.* For example, the debtor demonstrates that due to illness or disability, he or she can no longer work and therefore can no longer meet the terms of the plan. Loss of a job is not enough to merit a hardship discharge since it is assumed that the debtor can get another job.

2. *The unsecured creditors have received as much as they would have received under a straight liquidation bankruptcy, and a modification is not practical.*

To apply for a hardship discharge, your attorney will file a request with the court and a hearing will be held to determine if the requirements just outlined have been met. If they are, then all of your unsecured debts will be discharged or wiped out. Those that are not discharged, as in a straight liquidation bankruptcy, are: long-term debts, like mortgage payments on your house; purchase-money secured debts, like a car; debts for alimony, maintenance or support; priority claims, like taxes; and some consumer debts incurred after you filed Chapter 13.

If you have problems meeting the terms of your reorganization plan, consult the trustee and your attorney as soon as possible. You do not want to wait too long. Otherwise, sooner or later, the trustee or one of your creditors will file a motion to dismiss your case because you are not meeting the terms of your plan. If this happens, you should consult with your attorney to determine whether a modification, conversion or hardship discharge is your best alternative. It is important to note that a judge is more inclined to favor your side when a creditor objects to a modification if it is obvious that you recognized you were having a problem with your plan and took the initiative to address the problem.

The Discharge Hearing

Once you make your last payment on your Chapter 13 plan you stand ready for the court's last act to end your responsibility under the plan and to start you on a fresh beginning. That last act is the discharge of your debts. If, under your Chapter 13, you have paid your unsecured creditors at least 70 percent of their allowed claims, and the plan was your best effort proposed in good faith, you will retain the right to file a Chapter 7 liquidation bankruptcy, if needed, within the next six years. Of course, by the time you reach a discharge hearing in a Chapter 13 reorganization, you surely are saying to yourself, "I will never get into that trouble again." Unfortunately, it happens on occasion, and retaining the right to file a Chapter 7 liquidation bankruptcy has some value. Even if you were not able to pay 70 percent, you can still file another Chapter 13 reorganization at any time.

Comprehensive Chapter 13 Discharge

As mentioned before, a discharge under a Chapter 13 is more comprehensive than a discharge in a Chapter 7 bankruptcy. The only exceptions to discharge for a Chapter 13 debtor are child support, maintenance and alimony; long-term debts specified in the plan, such as home mortgages; and priority debts, such as taxes, student loans and personal injury and death claims that resulted because the debtor was driving a vehicle while intoxicated or under the influence of drugs. Criminal fines were added as a debt that cannot be discharged, according to the Bankruptcy Reform Act of

1994. Debts arising from fraudulent conduct, conversion or embezzlement are discharged in Chapter 13 at this time, although this may change in the future.

In a Chapter 13 discharge, the court will mail you a notice of your discharge. Generally, there will not be a discharge hearing. If there is, the judge will notify you of the hearing by mail, explaining when and where it is to take place. You may or may not have to attend this hearing. If you do, it is likely that you will be there with other debtors. After a roll call to make sure all debtors are present, the judge will speak with you. Afterwards, you will either receive a document signed by the judge, discharging you of all the debts you listed, with the exception of those listed earlier, or you will get it in the mail.

One last point is relevant at this time. If, for any reason, a discharge was granted through some fraud on the debtor's part, a creditor has up to one year after the discharge to bring this to the court's attention and to ask that the discharge be revoked.

Enough on the technical part of the discharge. If you have gotten this far, congratulations! You have accomplished a worthwhile feat. You have, through hard work and concentration on your responsibilities, satisfied your debts. You are ready to begin a new part of your life with a clear horizon.

CHAPTER
ELEVEN

Understanding Taxes and Bankruptcy

Wallace Stevens, an American poet who died in 1955, once wrote that money was a kind of poetry. That may be so. However, if you don't have any but you owe the tax man, your lack of money can be a kind of bad poem. When you owe money to the Internal Revenue Service (IRS) and have no means of paying your debt, filing for bankruptcy can offer the best relief. Only in bankruptcy court can you possibly stop an IRS collector, who is in hot pursuit, or wipe out taxes!

The changes in bankruptcy law brought about by the Bankruptcy Reform Act of 1994 make the bankruptcy court an even more attractive arena to do battle with the IRS. For example, the waiver of the government's sovereign immunity in bankruptcy court is a big help to debtors. However, some of the changes favor creditors who loan money to a debtor who uses the money to pay taxes. Now, after the 1994 changes in the law, this kind of debt will no longer be wiped out by bankruptcy. This chapter discusses common tax problems that can lead to bankruptcy and explains how taxes are treated in a bankruptcy and how bankruptcy can be used to limit the powers of the IRS and other taxing bodies.

Tax-Related Problems That Commonly Lead to Bankruptcy

Who files bankruptcy when they owe taxes? Here are some common examples:

- Small business owners who have closed their businesses and who were unable to pay their payroll taxes when things were really bad for their business. The amount they owe may be more than they can pay, and the IRS may be threatening to take their property.

- People whose income drops and who, as a result, are unable to pay the property taxes on their home. Or, people whose property taxes increase faster than their income. The taxing authority may be threatening to sue these people and to take and sell their property in order to wipe out their property tax debt.

- Business owners struggling to stay in business who just need a little time to pay back taxes—time enough to turn their business around. The IRS likes to close down businesses who get behind on payroll taxes.

- Women who become divorced and who are asked to pay the IRS taxes that their ex-spouse's business accumulated while they were married. Even if a woman had nothing to do with the business, if the former couple filed joint returns during their marriage, the IRS will go after the former wife if they are unable to collect from her ex-spouse.

Obviously, there are many different types of tax-related problems that can force a person into bankruptcy. No matter what the problem, however, all tax-related problems have one thing in common when bankruptcy becomes the best solution—the problem has reached a crisis point. This usually means that the taxing authority—federal, state or local—will no longer work with the person who owes the taxes and is threatening to either take some of the debtor's property away or to levy against his or her paycheck or bank account.

Stopping the IRS

Filing bankruptcy will stop all the IRS's collection efforts. The automatic stay that is invoked when you file for any type of bankruptcy will stop the agency from levying your account or paycheck, taking your property and from closing down your business.

WARNING

If the IRS levied against your bank account before you filed for bankruptcy, the agency will be able to take from your account the money you owed it. However, it won't be able to collect any new monies from you related to old taxes.

Once the automatic stay is in effect, the IRS is prohibited from taking a number of other actions. These actions include:

- *Offsetting tax refunds that may come to you in the future against tax liabilities.* This means that the IRS cannot apply future tax refunds to existing tax liabilities.

- *Attaching a tax lien to your property.* This is especially important in a Chapter 13 reorganization bankruptcy since it may mean you will pay less interest to the IRS.

- *Continuing to prosecute you in tax court.*

Beware of Actions That the IRS Can Still Take

The Bankruptcy Reform Act of 1994 describes some actions by the IRS that will not be stopped by the automatic stay. These include:

- *A tax audit.* If you are scheduled for an audit or are presently being audited, filing bankruptcy will not stop the audit. This was the case before the 1994 changes and continues to be the case. However, if you do file for bankruptcy, unlike other audits, the IRS cannot ask you for any money that the audit may have shown to be due. If you have filed a Chapter 7 and the taxes that are due are not dischargeable, the IRS may begin collection action once the bankruptcy has been discharged. If you filed Chapter 13 and you were audited for previous years' taxes, your Chapter 13 reorganization plan can be modified to include them so they can be paid off through the plan.

- *The assessment of taxes.* Before the 1994 changes in the law, the IRS couldn't assess taxes against a debtor once that person had filed for bankruptcy. This limitation affected how a person's tax debt would be treated in bankruptcy. Now, however, the IRS *can* assess any tax liability that is not contested by the debtor without getting the bankruptcy court's permission. But the agency cannot take collection action.

- *Demand the filing of tax returns.* The IRS can demand that you file any of the tax returns you have not filed.

Can Taxes Be Discharged in Bankruptcy?

Some kinds of taxes can be wiped out through bankruptcy. For example, income taxes that became due more than three years before a bankruptcy was filed can be discharged as long as certain requirements are met. These requirements include:

1. The income tax return had to be filed on time. If it wasn't, then it had to have been filed more than two years before the bankruptcy was filed.

2. The taxes had to be assessed more than 240 days before the filing of the bankruptcy. The tax is assessed when the IRS establishes the amount owed.

3. The filed tax return cannot be fraudulent. And the debtor cannot be willfully attempting to evade taxes.

4. The IRS cannot have taken a lien on the debtor's property.

Any IRS tax situations that don't meet these four stringent requirements will not be discharged.

It is important to know that the Bankruptcy Reform Act of 1994 includes a provision that says if a debtor borrowed money to pay taxes and if the taxes won't be wiped out through bankruptcy, then the borrowed money won't be discharged either. For example, if you got a cash advance on your credit card to pay your tax bill and you later filed bankruptcy, and if the credit card company can prove that you borrowed the money to pay taxes, then that company can ask the bankruptcy court to declare that the borrowed money will not be discharged. Also, the company would have the right to collect that money from you after you completed your Chapter 7 bankruptcy.

How You Can Benefit from the IRS's Loss of Sovereign Immunity

Before the new bankruptcy law was passed, one of the most frustrating aspects of dealing with the IRS was not being able to punish the agency if it violated bankruptcy rules. For instance, if a person filed for bankruptcy and the court invoked the automatic stay to stop further collection efforts by all of the debtor's creditors, including the IRS, and if the IRS continued to try to collect its taxes despite the automatic stay, in the past, the court could do very little to punish the agency for its transgression. Just about the most a bankruptcy judge could do was go "tsk, tsk." Now, however, with the 1994 changes, Congress has taken away the government's right of sovereign immunity in bankruptcy court matters. *Sovereign immunity* means that you cannot sue a government agency unless the government gives you permission.

When other entities violate the automatic stay, the courts usually punish them by ordering a money judgment. The court's theory in doing this is that hurting the pocketbook of the violator will make that entity less inclined to ignore the automatic stay again. But, before the 1994 change in the law, the court was prohibited from ordering a money judgment against the IRS for the same infraction.

Now that Congress has said sovereign immunity does not apply in bankruptcy court, a bankruptcy judge can order the government to pay for damages caused by any violation of the automatic stay. In other words, a debtor can get a money judgment against the IRS. This is a significant change in the law. Before this change, the Supreme Court had ruled in two cases that the IRS, as an agency of the government, was protected from damage actions unless it had somehow waived its right of sovereign immunity.

The real significance of this change will become apparent over time. At the very least we should see the government compensating individuals for any harm the IRS may do to them should it violate the stay. More importantly, we may see the IRS violate the rules less often.

However, you need to know that there are some restrictions on this important change. They are as follows:

1. Although a bankruptcy judge can issue any legal or equitable order against a government unit such as the IRS, the judge cannot enter an award for punitive damages on behalf of a debtor. This means an award for more than actual damages.

2. Awards by the court are limited by the hourly rate specified in the United States Code. This means, for example, that if actual damages

include paying for the debtor's attorney, that amount will be limited to the rate set by the government for attorneys, now $75 an hour.

3. The order issued by a bankruptcy judge cannot be enforced through the seizure of government property. So, if you get a money judgment against the IRS, you can't drive your truck up to an IRS office and haul off all of its computers to satisfy that judgment.

How Taxes Are Classified in Bankruptcy

When a Chapter 7 or Chapter 13 bankruptcy is filed, any taxes owed by the debtor are assigned to one of three different classifications. These classifications are important because they will determine how each tax debt will be treated in bankruptcy. In many cases, a debtor will owe all three types of taxes. These are the three main classifications:

1. *Secured.* If the IRS places a lien on your property to secure the taxes you owe, those taxes are secured taxes and cannot be discharged in bankruptcy. You will have three options to deal with this problem: 1. you can pay the IRS the value of its lien to get the lien released; 2. you can make arrangements to pay what you owe directly to the IRS in monthly payments; or 3. you can file a Chapter 13 bankruptcy so you will have three to five years to pay your tax debt.

2. *Priority.* This class of taxes is not secured by a property lien and cannot be discharged through bankruptcy. That means they will survive a Chapter 7 bankruptcy. To wipe out that debt, debtors must either make payments directly to the IRS or file a Chapter 13 and get three to five years to pay them off.

3. *General Unsecured.* This type of tax debt can be discharged through bankruptcy.

Which Bankruptcy Option Is Best When You Owe Taxes

If all of your taxes can be discharged and you have very little property, your bankruptcy decision is an easy one. You should file a Chapter 7 bankruptcy in order to wipe out your tax debt. Unfortunately most bankruptcy cases are not this simple.

For instance, what do you do when the IRS files a lien on your property for taxes that would otherwise be dischargeable? It depends. If the value of the property the IRS has a lien against is not much, you may still want to file a Chapter 7 bankruptcy and then pay the IRS the value of its lien in order to get it removed from your property.

Or, what happens if the value of the property the IRS takes a lien against is significant and you can't come up with the money necessary to get the lien removed? You could file a Chapter 13 bankruptcy and pay the value of the secured portion over the length of the plan—three to five years. The portion that is dischargeable would be treated like other unsecured creditors. And, because in a Chapter 13 you may only pay a portion of your unsecured creditors some of the taxes you owe, the IRS would be discharged. If you file a Chapter 13 to pay secured taxes, you will be required to pay interest on those taxes over the length of your plan. The interest is set by the bankruptcy court and is usually much lower than the interest rate charged by the IRS.

Occasionally, debtors have so much nondischargeable debt, including taxes, that they do not qualify for a Chapter 13. If this happens, some debtors file a Chapter 7 bankruptcy to wipe out as much debt as possible and then immediately file Chapter 13 in order to pay out the debts that couldn't be wiped out. Some attorneys call this a "Chapter 20."

Dealing with Past Due Trust Fund Taxes

If you had a business and you collected taxes from third parties for the IRS, like payroll taxes, those taxes are called *trust fund taxes* and cannot be discharged in bankruptcy. If you are a small business owner who owes trust fund taxes and if you are being pressed by the IRS to pay them, you can file a Chapter 13 that will stop IRS collection activities and will give you a three- to five-year period to pay off those taxes. If you have already shut down your business and you did not pay trust fund taxes while your business was operating, a Chapter 13 is also appropriate. It will protect you from the collection actions of the IRS while giving you a chance to pay your tax debt.

Owners of corporations are not necessarily safe from the IRS if the corporation owes trust fund taxes. Most likely, the IRS will assess each of the owners for the taxes owed. When the individual owners are assessed the taxes, the IRS terms it a penalty. That penalty (or tax debt) will not be discharged in bankruptcy.

Handling Property Taxes

Sometimes, property taxes on a house or land can cause problems for a debtor. If you do not pay these taxes, the taxing authority can usually take your house away from you and sell it in order to get its money. If you can't pay what you owe in property taxes and if you are in jeopardy of losing your house or land, filing Chapter 13 can help you. In Chapter 13 you can keep your property, and you'll have up to five years to pay your back property taxes.

Prior to the 1994 changes in the bankruptcy law, if a person filed Chapter 13 due to tax problems and if, while the debtor was paying off his old tax debt he was unable to stay current on the taxes that came due after he filed, the automatic stay prevented the taxing authority from placing a lien on the debtor's property for the new tax debt. Now, however, a taxing authority can place a lien on the debtor's property for taxes that come due after the bankruptcy has been filed, and it will not be violating the automatic stay.

If You Disagree with the IRS About Taxes Owed

If the IRS says that you owe back taxes and you disagree with the agency about the amount they say you owe or assert that you don't owe anything to the IRS, your attorney can litigate this issue in bankruptcy court when you file a Chapter 7 or Chapter 13 bankruptcy. To do this, you will need to file a motion objecting to the claim of the IRS. After you do so, the bankruptcy judge will rule on whether or not you owe taxes or on the amount of the taxes you owe. If the court rules that you owe taxes, it will also determine whether they are a secured, priority or general unsecured debt.

CHAPTER TWELVE

Divorce and Bankruptcy

Divorce and bankruptcy often go hand-in-hand. For example, it is not uncommon for divorced individuals, usually women, to be forced into bankruptcy after their divorce because their financial situation has deteriorated due to the change in their marital status. In addition, many men as well as an increasing number of women file for bankruptcy after a divorce because they are unable to meet the terms of their divorce agreement. Then, there are those who deliberately use bankruptcy as a way to get out of obligations they assumed when they signed their divorce agreement. The close relationship between divorce and bankruptcy has meant that many ex-spouses, usually women, become economically disadvantaged after their divorce.

In an effort to address the relationship between divorce and bankruptcy and to correct some of the social problems the relationship has helped create, the Bankruptcy Reform Act of 1994 made a number of changes related to divorce. (Many of the changes relate to separation as well although this chapter will focus just on divorce. Therefore, if you are separated or about to separate from your spouse, you may want to schedule an appointment with a certified bankruptcy attorney so that you understand how the 1994 changes in the law could affect you.) The main goals of the changes are to

- provide greater protection to persons whose ex-spouses file for bankruptcy and in the process wipe out their divorce obligations and other related debts they agreed to at the time of their divorce.

- provide greater protection to spouses, ex-spouses and to the children who are due support money.

This chapter will examine how Congress chose to achieve these goals by reviewing the most important divorce-related changes it made to the Bankruptcy Code and by discussing the implications of these changes.

The most important changes are the following:

- Adds a new category of nondischargeable debt to the Bankruptcy Code.

- Makes some divorce-related debts nondischargeable in certain circumstances and under certain conditions.

- Makes debts related to alimony, maintenance or support priority debts.

- Adds exceptions to the automatic stay.

- Changes the status of alimony, maintenance and support payments in regard to preferential transfers.

- Says that debtors may no longer use section 522(f)(I) of the Bankruptcy Code to avoid a judicial lien created to secure obligations that resulted from a division of property.

- Allows child support creditors and other representatives to appear at Bankruptcy Court proceedings.

Exceptions to the Nondischargeability of Alimony, Maintenance and Support Obligations

Alimony, maintenance and support obligations are treated as nondischargeable debts in both a Chapter 7 and a Chapter 13 bankruptcy. This means that if a divorced person files for bankruptcy, he cannot wipe out past due payments for these obligations. However, the former spouse who is owed these past due payments should not expect to begin receiving them as soon as the debtor has filed for bankruptcy.

If the bankrupt ex-spouse files Chapter 7, the former spouse can try to collect the past due payments from assets that are not part of the debtor's bankruptcy estate. The ex-spouse can also wait to collect until the debtor's bankruptcy has been discharged and the automatic stay has been lifted.

If the debtor is in Chapter 13, the debtor must pay all the past due alimony, maintenance or support payments he owes his ex-spouse during the life of his reorganization plan—usually three to five years. It is important to note that the filing of a bankruptcy will in no way affect a debtor's obligation to make all alimony, maintenance or child support payments that come due while he is in bankruptcy. The debtor will be expected to continue making those payments directly to his ex-spouse as they come due throughout his bankruptcy.

The Bankruptcy Reform Act of 1994 creates two exceptions to the nondischargeability of alimony, maintenance and support obligations:

1. If the person owed the alimony, maintenance or support voluntarily assigns the debt to another person or entity such as a private collection agency, the debt can be discharged through a Chapter 7 or a Chapter 13 bankruptcy.

2. If the court rules at the request of the debtor that although a debt is designated as alimony, maintenance or support, it really should be classified as another type of debt related to the debtor's change in marital status, a property settlement obligation, for example, the debt will be discharged. This applies to both Chapter 7 and Chapter 13 bankruptcies.

New Exception to Discharge of Debt

Prior to the changes in the law, "hold harmless" and property settlement obligations could be discharged through bankruptcy. This meant that if as part of their divorce agreement the nondebtor spouse agreed to let the debtor keep an asset or assets in exchange for a promise to pay her a set amount of money in installment payments, or to pay the third-party debts of the nondebtor spouse, or if the nondebtor spouse agreed to accept smaller alimony payments in exchange for being held harmless for debts incurred by both parties during their marriage, the debtor could use bankruptcy to wipe out the obligations he incurred by signing that agreement. As a result, it was not uncommon for the nondebtor spouse to end up with substantial debt to pay and with little or no alimony, maintenance or support. Now however, as a result of the 1994 changes to the Bankruptcy Code, "hold harmless" and property settlement obligations are nondischargeable under two conditions:

1. The debt will not be discharged if the court believes that the resources of the debtor are sufficient to allow the debtor to meet both the nonalimony, maintenance and support obligations as well

as his alimony, maintenance and support obligations. If the debtor can prove that he won't be able to meet both, all or a portion of the "hold harmless" and property settlements obligations will be discharged. Also, if the debtor can prove that not getting his alimony, maintenance and support obligations discharged will mean that he will not have enough resources to operate his business, the court can opt for a discharge.

2. The debt will not be discharged if the harm done to the nondebtor spouse should the debtor's "hold harmless" and property obligations be discharged outweighs the benefits the debtor would realize from having them erased.

This new exception to discharge contains an important catch for the former spouse of the person in bankruptcy. In order for the court to consider making an obligation of the debtor nondischargeable, the nondebtor spouse must file an adversary proceeding against the debtor within 60 days of the date of the first creditors' meeting. Such a proceeding is essentially a mini-law suit. What this requirement means is that unless the nondebtor spouse knows the law or retains an attorney once the debtor files for bankruptcy, the adversary proceeding will not be filed and the debtor's property obligations will be discharged. In addition, this stipulation in the law assumes that the nondebtor has the resources necessary to hire an attorney. Therefore, the true impact of this exception to discharge remains to be seen.

New Status for Alimony, Maintenance and Support Debts

Alimony, maintenance and support obligations have been elevated to priority status with the 1994 changes in the law. These debts will now enjoy a higher priority than tax debts and most unsecured debts. This new status means that such debts must be paid in full during a Chapter 13 and in a Chapter 7. They will get paid before most other creditors if there is any money to distribute. However, there are a few categories ahead of these kind of debts. This change increases the likelihood that an individual whose ex-spouse files for bankruptcy will receive the alimony, maintenance and support payments stipulated in the divorce agreement.

Alimony, maintenance and support debts that have been assigned to another individual or entity as well as debts arising from a marriage that are not in the nature of alimony, maintenance and support are not given priority status.

The Automatic Stay

Usually, when a debtor files for bankruptcy the first thing that happens is that the automatic stay is invoked to stop a debtor's creditors from continuing their collection efforts. However, bankruptcy law says that someone who is owed alimony, maintenance or support obligations can continue to collect these payments from the bankrupt debtor as long as they come from exempt assets—not part of the debtor's bankruptcy estate. In many states, these assets include future wages.

Also exempted from the automatic stay by the Bankruptcy Reform Act of 1994 are any actions necessary to establish the paternity of a child after a bankruptcy has been filed. So, if a divorced, separated or unwed woman had asked her state's attorney general to help her get child support and the alleged father of the child files for bankruptcy, the attorney general's actions can continue despite the bankruptcy. And, if the debtor is identified as the child's father, the debtor will be responsible for making child support payments.

Another exemption to the automatic stay allows a former spouse to establish or modify an order for alimony, maintenance or support without getting the bankruptcy court's permission first. Prior to the 1994 changes in the bankruptcy law, establishing or modifying an order required that the former spouse file a motion with the bankruptcy court requesting the court's permission to do so. Often this involved considerable expense for the former spouse and also created delays. However, if a person wants to begin or continue divorce proceedings and the proceedings involve the division of the property and debt the couple acquired during their marriage, should one of the parties to the divorce file for bankruptcy, the proceedings cannot continue until the nonfiling spouse files a motion to lift stay and gets the bankruptcy court's permission to go forward.

Preferential Transfers

Prior to filing a Chapter 7, if a debtor treats one creditor better than other creditors by making payments to that creditor and not to the others up to a year before filing bankruptcy, the court may view those payments as "preferential." In such an instance, the bankruptcy trustee will go after the money and return it to the bankruptcy estate so that it can be more equitably distributed among all eligible creditors. Under the old law, payments to a former spouse made prior to filing for bankruptcy could be treated as preferential. Now, however, the Bankruptcy Reform Act of 1994 says that those payments cannot be treated as "preferential transfers" in a Chapter 7.

Judicial Liens

In some divorce cases, under a division of property agreement, one spouse will secure the other spouse's promise to pay on a debt related to a division of property with a judicial lien against an asset of the other spouse. Under the old law, if the former spouse with the asset filed for bankruptcy, the law allowed that debtor to wipe out the lien if the lien was on exempt property. However, the 1994 changes to the law created an exception to this provision. The exception says that if the lien secures the obligation of one spouse under a division of property agreement, it cannot be wiped out through bankruptcy. This exception supplements and codifies the Supreme Court ruling in *Farrey v. Sanderfoot*. This ruling said that a former husband could not avoid a judicial lien on a house he used to own with his wife.

CHAPTER THIRTEEN

Conclusion: Making a Fresh Start

After you have completed your Chapter 13 reorganization plan or have been discharged in a Chapter 7 liquidation bankruptcy, you naturally want to know how to begin reestablishing your credit. Your credit record will probably show that you filed a Chapter 13 or a Chapter 7 and will also contain negative reports that might have been added by creditors at the time you were having trouble. Those notations will make it difficult to reestablish credit for seven to ten years. That is how long they are permitted to stay on your record. Since your Chapter 13 plan usually ends after three years, you face several more years with a bad credit history.

Do You Really Want More Credit?

Before telling you how to improve that situation, I would like to say that I think you should not be too anxious to obtain new credit. I believe people's lives would be happier if they lived more simply; this means not on credit. You secure a certain peace of mind when you spend only what you earn and do not work to satisfy continuous future obligations.

Since that opinion will be scoffed at by economists and ignored by most readers, who will find innumerable ways to rationalize the necessity of new credit, I will describe methods of reestablishing your credit. Remember, while you try these methods, that rebuilding credit is really rebuilding creditor confidence in your ability to pay your bills. You must meet your obligations promptly if you hope to obtain the good credit status you once had.

The Traditional Method of Rehabilitating Credit

Traditionally, the first part of starting over is finding a bank to do business with, a bank from which you have not previously borrowed money. Open a savings account at this bank, and when you have $500 in the account, approach the loan officer about borrowing a sum of money, using your savings account as collateral.

When you talk to the loan officer, be honest about your past credit problems and explain what you are trying to do, which is rebuild your credit. In most cases, the loan will be granted because the bank cannot lose. Most likely, it will charge the highest interest the law allows, and if you fail to pay, it can take your savings account.

After the loan is granted, do the same thing at another bank. Make the loan payments five days in advance of the date they come due. When the loans are paid off, go for larger loans. After a while you will have demonstrated to the bank that you are now a good credit risk. Then you will be able to use the bank to finance future purchases, like an automobile or furniture, on credit. You also will be able to use the bank as a credit reference.

When you have been paying on your loan for several months, contact the credit bureau in your area to make sure it has a history of your new credit. If it does not, ask your creditor to supply the information. The bureau will check out the information, then put it on your record.

The next step toward improving your credit is to obtain a national credit card, like Visa or MasterCard. Some savings and loans and banks will provide you with a Visa or MasterCard on a secured basis if you open a savings account at their institution. Your credit limit is a reflection of the amount you keep in the savings account. Companies that do this advertise in newspapers in the larger cities. You may even want to check with your local bank.

If you are unable to obtain a regular bankcard, an alternative is to apply for a secured bankcard. These cards were devised to meet the credit needs of people like you who are recovering from bankruptcy or from serious money troubles that damaged their credit history. Although you can use a secured bankcard just like a regular card, you must collateralize your credit purchases by opening a savings account at the bank issuing you the card or by purchasing a certificate of deposit from that bank. Using a secured bankcard responsibly over time is an excellent way of demonstrating that you are ready to have a regular bankcard.

After you have established credit with two banks and have national credit cards, you can begin to apply to local department stores that offer credit. When you have several of these, then apply for major gasoline credit cards.

Your success in obtaining new credit relates to your ability to convince creditors that you are now a good credit risk. Demonstrate this by paying your present obligations on time, by showing a stable job situation and by providing larger than normal down payments for large purchases.

The method we described is the most common approach to obtaining new credit. However, this method may not work for you. Remember, credit is a privilege that creditors give you. Some will never allow you that privilege again if you have had problems. Others will want you to obtain credit with them as soon as possible, on the theory that the sooner you start spending money with them again, the sooner they can recoup any loss they may have sustained in past dealings with you. There will be creditors who want you to prove yourself again.

Whether you live in a small town or a large one, your own initiative and luck all play a part in your ability to obtain new credit. Some people will be more successful than others. I hope that they will ever afterwards use their credit wisely, so they do not need to reread this book.

Appendix A
Chapter 7 Bankruptcy Forms

The forms that follow represent the basic forms that are filed with the court. In addition to these forms, each bankruptcy district in the United States may have local forms that also must be filed. There are so many different local forms that it is not practical to present all of them here. Your attorney should be familiar with the local rules in your area and with the additional forms required.

Forms may be purchased from Julius Blumberg, Inc., NYC 10013, or any of its dealers. Reproduction prohibited.

Form B1, P1 (12-94)

Julius Blumberg, Inc. NYC 10013

FORM 1 VOLUNTARY PETITION

United States Bankruptcy Court District of	**VOLUNTARY PETITION**
IN RE (Name of debtor-If individual, enter Last, First, Middle)	NAME OF JOINT DEBTOR (Spouse) (Last, First, Middle)
ALL OTHER NAMES used by the debtor in the last 6 years (including married, maiden and trade names)	ALL OTHER NAMES used by the joint debtor in the last 6 years (include married, maiden and trade names)
SOC. SEC./TAX I.D. NO. (If more than one, state all)	SOC. SEC./TAX I.D. NO. (If more than one, state all)
STREET ADDRESS OF DEBTOR (No. and street, city, state, zip)	STREET ADDRESS OF JOINT DEBTOR (No. and street, city, state, zip)
COUNTY OF RESIDENCE OR PRINCIPAL PLACE OF BUSINESS	COUNTY OF RESIDENCE OR PRINCIPAL PLACE OF BUSINESS
MAILING ADDRESS OF DEBTOR (If different from street address)	MAILING ADDRESS OF JOINT DEBTOR (If different from street address)

LOCATION OF PRINCIPLE ASSETS OF BUSINESS DEBTOR (If different from addresses listed above)	VENUE (Check one box)
	☐ Debtor has been domiciled or has had a residence, principal place of business or principal assets in this District for 180 days immediately preceding the date of this petition or for a longer part of such 180 days than in any other District. ☐ There is a bankruptcy case concerning debtor's affiliate, general partner or partnership pending in this district

INFORMATION REGARDING DEBTOR (Check Applicable boxes)

TYPE OF DEBTOR (Check one box) ☐ Individual ☐ Corporation Publicly Held ☐ Joint (H&W) ☐ Corporation Not Publicly Held ☐ Partnership ☐ Municipality ☐ Other _____ NATURE OF DEBT (Check one box) ☐ Non-Business Consumer ☐ Business - Complete A&B below A. TYPE OF BUSINESS (Check one box) ☐ Farming ☐ Transportation ☐ Commodity Broker ☐ Professional ☐ Manufacturing/Mining ☐ Construction ☐ Retail/Wholesale ☐ Stockbroker ☐ Real Estate ☐ Railroad ☐ Other Business B. BRIEFLY DESCRIBE NATURE OF BUSINESS	CHAPTER OR SECTION OF BANKRUPTCY CODE UNDER WHICH THE PETITION IS FILED (Check one box) ☐ Chapter 7 ☐ Chapter 11 ☐ Chapter 13 ☐ Chapter 9 ☐ Chapter 12 ☐ § 304-Case Ancillary to Foreign Proceeding SMALL BUSINESS (Ch.11 only) ☐ Debtor is a small business as defined in 11 U.S.C. § 101. ☐ Debtor is and elects to be considered a small business under 11 U.S.C. § 1121(e). (optional) FILING FEE (Check one box) ☐ Filing fee attached. ☐ Filing fee to be paid in installments. (Applicable to individuals only) Must attach signed application for the court's consideration certifying that the debtor is unable to pay fee except in installments. Rule 1006(b); see Official Form Number 3 NAME AND ADDRESS OF LAW FIRM OR ATTORNEY Telephone No.

STATISTICAL ADMINISTRATIVE INFORMATION (28 U.S.C. § 604) (Estimates only) (Check applicable boxes)	NAME(S) OF ATTORNEY(S) DESIGNATED TO REPRESENT THE DEBTOR (Print or Type)
☐ Debtor estimates that funds will be available for distribution to unsecured creditors. ☐ Debtor estimates that after any exempt property is excluded and administrative expenses paid, there will be no funds available for distribution to unsecured creditors.	☐ Debtor is not represented by an attorney. Telephone no. of debtor not represented by an attorney: ( )

	THIS SPACE FOR COURT USE ONLY
ESTIMATED NUMBER OF CREDITORS ☐ 1-15 ☐ 16-49 ☐ 50-99 ☐ 100-199 ☐ 200-999 ☐ 1000-over	
ESTIMATED ASSETS (in thousands of dollars) ☐ Under 50 ☐ 50-99 ☐ 100-499 ☐ 500-999 ☐ 1000-9999 ☐ 10,000-99,000 ☐ 100,000-over	
ESTIMATED LIABILITIES (in thousands of dollars) ☐ Under 50 ☐ 50-99 ☐ 100-499 ☐ 500-999 ☐ 1000-9999 ☐ 10,000-99,000 ☐ 100,000-over	
ESTIMATED NUMBER OF EMPLOYEES - CH 11 & 12 ONLY ☐ 0 ☐ 1-19 ☐ 20-99 ☐ 100-999 ☐ 1000-over	
ESTIMATED NO. OF EQUITY SECURITY HOLDERS - CH 11 & 12 ONLY ☐ 0 ☐ 1-19 ☐ 20-99 ☐ 100-999 ☐ 1000-over	

Julius Blumberg, Inc. NYC 10013

Form B1, P2 (12-94)

Name of Debtor: _____   Case No. _____
(Court use only)

FILING OF PLAN   For Chapter 7, 11, 12 and 13 cases only. Check appropriate box.

☐ A Copy of debtor's proposed plan dated _____ is attached.   ☐ Debtor intends to file a plan within the time allowed by statute, rule, or order of the court.

PRIOR BANKRUPTCY CASE FILED WITHIN LAST 6 YEARS (If more than one, attach additional sheet)

Location Where Filed	Case Number	Date Filed

PENDING BANKRUPTCY CASE FILED BY ANY SPOUSE, PARTNER, OR AFFILIATE OF THIS DEBTOR (If more than one, attach additional sheet.)

Name of Debtor	Case Number	Date
Relationship	District	Judge

REQUEST FOR RELIEF   Debtor is eligible for and requests relief in accordance with the chapter of title 11, United States Code, specified in this petition.

SIGNATURES

ATTORNEY   Signature X _____   Date _____

INDIVIDUAL/JOINT DEBTOR(S)

I declare under penalty of perjury that the information provided in this petition is true and correct

X _____
Signature of Debtor

_____
Date

X _____
Signature of Joint Debtor

_____
Date

CORPORATE OR PARTNERSHIP DEBTOR

I declare under penalty of perjury that the information provided in this petition is true and correct, and that I have been authorized to file this petition on behalf of the debtor.

X _____
Signature of Authorized Individual

_____
Print or Type Name of Authorized Individual

_____
Title of Individual Authorized by Debtor to File this Petition

_____
Date

If debtor is a corporation filing under chapter 11, Exhibit "A" is attached and made part of this petition.

TO BE COMPLETED BY INDIVIDUAL CHAPTER 7 DEBTOR WITH PRIMARILY CONSUMER DEBTS (See P.L. 98-353 § 322)

I am aware that I may proceed under chapter 7, 11, or 12, or 13 of title 11, United States Code, understand the relief available under each such chapter, and choose to proceed under chapter 7 of such title.

If I am represented by an attorney, exhibit "B" has been completed.

X _____   _____
Signature of Debtor   Date

X _____   _____
Signature of Joint Debtor   Date

CERTIFICATION AND SIGNATURE OF NON-ATTORNEY BANKRUPTCY PETITION PREPARER (See 11 U.S.C. § 110)

I certify that I am a bankruptcy petition preparer as defined in 11 U.S.C. § 110, that I have prepared this document for compensation, and that I have provided the debtor with a copy of this document.

_____
Printed or Typed Name of Bankruptcy Petition Preparer

_____
Social Security Number

_____
Address   Tel. No.

Names and Social Security numbers of all other individuals who prepared or assisted in preparing this document:

EXHIBIT "B"

(To be completed by attorney for individual chapter 7 debtor(s) with primarily consumer debts.)

I, the attorney for the debtor(s) named in the foregoing petition, declare that I have informed the debtor(s) that (he, she, or they) may proceed under chapter 7, 11, 12, or 13 of title 11, United States Code, and have explained the relief available under such chapter.

X _____   _____
Signature of Attorney   Date

If more than one person prepared this document, attach additional signed sheets conforming to the appropriate Official Form for each person.

X _____
Signature of Bankruptcy Petition Preparer

A bankruptcy petition preparer's failure to comply with the provisions of title 11 and the Federal Rules of Bankruptcy Procedure may result in fines or imprisonment or both. 11 U.S.C. § 110; 18 U.S.C. § 156.

BK 122
(8/84)

United States Bankruptcy Court

NOTICE TO INDIVIDUAL CONSUMER DEBTOR(S)

If you intend to file a petition for relief under the bankruptcy laws of the United States, and your debts are primarily consumer debts, the Clerk of Court is required to notify you of each chapter of the Bankruptcy Code under which you may seek relief. You may proceed under:

Chapter 7—Liquidation, or
Chapter 11—Reorganization, or
Chapter 13—Adjustment of Debts of an Individual
with Regular Income

If you have any questions regarding the information contained in this notice, you should consult with your attorney.

Clerk of Court

ACKNOWLEDGMENT

I hereby certify that I have read this notice.

DATED: _____

_____,
Debtor

_____,
Joint Debtor, if any

INSTRUCTIONS: *If the debtor is an individual, a copy of this notice personally signed by the debtor must accompany any bankruptcy petition filed with the Clerk. If filed by joint debtors, the notice must be personally signed by each. Failure to comply may result in the petition not being accepted for filing.*

3092 Clerk's notice. 10-84

Julius Blumberg, Inc. NYC 10013

Form B6 (6-90)

UNITED STATES BANKRUPTCY COURT

DISTRICT OF

In re: Debtor(s)   Case No.   (If Known)

See summary below for the list of schedules. Include Unsworn Declaration under Penalty of Perjury at the end.

GENERAL INSTRUCTIONS: Schedules D, E and F have been designed for the listing of each claim only once. Even when a claim is secured only in part, or entitled to priorityonly in part, it still should be listed only once. A claim which is secured in whole or in part should be listed on Schedule D only, and a claim which is entitled to priority in whole or in part should be listed in Schedule E only. Do not list the same claim twice. If a creditor has more than one claim, such as claims arising from separate transactions, each claim should be scheduled separately.

Review the specific instructions for each schedule before completing the schedule.

SUMMARY OF SCHEDULES

Indicate as to each schedule whether that schedule is attached and state the number of pages in each. Report the totals from Schedules A, B, D, E, F, I and J in the boxes provided. Add the amounts from Schedules A and B to determine the total amount of the debtor's assets. Add the amounts from Schedules D, E, and F to determine the total amount of the debtor's liabilities.

Name of Schedule	Attached (Yes No)	Number of sheets	Assets	Liabilities	Other
A - Real Property					
B - Personal Property					
C - Property Claimed as Exempt					
D - Creditors Holding Secured Claims					
E - Creditors Holding Unsecured Priority Claims					
F - Creditors Holding Unsecured Nonpriority Claims					
G - Executory Contracts and Unexpired Leases					
H - Codebtors					
I - Current Income of Individual Debtor(s)					
J - Current Expenditures of Individual Debtor(s)					
Total Number of Sheets of All Schedules					
Total Assets					
Total Liabilities					

Amounts Scheduled above columns Assets / Liabilities / Other

3072 · 1991 JULIUS BLUMBERG. INC., NYC 10013

Form B6 A/B, P1(6-90)   Julius Blumberg, Inc. NYC 10013

In re:

| | Debtor(s) | Case No. | (if known) |

SCHEDULE A - REAL PROPERTY

DESCRIPTION AND LOCATION OF PROPERTY	NATURE OF DEBTOR'S INTEREST IN PROPERTY	H W J C	CURRENT MARKET VALUE OF DEBTOR'S INTEREST IN PROPERTY WITHOUT DEDUCTING ANY SECURED CLAIM OR EXEMPTION	AMOUNT OF SECURED CLAIM

Total -> $ _____   (Report also on Summary of Schedules.)

SCHEDULE B - PERSONAL PROPERTY

TYPE OF PROPERTY	N O N E	DESCRIPTION AND LOCATION OF PROPERTY	H W J C	CURRENT MARKET VALUE OF DEBTOR'S INTEREST IN PROPERTY WITHOUT DEDUCTING ANY SECURED CLAIM OR EXEMPTION
1. Cash on hand				
2. Checking, savings or other financial accounts, certificates of deposit, or shares in banks, savings and loan, thrift, building and loan, and homestead associations, or credit unions, brokerage houses, or cooperatives.				
3. Security deposits with public utilities, telephone companies, landlords, and others.				
4. Household goods and furnishings including audio, video and computer equipment.				
5. Books; pictures and other art objects; antiques; stamp, coin, record, tape, compact disc, and other collections or collectibles.				
6. Wearing apparel.				
7. Furs and jewelry.				
8. Firearms and sports, photographic, and other hobby equipment.				
9. Interests in insurance policies. Name insurance company of each policy and itemize surrender or refund value of each.				

3072 : 1991 JULIUS BLUMBERG. INC.. NYC 10013

Form B6B, P2 (6-90)　　　Julius Blumberg, Inc. NYC 10013

SCHEDULE B
PERSONAL PROPERTY

In re: 　　　　　　　　　　　　　　　Debtor(s)　　Case No.　　　　　(if known)

TYPE OF PROPERTY	N O N E	DESCRIPTION AND LOCATION OF PROPERTY	H W J C	CURRENT MARKET VALUE OF DEBTOR'S INTEREST IN PROPERTY WITHOUT DEDUCTING ANY SECURED CLAIM OR EXEMPTION
10. Annuities. Itemize and name each issuer.				
11. Interests in IRA, ERISA, Keogh, or other pension or profit sharing plans. Itemize				
12. Stock and interests in incorporated and unincorporated businesses. Itemize.				
13. Interest in partnerships or joint ventures. Itemize.				
14. Government and corporate bonds and other negotiable and nonegotiable instruments.				
15. Accounts receivable.				
16. Alimony, maintenance, support, and property settlements to which the debtor is or may be entitled. Give particulars.				
17. Other liquidated debts owing debtor including tax refunds. Give particulars.				
18. Equitable or future interests, life estates, and rights or powers exercisable for the benefit of the debtor other than those listed in Schedule of Real Property.				
19. Contingent and noncontingent interests in estate of a decedent, death benefit plan, life insurance policy, or trust.				
20. Other contingent and unliquidated claims of every nature, including tax refunds, counterclaims of the debtor, and rights to setoff claims. Give estimated value of each.				
21. Patents, copyrights, and other intellectual property. Give particulars.				
22. Licenses, franchises, and other general intangibles. Give particulars.				
23. Automobiles, trucks, trailers, and other vehicles and accessories.				
24. Boats, motors, and accessories.				
25. Aircraft and accessories.				
26. Office equipment, furnishings, and supplies.				
27. Machinery, fixtures, equipment, and supplies used in business.				
28. Inventory.				
29. Animals.				
30. Crops - growing or harvested. Give particulars.				
31. Farming equipment and implements.				
32. Farm supplies, chemicals, and feed.				
33. Other personal property of any kind not already listed. Itemize.				

(Include amounts from any continuation sheets attached. Report total also on Summary of Schedules)　　Total ->　$

_____ continuation sheets attached

A p p e n d i x   A

Form B6 C (6,90)   Julius Blumberg, Inc. NYC 10013

In re:

                                                 Debtor(s)   Case No.   (if known)

SCHEDULE C - PROPERTY CLAIMED AS EXEMPT

Debtor elects the exemptions to which debtor is entitled under (Check one box)

☐ 11 U.S.C. § 522(b)(1): Exemptions provided in 11 U.S.C. § 522(d). Note: These exemptions are available only in certain states.

☐ 11 U.S.C. § 522(b)(2): Exemptions available under applicable nonbankruptcy federal laws, state or local law.

DESCRIPTION OF PROPERTY	SPECIFY LAW PROVIDING EACH EXEMPTION	VALUE OF CLAIMED EXEMPTION	CURRENT MARKET VALUE OF PROPERTY WITHOUT DEDUCTING EXEMPTION

3072 · 1991 JULIUS BLUMBERG, INC., NYC 10013

Form B6 D (6-90)   Julius Blumberg, Inc. NYC 10013

In re: _____   Debtor(s)   Case No. _____   (if known)

SCHEDULE D - CREDITORS HOLDING SECURED CLAIMS

☐ Check this box if debtor has no creditors holding secured claims to report on this Schedule D.

CREDITOR'S NAME AND MAILING ADDRESS INCLUDING ZIP CODE	CODEBTOR	HWJC	DATE CLAIM WAS INCURRED, NATURE OF LIEN, AND DESCRIPTION AND MARKET VALUE OF PROPERTY SUBJECT TO LIEN	CUD*	AMOUNT OF CLAIM WITHOUT DEDUCTING VALUE OF COLLATERAL	UNSECURED PORTION IF ANY
A/C #						
			VALUE $			
A/C #						
			VALUE $			
A/C #						
			VALUE $			
A/C #						
			VALUE $			
A/C #						
			VALUE $			
A/C #						
			VALUE $			
A/C #						
			VALUE $			
A/C #						
			VALUE $			
A/C #						
			VALUE $			

_____ continuation sheets attached

Subtotal -> (Total of this page) $ _____

Total -> (use only on last page) $ _____

*If contingent, enter C; if unliquidated, enter U; if disputed, enter D.

(Report total also on Summary of Schedules)

3072 · 1991 JULIUS BLUMBERG, INC., NYC 10013

Form B6 E (12/94)   Julius Blumberg, Inc. NYC 10013

In re: _____

                                    Debtor(s)   Case No. _____   (if known)

SCHEDULE E - CREDITORS HOLDING UNSECURED PRIORITY CLAIMS

☐ Check this box if debtor has no creditors holding unsecured priority claims to report on this Schedule E

TYPE OF PRIORITY CLAIMS (Check the appropriate box(es) below if claims in that category are listed on the attached sheets)

☐ **Extensions of credit in an involuntary case**   Claims arising in the ordinary course of the debtor's business or financial affairs after the commencement of the case but before the earlier of the appointment of a trustee or the order for relief. 11 U.S.C. § 507 (a) (2).

☐ **Wages, salaries, and commissions**   Wages, salaries, and commissions, including vacation, severance, and sick leave pay owing to employees, and commissions owing to qualifying independent sales representatives up to $4,000* per person, earned within 90 days immediately preceding the filing of the original petition, or the cessation of business, whichever occurred first, to the extent provided in 11 U.S.C. § 507 (a) (3).

☐ **Contributions to employee benefit plans**   Money owed to employee benefit plans for services rendered within 180 days immediately preceding the filing of the original petition, or the cessation of business, whichever occurred first, to the extent provided in 11 U.S.C. § 507 (a) (4).

☐ **Certain farmers and fishermen**   Claims of certain farmers and fishermen, up to $4,000* per farmer or fisherman, against the debtor, as provided in 11 U.S.C. § 507 (a) (5).

☐ **Deposits by individuals**   Claims of individuals up to $1,800* for deposits for the purchase, lease, or rental of property or services for personal, family, or household use, that were not delivered or provided. 11 U.S.C. § 507 (a) (6).

☐ **Alimony, Maintenance, or Support**   Claims of a spouse, former spouse, or child of the debtor for alimony, maintenance, or support, to the extent provided in 11 U.S.C. § 507 (a) (7).

☐ **Taxes and Certain Other Debts Owed to Governmental Units**   Taxes, customs duties, and penalties owing to federal, state, and local governmental units as set forth in 11 U.S.C. § 507 (a) (8).

☐ **Commitments to Maintain the Capital of an Insured Depository Institution**   Claims based on commitments to the FDIC, RTC, Director of the Office of Thrift Supervision, Comptroller of the Currency, or Board of Governors of the Federal Reserve System, or their predecessors or successors, to maintain the capital of an insured depository institution. 11 U.S.C. § 507 (a) (9).

*Amounts are subject to adjustment on April 1, 1998, and every three years thereafter with respect to cases commenced on or after the date of adjustment.

CREDITOR'S NAME AND MAILING ADDRESS INCLUDING ZIP CODE	CO DEBT	H W J C	DATE CLAIM WAS INCURRED AND CONSIDERATION FOR CLAIM	C U D *	TOTAL AMOUNT OF CLAIM	AMOUNT ENTITLED TO PRIORITY
A/C#						
A/C#						
A/C#						
A/C#						
A/C#						
				Subtotal -> (Total of this page)	$	
				Total -> (use only on last page of the completed Schedule E)	$	

_____ Continuation sheets attached.

* If contingent, enter C; if unliquidated., enter U; if disputed , enter D.

(Report total also on Summary of Schedules)

3072© 1991 JULIUS BLUMBERG, INC., NYC 10013

Form B6 F (6-90)   Julius Blumberg, Inc. NYC 10013

In re: Debtor(s)   Case No.   (if known)

SCHEDULE F - CREDITORS HOLDING UNSECURED NONPRIORITY CLAIMS

☐ Check this box if debtor has no creditors holding unsecured nonpriority claims to report on this Schedule F

CREDITOR'S NAME AND MAILING ADDRESS INCLUDING ZIP CODE	CODEBT	HWJC	DATE CLAIM WAS INCURRED AND CONSIDERATION FOR CLAIM. IF CLAIM IS SUBJECT TO SETOFF, SO STATE.	CUD*	AMOUNT OF CLAIM
A/C #					
A/C #					
A/C #					
A/C #					
A/C #					
A/C #					
A/C #					
A/C #					
A/C #					

_____ Continuation Sheets attached.

Subtotal -> $
(Total of this page)

*If contingent, enter C; if unliquidated, enter U; if disputed, enter D.

Total -> $
(use only on last page of completed Schedule F.)
(Report total also on Summary of Schedules)

3072 © 1991 JULIUS BLUMBERG, INC., NYC 10013

Form B6 G (6-90)   Julius Blumberg, Inc. NYC 10013

In re: Debtor(s)   Case No.   (if known)

SCHEDULE G - EXECUTORY CONTRACTS AND UNEXPIRED LEASES

☐ Check this box if debtor has no executory contracts or unexpired leases.

NAME AND MAILING ADDRESS, INCLUDING ZIP CODE, OF OTHER PARTIES TO LEASE OR CONTRACT.	DESCRIPTION OF CONTRACT OR LEASE AND NATURE OF DEBTOR'S INTEREST. STATE WHETHER LEASE IS FOR NONRESIDENTIAL REAL PROPERTY. STATE CONTRACT NUMBER OF ANY GOVERNMENT CONTRACT.

Form B6 H, (6-90)   Julius Blumberg, Inc. NYC 10013

In re: Debtor(s)   Case No.   (if known)

SCHEDULE H - CODEBTORS

☐ Check this box if debtor has no codebtors.

NAME AND ADDRESS OF CODEBTOR	NAME AND ADDRESS OF CREDITOR

Form B6I (6-90)   Julius Blumberg, Inc. NYC 10013

In re: Debtor(s)   Case No.   (if known)

SCHEDULE I - CURRENT INCOME OF INDIVIDUAL DEBTOR(S)

The column labeled "Spouse" must be completed in all cases filed by joint debtors and by a married debtor in a chapter 12 or 13 case whether or not a joint petition is filed, unless the spouses are separated and a joint petition is not filed.

Debtor's Marital Status:	DEPENDENTS OF DEBTOR AND SPOUSE		
	NAMES	AGE	RELATIONSHIP

Employment:	DEBTOR	SPOUSE
Occupation		
Name of Employer		
How long employed		
Address of Employer		

Income: (Estimate of average monthly income)   DEBTOR   SPOUSE

Current monthly gross wages, salary, and commissions (pro rate if not paid monthly.) .... $ $

Estimate monthly overtime ....

SUBTOTAL .... $ _____ $ _____

    LESS PAYROLL DEDUCTIONS

      a. Payroll taxes and social security ....

      b. Insurance ....

      c. Union dues ....

      d. Other (Specify)

    SUBTOTAL OF PAYROLL DEDUCTIONS .... $ _____ $ _____

TOTAL NET MONTHLY TAKE HOME PAY .... $ _____ $ _____

Regular income from operation of business or profession or farm

(attach detailed statement)

Income from real property ....

Interest and dividends ....

Alimony, maintenance or support payments payable to the debtor for the debtor's

    use or that of dependents listed above. ....

Social security or other government assistance (Specify) ....

Pension or retirement income ....

Other monthly income (Specify) ....

TOTAL MONTHLY INCOME .... $ _____ $ _____

TOTAL COMBINED MONTHLY INCOME $ _____   (Report also on Summary of Schedules)

Describe any increase or decrease of more than 10% in any of the above categories anticipated to occur within the year following the filing of this document:

Form B6 J, Cont. (6-90)   Julius Blumberg, Inc. NYC 10013

In re: Debtor(s)   Case No.   (if known)

SCHEDULE J - CURRENT EXPENDITURES OF INDIVIDUAL DEBTOR(S)

Complete this schedule by estimating the average monthly expenses of the debtor and the debtor's family. Pro rate any payments made bi-weekly, quarterly, semi-annually, or annually to show monthly rate.

☐ Check this box if a joint petition is filed and debtor's spouse maintains a separate household. Complete a separate schedule of expenditures labeled "Spouse".

Rent or home mortgage payment (include lot rented for mobile home) .... $

Are real estate taxes included? ☐ Yes ☐ No   Is property insurance included? ☐ Yes ☐ No

Utilities Electricity and heating fuel ....

     Water and sewer ....

     Telephone ....

     Other

Home maintenance (repairs and upkeep) ....

Food ....

Clothing ....

Laundry and dry cleaning ....

Medical and dental expenses ....

Transportation (not including car payments) ....

Recreation, clubs and entertainment, newspapers, magazines, etc. ....

Charitable contributions ....

Insurance (not deducted from wages or included in home mortgage payments)

     Homeowner's or renter's ....

     Life ....

     Health ....

     Auto ....

     Other

Taxes (not deducted from wages or included in home mortgage payments)

(Specify)

Installment payments: (In chapter 12 and 13 cases, do not list payments to be included in the plan)

     Auto ....

     Other

Alimony, maintenance, and support paid to others ....

Payments for support of additional dependents not living at your home ....

Regular expenses from operation of business, profession, or farm (attach detailed statement) ....

Other

TOTAL MONTHLY EXPENSES (Report also on Summary of Schedules) .... $ _____

(FOR CHAPTER 12 AND 13 DEBTORS ONLY)

Provide the information requested below, including whether plan payments are to be made bi-weekly, monthly, annually, or at some other regular interval.

A. Total projected monthly income .... $ _____

B. Total projected monthly expenses ....

C. Excess income (A minus B) .... $ _____

D. Total amount to be paid into plan each .... $ _____

                            (interval)

A p p e n d i x   A

Blumberg Law Products Form B6 Cont. (6-90)

Julius Blumberg, Inc. N Y C 10013

In re: _____   Debtor(s)   Case No. _____

                                                                                    (if known)

DECLARATION CONCERNING DEBTOR'S SCHEDULES

DECLARATION UNDER PENALTY OF PERJURY BY INDIVIDUAL DEBTOR

I declare under penalty of perjury that I have read the foregoing summary and schedules, consisting of _____ sheets, and that they are true and correct to the best of my knowledge, information, and belief.

(Total shown on summary page plus 1.)

Date _____

Signature: _____

Debtor

Date _____

Signature: _____

(Joint Debtor, if any)

(If joint case, both spouses must sign.)

DECLARATION UNDER PENALTY OF PERJURY ON BEHALF OF CORPORATION OR PARTNERSHIP

I, the _____ (the president or other officer or an authorized agent of the corporation or a member or an authorized agent of the partnership) of the _____ (corporation or partnership) named as debtor in this case, declare under penalty of perjury that I have read the foregoing summary and schedules, consisting of _____ sheets, and that they are true and correct to the best of my knowledge, information, and belief.

(Total shown on summary page plus 1.)

Date _____

Signature: _____

(Pint or type name of individual signing on behalf of debtor.)

(An individual signing on behalf of a partnership or corporation must indicate position or relationship to debtor.)

Penalty for making a false statement or concealing property: Fine of up to $500,000 or imprisonment for up to 5 years or both. 18 U.S.C. §§ 152 and 3571.

Form 7 Stmt. of Financial
Affairs (11-92)

Julius Blumberg, Inc.
NYC 10013

UNITED STATES BANKRUPTCY COURT

DISTRICT OF

In re:

Debtor(s)   *Case No.*

STATEMENT OF FINANCIAL AFFAIRS

This statement is to be completed by every debtor. Spouses filing a joint petition may file a single statement on which the information for both spouses is combined. If the case is filed under chapter 12 or chapter 13, a married debtor must furnish information for both spouses whether or not a joint petition is filed, unless the spouses are separated and a joint petition is not filed. An individual debtor engaged in business as a sole proprietor, partner, family farmer, or self-employed professional, should provide the information requested on this statement concerning all such activities as well as the individual's personal affairs.

Questions 1-15 are to be completed by all debtors. Debtors that are or have been in business, as defined below, also must complete Questions 16-21. **If the answer to any question is "None," or the question is not applicable, mark the box labeled "None."** If additional space is needed for the answer to any question, use and attach a separate sheet properly identified with the case name, case number (if known), and the number of the question.

DEFINITIONS

"In business." A debtor is "in business" for the purpose of this form if the debtor is a corporation or partnership. An individual debtor is "in business" for the purpose of this form if the debtor is or has been, within the two years immediately preceding the filing of this bankruptcy case, any of the following: an officer, director, managing executive, or person in control of a corporation; a partner, other than a limited partner, of a partnership; a sole proprietor or self-employed.

"Insider." The term "insider" includes but is not limited to: relatives of the debtor; general partners of the debtor and their relatives; corporations of which the debtor is an officer, director, or person in control; officers, directors, and any person in control of a corporate debtor and their relatives; affiliates of the debtor and insiders of such affiliates; any managing agent of the debtor. 11 U.S.C. §101(30).

__ None   **1. Income from Employment or Operation of Business**

State the gross amount of income the debtor has received from employment, trade, or profession, or from operation of the debtor's business from the beginning of this calendar year to the date this case was commenced. State also the gross amounts received during the **two years** immediately preceding this calendar year. (A debtor that maintains, or has maintained, financial records on the basis of a fiscal rather than a calendar year may report fiscal year income. Identify the beginning and ending dates of the debtor's fiscal year.) If a joint petition is filed, state income for each spouse separately. (Married debtors filing under chapter 12 or chapter 13 must state income of both spouses whether or not a joint petition is filed, unless the spouses are separated and a joint petition is not filed.)
Give AMOUNT and SOURCE (If more than one).

__ None   **2. Income Other than from Employment or Operation of Business**

State the amount of income received by the debtor other than from employment, trade, profession, or operation of the debtor's business during the **two years** immediately preceding the commencement of this case. Give particulars. If a joint petition is filed, state income for each spouse separately. (Married debtors filing under chapter 12 or chapter 13 must state income for each spouse whether or not a joint petition is filed, unless the spouses are separated and a joint petition is not filed.) Give AMOUNT and SOURCE.

3. Payments to Creditors

__ None   a. List all payments on loans, installment purchases of goods or services, and other debts, aggregating more than $600 to any creditor, made within **90 days** immediately preceding the commencement of this case. (Married debtors filing under chapter 12 or chapter 13 must include payments by either or both spouses whether or not a joint petition is filed, unless the spouses are separated and a joint petition is not filed.)
Give NAME AND ADDRESS OF CREDITOR, DATES OF PAYMENTS, AMOUNT PAID and AMOUNT STILL OWING.

__ None   b. List all payments made within **one year** immediately preceding the commencement of this case to or for the benefit of creditors who are or were insiders. (Married debtors filing under chapter 12 or chapter 13 must include payments by either or both spouses whether or not a joint petition is filed, unless the spouses are separated and a joint petition is not filed.)
Give NAME AND ADDRESS OF CREDITOR AND RELATIONSHIP TO DEBTOR, DATE OF PAYMENT, AMOUNT PAID and AMOUNT STILL OWING.

4. Suits and Administrative Proceedings, Executions, Garnishments and Attachments

__ None   a. List all suits and administrative proceedings to which the debtor is or was a party within **one year** immediately preceding the filing of this bankruptcy case. (Married debtors filing under chapter 12 or chapter 13 must include information concerning either or both spouses whether or not a joint petition is filed, unless the spouses are separated and a joint petition is not filed.)
Give CAPTION OF SUIT AND CASE NUMBER, NATURE OF PROCEEDING, COURT OR AGENCY AND LOCATION and STATUS OR DISPOSITION.

__ None   b. Describe all property that has been attached, garnished, or seized under any legal or equitable process within **one year** immediately preceding the commencement of this case. (Married debtors filing under chapter 12 or chapter 13 must include information concerning property of either or both spouses whether or not a joint petition is filed, unless the spouses are separated and a joint petition is not filed.)

Give NAME AND ADDRESS OF PERSON FOR WHOSE BENEFIT PROPERTY WAS SEIZED, DATE OF SEIZURE and DESCRIPTION AND VALUE OF PROPERTY.

☐ None   **5. Repossessions, Foreclosures, and Returns**

List all property that has been repossessed by a creditor, sold at a foreclosure sale, transferred through a deed in lieu of foreclosure or returned to the seller, within **one year** immediately preceding the commencement of this case. (Married debtors filing under chapter 12 or chapter 13 must include information concerning property of either or both spouses whether or not a joint petition is filed, unless the spouses are separated and a joint petition is not filed.)

Give NAME AND ADDRESS OF CREDITOR OR SELLER, DATE OF REPOSSESSION, FORECLOSURE SALE, TRANSFER OR RETURN and DESCRIPTION AND VALUE OF PROPERTY.

6. Assignments and Receiverships

☐ None   a. Describe any assignment of property for the benefit of creditors made within **120 days** immediately preceding the commencement of this case. (Married debtors filing under chapter 12 or chapter 13 must include any assignment by either or both spouses whether or not a joint petition is filed, unless the spouses are separated and a joint petition is not filed.)

Give NAME AND ADDRESS OF ASSIGNEE, DATE OF ASSIGNMENT and TERMS OF ASSIGNMENT OR SETTLEMENT.

☐ None   b. List all property which has been in the hands of a custodian, receiver, or court-appointed official within **one year** immediately preceding the commencement of this case. (Married debtors filing under chapter 12 or chapter 13 must include information concerning property of either or both spouses whether or not a joint petition is filed, unless the spouses are separated and a joint petition is not filed.)

Give NAME AND ADDRESS OF CUSTODIAN, NAME AND LOCATION OF COURT, CASE TITLE & NUMBER, DATE OF ORDER and DESCRIPTION AND VALUE OF PROPERTY.

☐ None   **7. Gifts**

List all gifts or charitable contributions made within **one year** immediately preceding the commencement of this case except ordinary and usual gifts to family members aggregating less than $200 in value per individual family member and charitable contributions aggregating less than $100 per recipient. (Married debtors filing under chapter 12 or chapter 13 must include gifts or contributions by either or both spouses whether or not a joint petition is filed, unless the spouses are separated and a joint petition is not filed.)

Give NAME AND ADDRESS OF PERSON OR ORGANIZATION, RELATIONSHIP TO DEBTOR, IF ANY, DATE OF GIFT, and DESCRIPTION AND VALUE OF GIFT.

☐ None   **8. Losses**

List all losses from fire, theft, other casualty or gambling within **one year** immediately preceding the commencement of this case **or since the commencement of this case.** (Married debtors filing under chapter 12 or chapter 13 must include losses by either or both spouses whether or not a joint petition is filed, unless the spouses are separated and a joint petition is not filed.)

Give DESCRIPTION AND VALUE OF PROPERTY, DESCRIPTION OF CIRCUMSTANCES AND, IF LOSS WAS COVERED IN WHOLE OR IN PART BY INSURANCE, GIVE PARTICULARS and DATE OF LOSS.

☐ None   **9. Payments Related to Debt Counseling or Bankruptcy**

List all payments made or property transferred by or on behalf of the debtor to any persons, including attorneys, for consultation concerning debt consolidation, relief under the bankruptcy law or preparation of a petition in bankruptcy within **one year** immediately preceding the commencement of this case.

Give NAME AND ADDRESS OF PAYEE, DATE OF PAYMENT, NAME OF PAYOR IF OTHER THAN DEBTOR and AMOUNT OF MONEY OR DESCRIPTION AND VALUE OF PROPERTY.

☐ None   **10. Other Transfers**

List all other property, other than property transferred in the ordinary course of the business or financial affairs of the debtor, transferred either absolutely or as security within **one year** immediately preceding the commencement of this case. (Married debtors filing under chapter 12 or chapter 13 must include transfers by either or both spouses whether or not a joint petition is filed, unless the spouses are separated and a joint petition is not filed.)

Give NAME AND ADDRESS OF TRANSFEREE, RELATIONSHIP TO DEBTOR, DATE, and DESCRIBE PROPERTY TRANSFERRED AND VALUE RECEIVED

☐ None   **11. Closed Financial Accounts**

List all financial accounts and instruments held in the name of the debtor or for the benefit of the debtor which were closed, sold, or otherwise transferred within **one year** immediately preceding the commencement of this case. Include checking, savings, or other financial accounts, certificates of deposit, or other instruments; shares and share accounts held in banks, credit unions, pension funds, cooperatives, associations, brokerage houses and other financial institutions. (Married debtors filing under chapter 12 or chapter 13 must include information concerning accounts or instruments held by or for either or both spouses whether or not a joint petition is filed, unless the spouses are separated and a joint petition is not filed.)

Give NAME AND ADDRESS OF INSTITUTION, TYPE AND NUMBER OF ACCOUNT AND AMOUNT OF FINAL BALANCE and AMOUNT AND DATE OF SALE OR CLOSING.

☐ None   **12. Safe Deposit Boxes**

List each safe deposit or other box or depository in which the debtor has or had securities, cash, or other valuables within **one year** immediately preceding the commencement of this case. (Married debtors filing under chapter 12 or chapter 13 must include boxes or depositories of either or both spouses whether or not a joint petition is filed, unless the spouses are separated and a joint petition is not filed.)

Give NAME AND ADDRESS OF BANK OR OTHER DEPOSITORY, NAMES AND ADDRESSES OF THOSE WITH ACCESS TO BOX OR DEPOSITORY, DESCRIPTION OF CONTENTS and DATE OF TRANSFER OR SURRENDER, IF ANY.

☐ None   **13. Setoffs**

List all setoffs made by any creditor, including a bank, against a debt or deposit of the debtor within **90 days** preceding the commencement of this case. (Married debtors filing under chapter 12 or chapter 13 must include information concerning either or both spouses whether or not a joint petition is filed, unless the spouses are separated and a joint petition is not filed.)

Give NAME AND ADDRESS OR CREDITOR, DATE OF SETOFF and AMOUNT OF SETOFF.

☐ None   **14. Property Held for Another Person**

List all property owned by another person that the debtor holds or controls.

Give NAME AND ADDRESS OF OWNER, DESCRIPTION AND VALUE OF PROPERTY and LOCATION OF PROPERTY.

☐ None   **15. Prior Address of Debtor**

If the debtor has moved within the two years immediately preceding the commencement of this case, list all premises which the debtor occupied during that period and vacated prior to the commencement of this case. If a joint petition is filed, report also any separate address of either spouse.

Give ADDRESS, NAME USED and DATES OF OCCUPANCY.

Unsworn Declaration under Penalty of Perjury.

I declare under penalty of perjury that I have read the answers contained in the foregoing statement of financial affairs and any attachments thereto and that they are true and correct.

Date _____   Signature of Debtor _____

Date _____   Signature of Joint Debtor (if any) _____

_____ continuation sheets attached

Penalty for making a false statement: Fine of up to $500,000 or imprisonment for up to 5 years, or both. 18 U.S.C.§§152 and 3571.

3076-3A ©1991 Julius BLumberg, Inc.

[If completed by an individual or individual and spouse]

I declare under penalty of perjury that I have read the answers contained in the foregoing statement of financial affairs and any attachments thereto and that they are true and correct.

Date ———————————————   Signature ———————————————————————
                                       of Debtor

Date ———————————————   Signature ———————————————————————
                                       of Joint Debtor
                                       (if any)

CERTIFICATION AND SIGNATURE OF NON-ATTORNEY BANKRUPTCY PETITION PREPARER (See 11 U.S.C. § 110)

I certify that I am a bankruptcy petition preparer as defined in 11 U.S.C. § 110, that I prepared this document for compensation, and that I have provided the debtor with a copy of this document.

————————————————————————————
Printed or Typed Name of Bankruptcy Petition Preparer   Social Security No.

————————————————————————————

Address

Names and Social Security numbers of all other individuals who prepared or assisted in preparing this document: If more than one person prepared this document, attach additional signed sheets conforming to the appropriate Official Form for each person.

X————————————————————————   ——————————————————
  Signature of Bankruptcy Petition Preparer   Date

A bankruptcy petition preparer's failure to comply with the provisions of title 11 and the Federal Rules of Bankruptcy Procedure may result in fines or imprisonment or both. 11 U.S.C § 110; 18 U.S.C. § 156.

[If completed on behalf of a partnership or corporation]

I, declare under penalty of perjury that I have read the answers contained in the foregoing statement of financial affairs and any attachments thereto and that they are true and correct to the best of my knowledge, information and belief.

Date ———————————————   Signature ———————————————————————

                                       ——————————————————————
                                       Print Name and Title

[An individual signing on behalf of a partnership or corporation must indicate position or relationship to debtor.]

Form B8 (6-90)   Julius Blumberg, Inc. NYC 10013

UNITED STATES BANKRUPTCY COURT   **DISTRICT OF**

In re: Debtor(s)   Case No.
                                                           Chapter

CHAPTER 7 INDIVIDUAL DEBTOR'S STATEMENT OF INTENTION

1. I, the debtor, have filed a schedule of assets and liabilities which includes consumer debts secured by property of the estate.
2. My intention with respect to the property of the estate which secures those consumer debts is as follows:
   a. *Property to Be Surrendered.*

Description of property	Creditor's name	H,W or J

   b. *Property to Be Retained (Specify Reaff'd, Red'd or Exempt to state debtor's intention concerning reaffirmation, redemption, or lien avoidance*.)*

Description of property	Creditor's name	Reaff'd Red'd Exempt

3. I understand that § 521(2)(B) of the Bankruptcy Code requires that I perform the above stated intention within 45 days of the filing of this statement with the court, or within such additional time as the court, for cause, within such 45-day period fixes.

Date:

....
Signature of Debtor

* Reaff'd - Debt will be reaffirmed pursuant to § 524(c)

Red'd - Property is claimed as exempt and will be redeemed pursuant to § 722

Exempt - Lien will be avoided pursuant to § 522(f) and property will be claimed as exempt

....
Signature of Debtor

3073 · 1991 JULIUS BLUMBERG, INC. NYC 10013

3085   Statement of compensation: Rule 2016(b), 8-91

UNITED STATES BANKRUPTCY COURT   **DISTRICT OF**

In re   Debtor(s)   Case No.   (If Known)

STATEMENT
Pursuant to Rule 2016(b)

The undersigned, pursuant to Rule 2016(b) Bankruptcy Rules, states that:

(1) The undersigned is the attorney for the debtor(s) in this case.
(2) The compensation paid or agreed to be paid by the debtor(s) to the undersigned is:
    (a) for legal services rendered or to be rendered in contemplation of and in connection
        with this case $ ....
    (b) prior to filing this statement, debtor(s) have paid $ ....
    (c) the unpaid balance due and payable is $ ....
(3) $ _____ of the filing fee in this case has been paid.
(4) The services rendered or to be rendered include the following:
    (a) analysis of the financial situation, and rendering advice and assistance to the debtor(s) in determining whether to file a
        petition under title 11 of the United States Code.
    (b) preparation and filing of the petition, schedules, statement of affairs and other documents required by the court.
    (c) representation of the debtor(s) at the meeting of creditors.

(5) The source of payments made by the debtor(s) to the undersigned was from earnings, wages and compensation for services
performed, and

(6) The source of payments to be made by the debtor(s) to the undersigned for the unpaid balance remaining, if any, will be from
earnings, wages and compensation for services performed, and

(7) The undersigned has received no transfer, assignment or pledge of property execept the following for the value stated:

(8) The undersigned has not shared or agreed to share with any other entity, other than with members of undersigned's law firm,
any compensation paid or to be paid except as follows:

Dated: _____   Respectfully submitted, ...*Attorney for Petitioner*

Attorney's name and address ....

Appendix B
Chapter 13 Bankruptcy Forms

The following forms represent the basic Chapter 13 petition and plan. The plan is used for individuals as well as for small businesses that are sole proprietorships. In addition to these forms, each bankruptcy district in the United States may have local forms that also must be filed. There are so many local forms that it is not practical to present all of them here. Your attorney should be familiar with the local rules in your area and with the additional forms required.

The plan provides for the mandatory provisions required by law. However, experienced bankruptcy attorneys will provide a plan that includes additional provisions to give the debtor other rights and safeguards.

Forms may be purchased from Julius Blumberg, Inc., NYC 10013, or any of its dealers. Reproduction prohibited.

Blumbergs Law Products   Julius Blumberg, Inc. NYC 10013

Form B1, P1 (12-94)   **FORM 1 VOLUNTARY PETITION**

United States Bankruptcy Court **District of**	**VOLUNTARY PETITION**
IN RE (Name of debtor-If individual, enter Last, First, Middle)	NAME OF JOINT DEBTOR (Spouse) (Last, First, Middle)
ALL OTHER NAMES used by the debtor in the last 6 years (including married, maiden and trade names)	ALL OTHER NAMES used by the joint debtor in the last 6 years (include married, maiden and trade names)
SOC. SEC./TAX I.D. NO. (If more than one, state all)	SOC. SEC./TAX I.D. NO. (If more than one, state all)
STREET ADDRESS OF DEBTOR (No. and street, city, state, zip)	STREET ADDRESS OF JOINT DEBTOR (No. and street, city, state, zip)
COUNTY OF RESIDENCE OR PRINCIPAL PLACE OF BUSINESS	COUNTY OF RESIDENCE OR PRINCIPAL PLACE OF BUSINESS
MAILING ADDRESS OF DEBTOR (If different from street address)	MAILING ADDRESS OF JOINT DEBTOR (If different from street address)

LOCATION OF PRINCIPLE ASSETS OF BUSINESS DEBTOR (If different from addresses listed above)	VENUE (Check one box)
	☐ Debtor has been domiciled or has had a residence, principal place of business or principal assets in this District for 180 days immediately preceding the date of this petition or for a longer part of such 180 days than in any other District. ☐ There is a bankruptcy case concerning debtor's affiliate, general partner or partnership pending in this district

INFORMATION REGARDING DEBTOR (Check Applicable boxes)

TYPE OF DEBTOR (Check one box) ☐ Individual ☐ Joint (H&W) ☐ Partnership ☐ Other _____	☐ Corporation Publicly Held ☐ Corporation Not Publicly Held ☐ Municipality

CHAPTER OR SECTION OF BANKRUPTCY CODE UNDER WHICH THE PETITION IS FILED (Check one box)		
☐ Chapter 7	☐ Chapter 11	☐ Chapter 13
☐ Chapter 9	☐ Chapter 12	☐ § 304-Case Ancillary to Foreign Proceeding

NATURE OF DEBT (Check one box)

☐ Non-Business Consumer   ☐ Business - Complete A&B below

A. TYPE OF BUSINESS (Check one box)

☐ Farming	☐ Transportation	☐ Commodity Broker
☐ Professional	☐ Manufacturing/Mining	☐ Construction
☐ Retail/Wholesale	☐ Stockbroker	☐ Real Estate
☐ Railroad	☐ Other Business	

B. BRIEFLY DESCRIBE NATURE OF BUSINESS

SMALL BUSINESS (Ch.11 only)

☐ Debtor is a small business as defined in 11 U.S.C. § 101.

☐ Debtor is and elects to be considered a small business under 11 U.S.C. § 1121(e). (optional)

FILING FEE (Check one box)

☐ Filing fee attached.

☐ Filing fee to be paid in installments. (Applicable to individuals only) Must attach signed application for the court's consideration certifying that the debtor is unable to pay fee except in installments. Rule 1006(b); see Official Form Number 3

NAME AND ADDRESS OF LAW FIRM OR ATTORNEY

Telephone No.

STATISTICAL ADMINISTRATIVE INFORMATION (28 U.S.C. § 604) (Estimates only) (Check applicable boxes)	NAME(S) OF ATTORNEY(S) DESIGNATED TO REPRESENT THE DEBTOR (Print or Type)
☐ Debtor estimates that funds will be available for distribution to unsecured creditors. ☐ Debtor estimates that after any exempt property is excluded and administrative expenses paid, there will be no funds available for distribution to unsecured creditors.	☐ Debtor is not represented by an attorney. Telephone no. of debtor not represented by an attorney: ( )

		THIS SPACE FOR COURT USE ONLY
ESTIMATED NUMBER OF CREDITORS ☐ 1-15 ☐ 16-49 ☐ 50-99 ☐ 100-199 ☐ 200-999 ☐ 1000-over		
ESTIMATED ASSETS (in thousands of dollars) ☐ Under 50 ☐ 50-99 ☐ 100-499 ☐ 500-999 ☐ 1000-9999 ☐ 10,000-99,000 ☐ 100,000-over		
ESTIMATED LIABILITIES (in thousands of dollars) ☐ Under 50 ☐ 50-99 ☐ 100-499 ☐ 500-999 ☐ 1000-9999 ☐ 10,000-99,000 ☐ 100,000-over		
ESTIMATED NUMBER OF EMPLOYEES - CH 11 & 12 ONLY ☐ 0 ☐ 1-19 ☐ 20-99 ☐ 100-999 ☐ 1000-over		
ESTIMATED NO. OF EQUITY SECURITY HOLDERS - CH 11 & 12 ONLY ☐ 0 ☐ 1-19 ☐ 20-99 ☐ 100-999 ☐ 1000-over		

Julius Blumberg, Inc. NYC 10013

Form B1, P2 (12-94)

Name of Debtor: _____ Case No. _____
(Court use only)

FILING OF PLAN   For Chapter 7, 11, 12 and 13 cases only. Check appropriate box.

☐ A Copy of debtor's proposed plan dated _____ is attached. ☐ Debtor intends to file a plan within the time allowed by statute, rule, or order of the court.

PRIOR BANKRUPTCY CASE FILED WITHIN LAST 6 YEARS (If more than one, attach additional sheet)

Location Where Filed	Case Number	Date Filed

PENDING BANKRUPTCY CASE FILED BY ANY SPOUSE, PARTNER, OR AFFILIATE OF THIS DEBTOR (If more than one, attach additional sheet.)

Name of Debtor	Case Number	Date
Relationship	District	Judge

REQUEST FOR RELIEF   Debtor is eligible for and requests relief in accordance with the chapter of title 11, United States Code, specified in this petition.

SIGNATURES

ATTORNEY   Signature X _____ Date _____

INDIVIDUAL/JOINT DEBTOR(S)

I declare under penalty of perjury that the information provided in this petition is true and correct

X _____
Signature of Debtor

_____
Date

X _____
Signature of Joint Debtor

_____
Date

CORPORATE OR PARTNERSHIP DEBTOR

I declare under penalty of perjury that the information provided in this petition is true and correct, and that I have been authorized to file this petition on behalf of the debtor.

X _____
Signature of Authorized Individual

_____
Print or Type Name of Authorized Individual

_____
Title of Individual Authorized by Debtor to File this Petition

_____
Date

If debtor is a corporation filing under chapter 11, Exhibit "A" is attached and made part of this petition.

TO BE COMPLETED BY INDIVIDUAL CHAPTER 7 DEBTOR WITH PRIMARILY CONSUMER DEBTS (See P.L. 98-353 § 322)

I am aware that I may proceed under chapter 7, 11, or 12, or 13 of title 11, United States Code, understand the relief available under each such chapter, and choose to proceed under chapter 7 of such title.

If I am represented by an attorney, exhibit "B" has been completed.

X _____ _____
Signature of Debtor   Date

X _____ _____
Signature of Joint Debtor   Date

EXHIBIT "B"

(To be completed by attorney for individual chapter 7 debtor(s) with primarily consumer debts.)

I, the attorney for the debtor(s) named in the foregoing petition, declare that I have informed the debtor(s) that (he, she, or they) may proceed under chapter 7, 11, 12, or 13 of title 11, United States Code, and have explained the relief available under such chapter.

X _____ _____
Signature of Attorney   Date

CERTIFICATION AND SIGNATURE OF NON-ATTORNEY BANKRUPTCY PETITION PREPARER (See 11 U.S.C. § 110)

I certify that I am a bankruptcy petition preparer as defined in 11 U.S.C. § 110, that I have prepared this document for compensation, and that I have provided the debtor with a copy of this document.

_____
Printed or Typed Name of Bankruptcy Petition Preparer

_____
Social Security Number

_____
Address   Tel.No.

Names and Social Security numbers of all other individuals who prepared or assisted in preparing this document:

If more than one person prepared this document, attach additional signed sheets conforming to the appropriate Official Form for each person.

X _____
Signature of Bankruptcy Petition Preparer

A bankruptcy petition preparer's failure to comply with the provisions of title 11 and the Federal Rules of Bankruptcy Procedure may result in fines or imprisonment or both. 11 U.S.C. § 110; 18 U.S.C. § 156.

3069-2 © 1991 JULIUS BLUMBERG, INC., NYC 10013

BK 122
(8/84)

United States Bankruptcy Court

NOTICE TO INDIVIDUAL CONSUMER DEBTOR(S)

If you intend to file a petition for relief under the bankruptcy laws of the United States, and your debts are primarily consumer debts, the Clerk of Court is required to notify you of each chapter of the Bankruptcy Code under which you may seek relief. You may proceed under:

> **Chapter 7**—Liquidation, or
> **Chapter 11**—Reorganization, or
> **Chapter 13**—Adjustment of Debts of an Individual
> with Regular Income

If you have any questions regarding the information contained in this notice, you should consult with your attorney.

Clerk of Court

ACKNOWLEDGMENT

I hereby certify that I have read this notice.

DATED: _____

_____,
Debtor

_____,
Joint Debtor, if any

INSTRUCTIONS: *If the debtor is an individual, a copy of this notice personally signed by the debtor must accompany any bankruptcy petition filed with the Clerk. If filed by joint debtors, the notice must be personally signed by each. Failure to comply may result in the petition not being accepted for filing.*

3092 Clerk's notice. 10-84

Julius Blumberg, Inc. NYC 10013

Blumbergs Law Products Form B6 (6-90)

UNITED STATES BANKRUPTCY COURT   **DISTRICT OF**

In re: Debtor(s)   Case No.   (If Known)

See summary below for the list of schedules. Include Unsworn Declaration under Penalty of Perjury at the end.

GENERAL INSTRUCTIONS: Schedules D, E and F have been designed for the listing of each claim only once. Even when a claim is secured only in part, or entitled to priority only in part, it still should be listed only once. A claim which is secured in whole or in part should be listed on Schedule D only, and a claim which is entitled to priority in whole or in part should be listed in Schedule E only. Do not list the same claim twice. If a creditor has more than one claim, such as claims arising from separate transactions, each claim should be scheduled separately.

Review the specific instructions for each schedule before completing the schedule.

SUMMARY OF SCHEDULES

Indicate as to each schedule whether that schedule is attached and state the number of pages in each. Report the totals from Schedules A, B, D, E, F, I and J in the boxes provided. Add the amounts from Schedules A and B to determine the total amount of the debtor's assets. Add the amounts from Schedules D, E, and F to determine the total amount of the debtor's liabilities.

Name of Schedule	Attached (Yes No)	Number of sheets	Amounts Scheduled		
			Assets	Liabilities	Other
A - Real Property					
B - Personal Property					
C - Property Claimed as Exempt					
D - Creditors Holding Secured Claims					
E - Creditors Holding Unsecured Priority Claims					
F - Creditors Holding Unsecured Nonpriority Claims					
G - Executory Contracts and Unexpired Leases					
H - Codebtors					
I - Current Income of Individual Debtor(s)					
J - Current Expenditures of Individual Debtor(s)					
Total Number of Sheets of All Schedules					
Total Assets					
Total Liabilities					

Form B6 A/B, P1(6-90)   Julius Blumberg, Inc. NYC 10013

In re:

                                       Debtor(s)   Case No.   (if known)

SCHEDULE A - REAL PROPERTY

DESCRIPTION AND LOCATION OF PROPERTY	NATURE OF DEBTOR'S INTEREST IN PROPERTY	H W J C	CURRENT MARKET VALUE OF DEBTOR'S INTEREST IN PROPERTY WITHOUT DEDUCTING ANY SECURED CLAIM OR EXEMPTION	AMOUNT OF SECURED CLAIM

Total -> $ (Report also on Summary of Schedules.)

SCHEDULE B - PERSONAL PROPERTY

TYPE OF PROPERTY	N O N E	DESCRIPTION AND LOCATION OF PROPERTY	H W J C	CURRENT MARKET VALUE OF DEBTOR'S INTEREST IN PROPERTY WITHOUT DEDUCTING ANY SECURED CLAIM OR EXEMPTION
1. Cash on hand				
2. Checking, savings or other financial accounts, certificates of deposit, or shares in banks, savings and loan, thrift, building and loan, and homestead associations, or credit unions, brokerage houses, or cooperatives.				
3. Security deposits with public utilities, telephone companies, landlords, and others.				
4. Household goods and furnishings including audio, video and computer equipment.				
5. Books; pictures and other art objects; antiques; stamp, coin, record, tape, compact disc, and other collections or collectibles.				
6. Wearing apparel.				
7. Furs and jewelry.				
8. Firearms and sports, photographic, and other hobby equipment.				
9. Interests in insurance policies. Name insurance company of each policy and itemize surrender or refund value of each.				

3072 · 1991 JULIUS BLUMBERG, INC., NYC 10013

Form B6B, P2 (6-90)   Julius Blumberg, Inc. NYC 10013

SCHEDULE B
PERSONAL PROPERTY

In re: Debtor(s)   Case No.   (if known)

TYPE OF PROPERTY	N O N E	DESCRIPTION AND LOCATION OF PROPERTY	H W J C	CURRENT MARKET VALUE OF DEBTOR'S INTEREST IN PROPERTY WITHOUT DEDUCTING ANY SECURED CLAIM OR EXEMPTION
10. Annuities. Itemize and name each issuer.				
11. Interests in IRA, ERISA, Keogh, or other pension or profit sharing plans. Itemize				
12. Stock and interests in incorporated and unincorporated businesses. Itemize.				
13. Interest in partnerships or joint ventures. Itemize.				
14. Government and corporate bonds and other negotiable and nonegotiable instruments.				
15. Accounts receivable.				
16. Alimony, maintenance, support, and property settlements to which the debtor is or may be entitled. Give particulars.				
17. Other liquidated debts owing debtor including tax refunds. Give particulars.				
18. Equitable or future interests, life estates, and rights or powers exercisable for the benefit of the debtor other than those listed in Schedule of Real Property.				
19. Contingent and noncontingent interests in estate of a decedent, death benefit plan, life insurance policy, or trust.				
20. Other contingent and unliquidated claims of every nature, including tax refunds, counterclaims of the debtor, and rights to setoff claims. Give estimated value of each.				
21. Patents, copyrights, and other intellectual property. Give particulars.				
22. Licenses, franchises, and other general intangibles. Give particulars.				
23. Automobiles, trucks, trailers, and other vehicles and accessories.				
24. Boats, motors, and accessories.				
25. Aircraft and accessories.				
26. Office equipment, furnishings, and supplies.				
27. Machinery, fixtures, equipment, and supplies used in business.				
28. Inventory.				
29. Animals.				
30. Crops - growing or harvested. Give particulars.				
31. Farming equipment and implements.				
32. Farm supplies, chemicals, and feed.				
33. Other personal property of any kind not already listed. Itemize.				

(Include amounts from any continuation sheets attached. Report total also on Summary of Schedules)   Total -> $

_____ continuation sheets attached

Form B6 C (6,90)   Julius Blumberg, Inc. NYC 10013

In re: Debtor(s)   Case No.   (if known)

SCHEDULE C - PROPERTY CLAIMED AS EXEMPT

Debtor elects the exemptions to which debtor is entitled under (Check one box)

☐ 11 U.S.C. § 522(b)(1): Exemptions provided in 11 U.S.C. § 522(d). Note: These exemptions are available only in certain **states.**

☐ 11 U.S.C. § 522(b)(2): Exemptions available under applicable nonbankruptcy federal laws, state or local law.

DESCRIPTION OF PROPERTY	SPECIFY LAW PROVIDING EACH EXEMPTION	VALUE OF CLAIMED EXEMPTION	CURRENT MARKET VALUE OF PROPERTY WITHOUT DEDUCTING EXEMPTION

Form B6 D (6-90)   Julius Blumberg, Inc. NYC 10013

In re: Debtor(s)   Case No.   (if known)

SCHEDULE D - CREDITORS HOLDING SECURED CLAIMS

☐ Check this box if debtor has no creditors holding secured claims to report on this Schedule D.

CREDITOR'S NAME AND MAILING ADDRESS INCLUDING ZIP CODE	CODEBTOR	HWJC	DATE CLAIM WAS INCURRED, NATURE OF LIEN, AND DESCRIPTION AND MARKET VALUE OF PROPERTY SUBJECT TO LIEN	CUD*	AMOUNT OF CLAIM WITHOUT DEDUCTING VALUE OF COLLATERAL	UNSECURED PORTION IF ANY
A/C #						
			VALUE $			
A/C #						
			VALUE $			
A/C #						
			VALUE $			
A/C #						
			VALUE $			
A/C #						
			VALUE $			
A/C #						
			VALUE $			
A/C #						
			VALUE $			
A/C #						
			VALUE $			
A/C #						
			VALUE $			

_____ continuation sheets attached

Subtotal -> (Total of this page) $

Total -> (use only on last page) $

*If contingent, enter C; if unliquidated, enter U; if disputed, enter D.

(Report total also on Summary of Schedules)

3072 · 1991 JULIUS BLUMBERG, INC., NYC 10013

Form B6 E (12/94)   Julius Blumberg, Inc. NYC 10013

In re: _____   Debtor(s)   Case No. _____   (if known)

SCHEDULE E - CREDITORS HOLDING UNSECURED PRIORITY CLAIMS

☐ Check this box if debtor has no creditors holding unsecured priority claims to report on this Schedule E

TYPE OF PRIORITY CLAIMS (Check the appropriate box(es) below if claims in that category are listed on the attached sheets)

☐ **Extensions of credit in an involuntary case**   Claims arising in the ordinary course of the debtor's business or financial affairs after the commencement of the case but before the earlier of the appointment of a trustee or the order for relief. 11 U.S.C. § 507 (a) (2).

☐ **Wages, salaries, and commissions**   Wages, salaries, and commissions, including vacation, severance. and sick leave pay owing to employees, and commissions owing to qualifying independent sales representatives up to $4,000* per person, earned within 90 days immediately preceding the filing of the original petition, or the cessation of business, whichever occurred first, to the extent provided in 11 U.S.C. § 507 (a) (3).

☐ **Contributions to employee benefit plans**   Money owed to employee benefit plans for services rendered within 180 days immediately preceding the filing of the original petition, or the cessation of business, whichever occurred first, to the extent provided in 11 U.S.C. § 507 (a) (4).

☐ **Certain farmers and fishermen**   Claims of certain farmers and fishermen, up to $4,000* per farmer or fisherman, against the debtor, as provided in 11 U.S.C. § 507 (a) (5).

☐ **Deposits by individuals**   Claims of individuals up to $1,800* for deposits for the purchase, lease, or rental of property or services for personal, family, or household use, that were not delivered or provided. 11 U.S.C. § 507 (a) (6).

☐ **Alimony, Maintenance, or Support**   Claims of a spouse, former spouse, or child of the debtor for alimony. maintenance, or support, to the extent provided in 11 U.S.C. § 507 (a) (7).

☐ **Taxes and Certain Other Debts Owed to Governmental Units**   Taxes, customs duties, and penalties owing to federal, state, and local governmental units as set forth in 11 U.S.C. § 507 (a) (8).

☐ **Commitments to Maintain the Capital of an Insured Depository Institution**   Claims based on commitments to the FDIC, RTC, Director of the Office of Thrift Supervision, Comptroller of the Currency, or Board of Governors of the Federal Reserve System, or their predecessors or successors, to maintain the capital of an insured depository institution. 11 U.S.C. § 507 (a) (9).

*Amounts are subject to adjustment on April 1, 1998, and every three years thereafter with respect to cases commenced on or after the date of adjustment.

CREDITOR'S NAME AND MAILING ADDRESS INCLUDING ZIP CODE	CO D E B T	H W J C	DATE CLAIM WAS INCURRED AND CONSIDERATION FOR CLAIM	C U D *	TOTAL AMOUNT OF CLAIM	AMOUNT ENTITLED TO PRIORITY
A/C#						
A/C#						
A/C#						
A/C#						
A/C#						

_____ Continuation sheets attached.

Subtotal -> (Total of this page) $ _____

Total -> (use only on last page of the completed Schedule E) $ _____

* If contingent, enter C; if unliquidated., enter U; if disputed , enter D.

(Report total also on Summary of Schedules)

3072© 1991 JULIUS BLUMBERG, INC., NYC 10013

Blumbergs Law Products Form B6 F (6-90)

Julius Blumberg, Inc. NYC 10013

In re: _____ Debtor(s)   Case No. _____ (if known)

SCHEDULE F - CREDITORS HOLDING UNSECURED NONPRIORITY CLAIMS

☐ Check this box if debtor has no creditors holding unsecured nonpriority claims to report on this Schedule F

CREDITOR'S NAME AND MAILING ADDRESS INCLUDING ZIP CODE	CO DEBT	H W J C	DATE CLAIM WAS INCURRED AND CONSIDERATION FOR CLAIM. IF CLAIM IS SUBJECT TO SETOFF, SO STATE.	C U D *	AMOUNT OF CLAIM
A/C #					
A/C #					
A/C #					
A/C #					
A/C #					
A/C #					
A/C #					
A/C #					
A/C #					

_____ Continuation Sheets attached.

Subtotal -> (Total of this page) $ _____

*If contingent, enter C; if unliquidated, enter U; if disputed, enter D.

Total -> (use only on last page of completed Schedule F.) $ _____

(Report total also on Summary of Schedules)

Form B6 G (6-90)   Julius Blumberg, Inc. NYC 10013

In re: Debtor(s)   Case No.   (if known)

SCHEDULE G - EXECUTORY CONTRACTS AND UNEXPIRED LEASES

☐ Check this box if debtor has no executory contracts or unexpired leases.

NAME AND MAILING ADDRESS, INCLUDING ZIP CODE, OF OTHER PARTIES TO LEASE OR CONTRACT.	DESCRIPTION OF CONTRACT OR LEASE AND NATURE OF DEBTOR'S INTEREST. STATE WHETHER LEASE IS FOR NONRESIDENTIAL REAL PROPERTY. STATE CONTRACT NUMBER OF ANY GOVERNMENT CONTRACT.

Form B6 H, (6-90)   Julius Blumberg, Inc. NYC 10013

Debtor(s)   Case No.   (if known)

In re:

SCHEDULE H - CODEBTORS

☐ Check this box if debtor has no codebtors.

NAME AND ADDRESS OF CODEBTOR	NAME AND ADDRESS OF CREDITOR

3072 © 1991 JULIUS BLUMBERG. INC.. NYC 10013

A p p e n d i x   B

Form B6I (6-90)   Julius Blumberg, Inc. NYC 10013

In re: _____

Debtor(s)   Case No. _____   (if known)

SCHEDULE I - CURRENT INCOME OF INDIVIDUAL DEBTOR(S)

The column labeled "Spouse" must be completed in all cases filed by joint debtors and by a married debtor in a chapter 12 or 13 case whether or not a joint petition is filed, unless the spouses are separated and a joint petition is not filed.

Debtor's Marital Status:	DEPENDENTS OF DEBTOR AND SPOUSE		
	NAMES	AGE	RELATIONSHIP

Employment:	DEBTOR	SPOUSE
Occupation		
Name of Employer		
How long employed		
Address of Employer		

Income: (Estimate of average monthly income)   DEBTOR   SPOUSE

Current monthly gross wages, salary, and commissions (pro rate if not paid monthly.) $ _____ $ _____

Estimate monthly overtime

SUBTOTAL $ _____ $ _____

    LESS PAYROLL DEDUCTIONS

      a. Payroll taxes and social security

      b. Insurance

      c. Union dues

      d. Other (Specify)

    SUBTOTAL OF PAYROLL DEDUCTIONS $ _____ $ _____

TOTAL NET MONTHLY TAKE HOME PAY $ _____ $ _____

Regular income from operation of business or profession or farm

(attach detailed statement)

Income from real property

Interest and dividends

Alimony, maintenance or support payments payable to the debtor for the debtor's

    use or that of dependents listed above.

Social security or other government assistance (Specify)

Pension or retirement income

Other monthly income (Specify)

TOTAL MONTHLY INCOME $ _____ $ _____

TOTAL COMBINED MONTHLY INCOME $ _____   (Report also on Summary of Schedules)

Describe any increase or decrease of more than 10% in any of the above categories anticipated to occur within the year following the filing of this document:

Form B6 J, Cont. (6-90)   Julius Blumberg, Inc. NYC 10013

In re: Debtor(s)   Case No.   (if known)

SCHEDULE J - CURRENT EXPENDITURES OF INDIVIDUAL DEBTOR(S)

Complete this schedule by estimating the average monthly expenses of the debtor and the debtor's family. Pro rate any payments made bi-weekly, quarterly, semi-annually, or annually to show monthly rate.

☐ Check this box if a joint petition is filed and debtor's spouse maintains a separate household. Complete a separate schedule of expenditures labeled "Spouse".

Rent or home mortgage payment (include lot rented for mobile home) $

Are real estate taxes included? ☐ Yes ☐ No   Is property insurance included? ☐ Yes ☐ No

Utilities Electricity and heating fuel ....

         Water and sewer ....

         Telephone ....

         Other ....

Home maintenance (repairs and upkeep) ....

Food ....

Clothing ....

Laundry and dry cleaning ....

Medical and dental expenses ....

Transportation (not including car payments) ....

Recreation, clubs and entertainment, newspapers, magazines, etc. ....

Charitable contributions ....

Insurance (not deducted from wages or included in home mortgage payments)

         Homeowner's or renter's ....

         Life ....

         Health ....

         Auto ....

         Other ....

Taxes (not deducted from wages or included in home mortgage payments)

(Specify)

Installment payments: (In chapter 12 and 13 cases, do not list payments to be included in the plan)

         Auto ....

         Other ....

Alimony, maintenance, and support paid to others ....

Payments for support of additional dependents not living at your home ...

Regular expenses from operation of business, profession, or farm (attach detailed statement) ...

Other

TOTAL MONTHLY EXPENSES (Report also on Summary of Schedules) .... $ _____

(FOR CHAPTER 12 AND 13 DEBTORS ONLY)
Provide the information requested below, including whether plan payments are to be made bi-weekly, monthly, annually, or at some other regular interval.

A. Total projected monthly income $

B. Total projected monthly expenses .... $ _____

C. Excess income (A minus B) .... $ _____

D. Total amount to be paid into plan each .... $ _____
                    (interval)

Form B6 Cont. (6-90)   Julius Blumberg, Inc. N Y C 10013

In re: _____

                                    Debtor(s)   Case No.

                                                          (if known)

DECLARATION CONCERNING DEBTOR'S SCHEDULES

DECLARATION UNDER PENALTY OF PERJURY BY INDIVIDUAL DEBTOR

I declare under penalty of perjury that I have read the foregoing summary and schedules, consisting of _____ sheets, and that
they are true and correct to the best of my knowledge, information, and belief.   (Total shown on summary page plus 1.)

Date _____

                          Signature: _____
                                                          Debtor

Date _____

                          Signature: _____
                                              (Joint Debtor, if any)
                          (If joint case, both spouses must sign.)

DECLARATION UNDER PENALTY OF PERJURY ON BEHALF OF CORPORATION OR PARTNERSHIP

I, the _____ (the president or other officer or an authorized agent of the corporation or a member or an
authorized agent of the partnership) of the _____ (corporation or partnership) named as debtor in this case,
declare under penalty of perjury that I have read the foregoing summary and schedules, consisting of _____ sheets, and
that they are true and correct to the best of my knowledge, information, and belief.   (Total shown on summary page plus 1.)

Date _____

                          Signature: _____

                          (Pint or type name of individual signing on behalf of debtor.)

(An individual signing on behalf of a partnership or corporation must indicate position or relationship to debtor.)

Penalty for making a false statement or concealing property: Fine of up to $500,000 or imprisonment for up to 5 years or both. 18 U.S.C. §§ 152 and 3571.

3082 Chapter 13 Plan. 8-91

Blumbergs
Law Products

UNITED STATES BANKRUPTCY COURT

In re

DISTRICT OF

Debtor(s)   Case No.   (If Known)

CHAPTER 13 PLAN

(If this form is used by joint debtors wherever the word "debtor" or words referring to debtor are used they shall be read as if in the plural.)

1. The future earnings of the debtor are submitted to the supervision and control of the trustee and the *debtor — debtor's employer* shall pay to the trustee the sum of $ *weekly — bi-weekly — semi-monthly — monthly*   for a period of

2. From the payments so received, the trustee shall make disbursements as follows:
   (*a*) Full payment in deferred cash payments of all claims entitled to priority under 11 U.S.C. §507.

   (*b*) Holders of allowed secured claims shall retain the liens securing such claims and shall be paid as follows:

   (*c*) *Subsequent to — pro rata with* dividends to secured creditors, dividends to unsecured creditors whose claims are duly allowed as follows:

3. The following executory contracts of the debtor are rejected:

   Title to the debtor's property shall revest in the debtor *on confirmation of a plan — upon dismissal of the case after confirmation pursuant to 11 U.S.C. §350.*

Dated:
....
                    Debtor   *Debtor*

Acceptances may be mailed to..   ....
                                                                          Post Office Address

Blumbergs Law Products — Form 7 Stmt. of Financial Affairs (11-92)

Julius Blumberg, Inc.
NYC 10013

UNITED STATES BANKRUPTCY COURT

DISTRICT OF

In re:

Debtor(s)   *Case No.*

STATEMENT OF FINANCIAL AFFAIRS

This statement is to be completed by every debtor. Spouses filing a joint petition may file a single statement on which the information for both spouses is combined. If the case is filed under chapter 12 or chapter 13, a married debtor must furnish information for both spouses whether or not a joint petition is filed, unless the spouses are separated and a joint petition is not filed. An individual debtor engaged in business as a sole proprietor, partner, family farmer, or self-employed professional, should provide the information requested on this statement concerning all such activities as well as the individual's personal affairs.

Questions 1-15 are to be completed by all debtors. Debtors that are or have been in business, as defined below, also must complete Questions 16-21. **If the answer to any question is "None," or the question is not applicable, mark the box labeled "None."** If additional space is needed for the answer to any question, use and attach a separate sheet properly identified with the case name, case number (if known), and the number of the question.

DEFINITIONS

"In business." A debtor is "in business" for the purpose of this form if the debtor is a corporation or partnership. An individual debtor is "in business" for the purpose of this form if the debtor is or has been, within the two years immediately preceding the filing of this bankruptcy case, any of the following: an officer, director, managing executive, or person in control of a corporation; a partner, other than a limited partner, of a partnership; a sole proprietor or self-employed.

"Insider." The term "insider" includes but is not limited to: relatives of the debtor; general partners of the debtor and their relatives; corporations of which the debtor is an officer, director, or person in control; officers, directors, and any person in control of a corporate debtor and their relatives; affiliates of the debtor and insiders of such affiliates; any managing agent of the debtor. 11 U.S.C. §101(30).

___ None   **1. Income from Employment or Operation of Business**

State the gross amount of income the debtor has received from employment, trade, or profession, or from operation of the debtor's business from the beginning of this calendar year to the date this case was commenced. State also the gross amounts received during the **two years** immediately preceding this calendar year. (A debtor that maintains, or has maintained, financial records on the basis of a fiscal rather than a calendar year may report fiscal year income. Identify the beginning and ending dates of the debtor's fiscal year.) If a joint petition is filed, state income for each spouse separately. (Married debtors filing under chapter 12 or chapter 13 must state income of both spouses whether or not a joint petition is filed, unless the spouses are separated and a joint petition is not filed.)
Give AMOUNT and SOURCE (If more than one).

___ None   **2. Income Other than from Employment or Operation of Business**

State the amount of income received by the debtor other than from employment, trade, profession, or operation of the debtor's business during the **two years** immediately preceding the commencement of this case. Give particulars. If a joint petition is filed, state income for each spouse separately. (Married debtors filing under chapter 12 or chapter 13 must state income for each spouse whether or not a joint petition is filed, unless the spouses are separated and a joint petition is not filed.) Give AMOUNT and SOURCE.

3. Payments to Creditors

___ None   a. List all payments on loans, installment purchases of goods or services, and other debts, aggregating more than $600 to any creditor, made within **90 days** immediately preceding the commencement of this case. (Married debtors filing under chapter 12 or chapter 13 must include payments by either or both spouses whether or not a joint petition is filed, unless the spouses are separated and a joint petition is not filed.)
Give NAME AND ADDRESS OF CREDITOR, DATES OF PAYMENTS, AMOUNT PAID and AMOUNT STILL OWING.

___ None   b. List all payments made within **one year** immediately preceding the commencement of this case to or for the benefit of creditors who are or were insiders. (Married debtors filing under chapter 12 or chapter 13 must include payments by either or both spouses whether or not a joint petition is filed, unless the spouses are separated and a joint petition is not filed.)
Give NAME AND ADDRESS OF CREDITOR AND RELATIONSHIP TO DEBTOR, DATE OF PAYMENT, AMOUNT PAID and AMOUNT STILL OWING.

4. Suits and Administrative Proceedings, Executions, Garnishments and Attachments

___ None   a. List all suits and administrative proceedings to which the debtor is or was a party within **one year** immediately preceding the filing of this bankruptcy case. (Married debtors filing under chapter 12 or chapter 13 must include information concerning either or both spouses whether or not a joint petition is filed, unless the spouses are separated and a joint petition is not filed.)
Give CAPTION OF SUIT AND CASE NUMBER, NATURE OF PROCEEDING, COURT OR AGENCY AND LOCATION and STATUS OR DISPOSITION.

___ None   b. Describe all property that has been attached, garnished, or seized under any legal or equitable process within **one year** immediately preceding the commencement of this case. (Married debtors filing under chapter 12 or chapter 13 must include information concerning property of either or both spouses whether or not a joint petition is filed, unless the spouses are separated and a joint petition is not filed.)

Give NAME AND ADDRESS OF PERSON FOR WHOSE BENEFIT PROPERTY WAS SEIZED, DATE OF SEIZURE and DESCRIPTION AND VALUE OF PROPERTY.

☐ None **5. Repossessions, Foreclosures, and Returns**

List all property that has been repossessed by a creditor, sold at a foreclosure sale, transferred through a deed in lieu of foreclosure or returned to the seller, within **one year** immediately preceding the commencement of this case. (Married debtors filing under chapter 12 or chapter 13 must include information concerning property of either or both spouses whether or not a joint petition is filed, unless the spouses are separated and a joint petition is not filed.)

Give NAME AND ADDRESS OF CREDITOR OR SELLER, DATE OF REPOSSESSION, FORECLOSURE SALE, TRANSFER OR RETURN and DESCRIPTION AND VALUE OF PROPERTY.

6. Assignments and Receiverships

☐ None   a. Describe any assignment of property for the benefit of creditors made within **120 days** immediately preceding the commencement of this case. (Married debtors filing under chapter 12 or chapter 13 must include any assignment by either or both spouses whether or not a joint petition is filed, unless the spouses are separated and a joint petition is not filed.)

Give NAME AND ADDRESS OF ASSIGNEE, DATE OF ASSIGNMENT and TERMS OF ASSIGNMENT OR SETTLEMENT.

☐ None   b. List all property which has been in the hands of a custodian, receiver, or court-appointed official within **one year** immediately preceding the commencement of this case. (Married debtors filing under chapter 12 or chapter 13 must include information concerning property of either or both spouses whether or not a joint petition is filed, unless the spouses are separated and a joint petition is not filed.)

Give NAME AND ADDRESS OF CUSTODIAN, NAME AND LOCATION OF COURT, CASE TITLE & NUMBER, DATE OF ORDER and DESCRIPTION AND VALUE OF PROPERTY.

☐ None **7. Gifts**

List all gifts or charitable contributions made within **one year** immediately preceding the commencement of this case except ordinary and usual gifts to family members aggregating less than $200 in value per individual family member and charitable contributions aggregating less than $100 per recipient. (Married debtors filing under chapter 12 or chapter 13 must include gifts or contributions by either or both spouses whether or not a joint petition is filed, unless the spouses are separated and a joint petition is not filed.)

Give NAME AND ADDRESS OF PERSON OR ORGANIZATION, RELATIONSHIP TO DEBTOR, IF ANY, DATE OF GIFT, and DESCRIPTION AND VALUE OF GIFT.

☐ None **8. Losses**

List all losses from fire, theft, other casualty or gambling within **one year** immediately preceding the commencement of this case **or since the commencement of this case.** (Married debtors filing under chapter 12 or chapter 13 must include losses by either or both spouses whether or not a joint petition is filed, unless the spouses are separated and a joint petition is not filed.)

Give DESCRIPTION AND VALUE OF PROPERTY, DESCRIPTION OF CIRCUMSTANCES AND, IF LOSS WAS COVERED IN WHOLE OR IN PART BY INSURANCE, GIVE PARTICULARS and DATE OF LOSS.

☐ None **9. Payments Related to Debt Counseling or Bankruptcy**

List all payments made or property transferred by or on behalf of the debtor to any persons, including attorneys, for consultation concerning debt consolidation, relief under the bankruptcy law or preparation of a petition in bankruptcy within **one year** immediately preceding the commencement of this case.

Give NAME AND ADDRESS OF PAYEE, DATE OF PAYMENT, NAME OF PAYOR IF OTHER THAN DEBTOR and AMOUNT OF MONEY OR DESCRIPTION AND VALUE OF PROPERTY.

☐ None **10. Other Transfers**

List all other property, other than property transferred in the ordinary course of the business or financial affairs of the debtor, transferred either absolutely or as security within **one year** immediately preceding the commencement of this case. (Married debtors filing under chapter 12 or chapter 13 must include transfers by either or both spouses whether or not a joint petition is filed, unless the spouses are separated and a joint petition is not filed.)

Give NAME AND ADDRESS OF TRANSFEREE, RELATIONSHIP TO DEBTOR, DATE, and DESCRIBE PROPERTY TRANSFERRED AND VALUE RECEIVED.

☐ None   **11. Closed Financial Accounts**

List all financial accounts and instruments held in the name of the debtor or for the benefit of the debtor which were closed, sold, or otherwise transferred within **one year** immediately preceding the commencement of this case. Include checking, savings, or other financial accounts, certificates of deposit, or other instruments; shares and share accounts held in banks, credit unions, pension funds, cooperatives, associations, brokerage houses and other financial institutions. (Married debtors filing under chapter 12 or chapter 13 must include information concerning accounts or instruments held by or for either or both spouses whether or not a joint petition is filed, unless the spouses are separated and a joint petition is not filed.)

Give NAME AND ADDRESS OF INSTITUTION, TYPE AND NUMBER OF ACCOUNT AND AMOUNT OF FINAL BALANCE and AMOUNT AND DATE OF SALE OR CLOSING.

☐ None   **12. Safe Deposit Boxes**

List each safe deposit or other box or depository in which the debtor has or had securities, cash, or other valuables within **one year** immediately preceding the commencement of this case. (Married debtors filing under chapter 12 or chapter 13 must include boxes or depositories of either or both spouses whether or not a joint petition is filed, unless the spouses are separated and a joint petition is not filed.)

Give NAME AND ADDRESS OF BANK OR OTHER DEPOSITORY, NAMES AND ADDRESSES OF THOSE WITH ACCESS TO BOX OR DEPOSITORY, DESCRIPTION OF CONTENTS and DATE OF TRANSFER OR SURRENDER, IF ANY.

☐ None   **13. Setoffs**

List all setoffs made by any creditor, including a bank, against a debt or deposit of the debtor within **90 days** preceding the commencement of this case. (Married debtors filing under chapter 12 or chapter 13 must include information concerning either or both spouses whether or not a joint petition is filed, unless the spouses are separated and a joint petition is not filed.)

Give NAME AND ADDRESS OR CREDITOR, DATE OF SETOFF and AMOUNT OF SETOFF.

☐ None   **14. Property Held for Another Person**

List all property owned by another person that the debtor holds or controls.

Give NAME AND ADDRESS OF OWNER, DESCRIPTION AND VALUE OF PROPERTY and LOCATION OF PROPERTY.

☐ None   **15. Prior Address of Debtor**

If the debtor has moved within the two years immediately preceding the commencement of this case, list all premises which the debtor occupied during that period and vacated prior to the commencement of this case. If a joint petition is filed, report also any separate address of either spouse.

Give ADDRESS, NAME USED and DATES OF OCCUPANCY.

Unsworn Declaration under Penalty of Perjury.

I declare under penalty of perjury that I have read the answers contained in the foregoing statement of financial affairs and any attachments thereto and that they are true and correct.

Date _____   Signature of Debtor _____

Date _____   Signature of Joint Debtor (if any) _____

_____ continuation sheets attached

Penalty for making a false statement: Fine of up to $500,000 or imprisonment for up to 5 years, or both. 18 U.S.C. §§152 and 3571.

[If completed by an individual or individual and spouse]

I declare under penalty of perjury that I have read the answers contained in the foregoing statement of financial affairs and any attachments thereto and that they are true and correct.

Date _____   Signature _____
                                                        of Debtor

Date _____   Signature _____
                                                        of Joint Debtor
                                                        (if any)

CERTIFICATION AND SIGNATURE OF NON-ATTORNEY BANKRUPTCY PETITION PREPARER (See 11 U.S.C. § 110)

I certify that I am a bankruptcy petition preparer as defined in 11 U.S.C. § 110, that I prepared this document for compensation, and that I have provided the debtor with a copy of this document.

_____   _____
Printed or Typed Name of Bankruptcy Petition Preparer   Social Security No.

_____

_____
Address

Names and Social Security numbers of all other individuals who prepared or assisted in preparing this document: If more than one person prepared this document, attach additional signed sheets conforming to the appropriate Official Form for each person.

X_____   _____
Signature of Bankruptcy Petition Preparer   Date

A bankruptcy petition preparer's failure to comply with the provisions of title II and the Federal Rules of Bankruptcy Procedure may result in fines or imprisonment or both. 11 U.S.C § 110; 18 U.S.C. § 156.

[If completed on behalf of a partnership or corporation]

I, declare under penalty of perjury that I have read the answers contained in the foregoing statement of financial affairs and any attachments thereto and that they are true and correct to the best of my knowledge, information and belief.

Date _____   Signature _____

                                         _____
                                          Print Name and Title

[An individual signing on behalf of a partnership or corporation must indicate position or relationship to debtor.]

A p p e n d i x   B

3085   Statement of compensation: Rule 2016(b). 8-91

Blumbergs Law Products

UNITED STATES BANKRUPTCY COURT   **DISTRICT OF**

In re   Debtor(s)   Case No.   (If Known)

STATEMENT
Pursuant to Rule 2016(b)

The undersigned, pursuant to Rule 2016(b) Bankruptcy Rules, states that:

(1) The undersigned is the attorney for the debtor(s) in this case.

(2) The compensation paid or agreed to be paid by the debtor(s) to the undersigned is:

    (a) for legal services rendered or to be rendered in contemplation of and in connection with this case $ ....

    (b) prior to filing this statement, debtor(s) have paid $ ....

    (c) the unpaid balance due and payable is $ ....

(3) $ of the filing fee in this case has been paid.

(4) The services rendered or to be rendered include the following:

    (a) analysis of the financial situation, and rendering advice and assistance to the debtor(s) in determining whether to file a petition under title 11 of the United States Code.

    (b) preparation and filing of the petition, schedules, statement of affairs and other documents required by the court.

    (c) representation of the debtor(s) at the meeting of creditors.

(5) The source of payments made by the debtor(s) to the undersigned was from earnings, wages and compensation for services performed, and

(6) The source of payments to be made by the debtor(s) to the undersigned for the unpaid balance remaining, if any, will be from earnings, wages and compensation for services performed, and

(7) The undersigned has received no transfer, assignment or pledge of property execept the following for the value stated:

(8) The undersigned has not shared or agreed to share with any other entity, other than with members of undersigned's law firm, any compensation paid or to be paid except as follows:

Dated: Respectfully submitted, ... *Attorney for Petitioner*

Attorney's name and address ....

Appendix C
Federal Bankruptcy Exemptions

Bankruptcy Code Section 522(d)

1. The debtor's aggregate interest, not to exceed $15,000 in value, in real property or personal property that the debtor or a dependent of the debtor uses as a residence, in a cooperative that owns property that the debtor or a dependent of the debtor uses as a residence, or in a burial plot for the debtor or a dependent of the debtor.

2. The debtor's interest, not to exceed $2,400 in value, in one motor vehicle. A couple filing can each have a car with $2,400 equity.

3. The debtor's interest, not to exceed $400 in value in any particular item or $8,000 in aggregate value, in household furnishings, household goods, wearing apparel, appliances, books, animals, crops, or musical instruments, that are held primarily for the personal, family, or household use of the debtor or a dependent of the debtor.

4. The debtor's aggregate interest, not to exceed $1,000 in value, in jewelry held primarily for the personal, family, or household use of the debtor or a dependent of the debtor.

5. The debtor's aggregate interest in any property, not to exceed in value $800 plus up to $7,500 of any unused amount of the exemption provided under paragraph (1) of this subsection.

6. The debtor's aggregate interest, not to exceed $1,500 in value, in any implements, professional books, or tools of the trade of the debtor or the trade of a dependent of the debtor.

7. Any unmatured life insurance contract owned by the debtor, other than a credit life insurance contract.

8. The debtor's aggregate interest, not to exceed in value $8,000 less any amount of property of the estate transferred in the manner specified in section 542(d) of this title, in any accrued dividend or interest under, or loan value of, any unmatured life insurance contract owned by the debtor under which the insured is the debtor or an individual of whom the debtor is a dependent.

9. Professionally prescribed health aids for the debtor or a dependent of the debtor.

10. The debtor's right to receive—

    (A) a social security benefit, unemployment compensation, or a local public assistance benefit;

    (B) a veterans' benefit;

    (C) a disability, illness, or unemployment benefit;

    (D) alimony, support, or separate maintenance, to the extent reasonably necessary for the support of the debtor and any dependent of the debtor;

    (E) a payment under a stock bonus, pension, profit sharing, annuity, or similar plan or contract on account of illness, disability, death, age, or length of service, to the extent reasonably necessary for the support of the debtor and any dependent of the debtor, unless—

    (i) such plan or contract was established by or under the auspices of an insider that employed the debtor at the time the debtor's rights under such plan or contract arose;

    (ii) such payment is on account of age or length of service; and

    (iii) such plan or contract does not qualify under section 401(a), 403(a), 403(b), 408, or 409 of the Internal Revenue Code of 1954 [26 U.S.C. 401(a), 403(a), 403(b), 408, or 409].

11. The debtor's right to receive, or property that is traceable to:

    (A) an award under a crime victim's reparation law;

    (B) a payment on account of the wrongful death of an individual of whom the debtor was a dependent, to the extent reasonably necessary for the support of the debtor and any dependent of the debtor;

    (C) a payment under a life insurance contract that insured the life of an individual of whom the debtor was a dependent on the date of such individual's death, to the extent reasonably necessary for the support of the debtor and any dependent of the debtor;

(D) a payment, not to exceed $15,000, on account of personal bodily injury, not including pain and suffering or compensation for actual pecuniary loss, of the debtor or an individual of whom the debtor is a dependent; or

(E) a payment in compensation of loss of future earnings of the debtor or an individual of whom the debtor is or was a dependent, to the extent reasonably necessary for the support of the debtor and any dependent of the debtor.

Appendix D
State Bankruptcy Exemptions

WARNING

The state exemptions listed here are not complete. Only the major parts of the law have been explained. Also, state laws change. Consult an attorney in your area to find out the most recent law in your area.

Alabama

The homestead exemption has a $5,000 limitation of value and cannot be more than 160 acres in size. If the homestead exemption is not claimed, the debtor may claim up to $5,000 in value in a mobile home.

Personal property may be exempted to a value of $3,000. All necessary wearing apparel, family portraits or pictures and books may be exempted, as well as a burial place and church pew. Seventy-five percent of wages earned but unpaid is exempt.

(Alabama Code Title 6 Sec. 10-2; Sec. 10-5; Sec. 10-6; Sec. 10-7. Alabama Constitution, Article X Sec. 204.)

Alaska

The homestead exemption has a $27,000 limitation of value. Personal property and tools of trade can be exempted to a total value of $1,500.

Wearing apparel, household goods, books, musical instruments, family heirlooms and portraits, jewelry to a value of $500, pets to a value of $500, a motor vehicle to a value of $1,500 (if its full value does not exceed $10,000) and a burial plot may be exempted. Tools of trade, implements and professional books may be exempt to a value of $1,400. Weekly net earnings to a value of $175 are exempt.

(Alaska Statutes Sec. 9.38.010; Sec. 9.30.020; Sec. 9.30.15; Sec. 9.38.030.)

Arizona

The homestead exemption has a $50,000 limitation of value.

Personal property that can be exempted to a value of $4,000 includes: specified household equipment and furniture, family portraits, and paintings and drawings made by the debtor. Exemptions can be taken for food, fuel and provisions for six months, wearing apparel to a value of $500, musical instruments to a value of $250, certain livestock and pets to a value of $500, engagement and wedding rings to a value of $1,000, motor vehicle to a value of $1,500, books to a value of $250 and a watch to a value of $100. Other exemptions may include: a typewriter, bicycle, sewing machine, family bible, burial plot, shotgun and rifle to a value of $500; life insurance proceeds to a value of $20,000; prepaid rent to a value of $1,000; and $100 deposit in a financial institution. Books and tools of trade may be exempted to a value of $2,500; farm equipment and utensils, feed, seed and farm animals to a value of $2,500. Seventy-five percent of earned but unpaid wages is exempt (exemption may be higher for low-income debtors).

(Arizona Revised Statutes Sec. 33-1101; Sec. 33-1123; Sec. 33-1124; Sec. 33-1125; Sec. 33-1126; Sec. 33-1130; Sec. 33-1131.)

Arkansas

The homestead exemption limitations of value for a head of family are: no limit if less than 1/4 acre in town or 80 acres elsewhere; $2,500 limit if between 1/4 and one acre in town or 80 and 160 acres elsewhere. No homestead may exceed one acre in a city or town or 160 acres elsewhere. A debtor may instead claim real or personal property used as a residence to a value of $1,250, if married, or $800, if single.

Personal property exemptions may include a motor vehicle to a value of $1,200 and wedding rings with diamonds not exceeding 1/2 carat. Exemptions of the debtor's choice may be taken to a limit of $500 (if married or head of family) or $200 (if single). At least $25 a week of earned but unpaid wages is exempt; more may be claimed as part of the $500/$200 limit. Books and tools of trade are exempt to a value of $750.

(Arkansas Statutes Sec. 30-207; Sec. 36-211. Arkansas Constitution Art. 9 Sec. 3-5; Sec. 1, 2.)

California

Either state exemption system may be used; both husband and wife must pick the same exemption system.

Exemption System #1

A person who is 65 or older or who is disabled and therefore unable to engage in substantial gainful employment, may claim a homestead exemption to a $55,000 limitation of value for a house, mobile home, boat or condominium in which he actually lives. A member of a family unit may claim such property to a value of $45,000. Others may claim this property to a value of $30,000.

Personal property exemptions may include: motor vehicle(s) to a value of $1,200; household furnishings and provisions, wearing apparel and personal effects necessary and personally used by the debtor; materials about to be applied to repair or improve the debtor's residence, to a value of $1,000; jewelry, art and heirlooms to a value of $2,500; health aids; $500 deposit in account in which Social Security payments are deposited directly; $1,000 in an inmate's trust account; wrongful death and personal injury causes of action and recoveries necessary to support the debtor and family; cash and bank accounts that can be traced to an exempt asset; family burial plot. Exemptions to a value of $2,500 may be taken for various books, tools, equipment and personal property necessary for the debtor to earn a livelihood. Also exempt is 75 percent of earnings paid in the preceding 30 days (100 percent if subject to earnings withholding or wage assignment for support), a minimum of 75 percent of earned but unpaid wages (higher amount for low-income debtors), and public employee's vacation credits.

(California Code of Civil Procedure Sec. 703.080; Sec. 704.010; Sec. 704.020; Sec. 704.030; Sec. 704.040; Sec. 704.050; Sec. 704.060; Sec. 704.070; Sec. 704.080; Sec. 704.090; Sec. 704.113; Sec. 704.140; Sec. 704.150; Sec. 704.200; Sec. 704.730; Sec. 706.050.)

Exemption System #2 (Modified Federal System)

A homestead exemption to a value of $7,500 may be taken for a residence.

Personal property exemptions may include: motor vehicle to a value of $1,200; household goods and furnishings, wearing apparel, appliances, books, animals, crops and musical instruments to a value of $200 per item; jewelry to a total value of $500; personal injury recoveries to a value of $7,500; wrongful death recoveries; other property to a value of $400 ($7,900, if the homestead exemption is not claimed). Books and tools of trade are exempt to a value of $750.

(California Code of Civil Procedure Sec. 703.140.)

Colorado

The homestead exemption for real property or a mobile home has a $20,000 limitation of value.

Personal property exemptions include: wearing apparel of the debtor and each dependent to a value of $750; jewelry and watches and articles of adornment of the debtor and each dependent to a value of $500; books and family pictures to a value of $750; one burial plot per family member; household goods to a value of $1,500; fuel and provisions to a value of $300; motor vehicles used for gainful employment to a value of $1,000; personal injury recoveries. Exemptions may be claimed for: business books, equipment, stock, supplies and tools used and kept for the purpose of carrying on any gainful occupation to a value of $1,500; professional person's library to a value of $1,500; in the case of a debtor engaged, as his principal occupation, in agriculture or livestock or poultry raising, livestock and poultry to a value of $3,000 and horses, mules, wagons, machinery and tools to a value of $2,000. A minimum of 75 percent of earned but unpaid wages is exempt (may be greater for low-income debtors).

(Colorado Revised Statutes Sec. 13-54-102; Sec. 13-54-104; Sec. 38-41-201; Sec. 38-41-201.6.)

Connecticut

Personal property exemptions include: necessary apparel, food, bedding, household appliances and furniture; burial plot; motor vehicle to a value of $1,500; wedding and engagement rings; residential security and utility deposits. Exemptions may be claimed for books, tools and farm animals necessary for the debtor's occupation; and arms, uniforms and musical instruments owned by a member of the armed forces. A minimum of 75 percent of earned but unpaid wages is exempt (may be higher for low-income debtors).

(Connecticut General Statutes Annotated Sec. 52-352b; Sec. 83-581.)

Delaware

All debtors may exempt school books, family bible, family library, church pew, burial plot, sewing machine and wearing apparel. A head of family may also exempt other personal property to a value of $500. Books and tools of trade necessary for a debtor's business or trade are exempt to a value of $75 in New Castle and Sussex Counties and to a value of $50 in Kent County. Eighty-five percent of earned but unpaid wages is exempt.

(Delaware Code Annotated Title 10 Sec. 4902; Sec. 4903; Sec. 4913.)

District of Columbia

Personal property that may be exempted includes: wearing apparel to a value of $300; household furnishings, beds, bedding, stove, radio, sewing machine, cooking utensils to a value of $300; horse or mule, cart or motor vehicle to a value of $500 if used mainly for debtor's business; provisions and fuel for three months; family pictures; family library to a value of $400.

Exemptions may be taken for: library, implements and office furniture of a professional or artist to a value of $300; mechanic's tools to a value of $200; stock and materials necessary for business to a value of $200. A maximum of $200 per month of earned but unpaid wages may be exempted by a debtor who is the principal family support. Other debtors may exempt only $60 per month.

(District of Columbia Code Sec.15-501; Sec. 15-503.)

Florida

The homestead exemption is limited to 1/2 acre within a municipality or 160 acres elsewhere, or to a modular or mobile home.

Personal property is exempt to a value of $1,000. A head of family may exempt 100 percent of earned but unpaid wages.

(Florida Statutes Annotated Sec. 222.05; Sec. 222-11. Florida Constitution Article 10 Sec. 4.)

Georgia

The homestead exemption has a $5,000 limit of value.

Personal property that may be exempted includes: motor vehicles to a value of $1,000; household goods and furnishings, wearing apparel, appliances, books, musical instruments, animals and crops to a value of $200 per item (total value $3,500); jewelry to a value of $500; other property to a value of $400 plus any unused amount of the homestead exemption; life insurance proceeds and wrongful death recoveries necessary for debtor's support and personal injury recoveries to a value of $7,500. Professional books and tools of trade are exempt to a value of $500.

(Georgia Code Annotated Sec. 44-13-100.)

Hawaii

The homestead exemption has a value limitation of $30,000 for a head of household or debtor age 65 or older. The value limitation for all others is $20,000.

Personal property that may be exempted includes: motor vehicle to a value of $1,000; household furnishings and appliances; wearing apparel and books; jewelry and watches to a value of $1,000; burial plot. Exemptions may be taken for tools of trade, books, uniforms, furnishings, tools, fishing boat and motor vehicle. All of earned but unpaid wages for services rendered during the past 31 days is exempt.

(Hawaii Revised Statutes Sec. 651-92; Sec. 651-121.)

Idaho

The homestead exemption has a value limitation of $25,000.

Personal property exemptions include: furnishings and appliances, including wearing apparel, books, musical instruments, pets, one firearm, family portraits and certain heirlooms to a value of $500 per item and a total value of $4,000 per household; jewelry to a value of $250; a motor vehicle to a value of $500; a burial plot; water rights to 160 inches for irrigation; crops to a value of $1,000; personal injury and wrongful death recoveries.

Professional books, implements and tools of trade are exempt to a value of $1,000. Arms and uniforms are exempt for peace officers and members of the national guard or military. Seventy-five percent of earned but unpaid wages may be exempted (may be higher for low-income debtors).

(Idaho Code Sec. 11-207; Sec. 11-603; Sec. 11-604; Sec. 11-605; Sec. 55-1201.)

Illinois

The homestead exemption has a $7,500 limit of value.

Personal property that may be exempted includes: necessary wearing apparel, school books, bible and family pictures; motor vehicle to a value of $1,200; other property to a value of $2,000; wrongful death recoveries and life insurance proceeds (if necessary to support the debtor) and personal injury recoveries to a value of $7,500. Professional books and tools of trade are exempt to a value of $750. Eighty-five percent of earned but unpaid wages may be exempted (may be more for low-income debtors).

(Illinois Code of Civil Procedure Sec. 12-803; Sec. 12-901; Sec. 12-1001.)

Indiana

The homestead exemption has a $7,500 limit of value for real estate or personal property that is the personal or family residence of debtor.

Personal property that may be exempted includes tangible property to a value of $4,000 and intangible property to a value of $100; total value of all exempted property (homestead, real and personal) cannot exceed $10,000. Seventy-five percent of earned but unpaid wages is exempt (may be higher for low-income debtors).

(Indiana Statutes Annotated Sec. 24-4.5-5-105; Sec. 34-2-28-1.)

Iowa

The homestead exemption limits real property to 1/2 acre in a city or town and 40 acres elsewhere.

Personal property exemptions include: wearing apparel to a value of $200 per item, $1,000 total; library, bibles, portraits, pictures and paintings to a value of $200 per item, $1,000 total; household furnishings, goods and appliances to a value of $200 per item, $2,000 total; shotgun and rifle; various farm animals; any combination, to a value of $5,000, of musical instruments, motor vehicle to a value of $1,200, books and tools of trade, team and wagon, wages and tax refunds to a value of $1,000. Seventy-five percent of earned but unpaid wages is exempt (may be higher for low-income debtors). (Iowa Code Annotated Sec. 561.2; Sec. 627.6; Sec. 642.21.)

Kansas

The homestead limitation is 160 acres of farming land or one acre within a town or city, or a mobile home.

Personal property exemptions include: furnishings, supplies and equipment (including clothing, food and fuel) for one year; personal ornaments to a value of $1,000; one means of conveyance not to exceed $20,000; a burial plot. Exemptions to a value of $7,500 may be taken for books, furniture, tools, equipment, breeding stock, seed or plant stock necessary for a profession or business. Seventy-five percent of earned but unpaid wages is exempt (may be more for low-income debtors). (Kansas Statutes Annotated Sec. 60-2301; Sec. 60-2304.)

Kentucky

The homestead exemption has a $5,000 limitation of value.

Personal property exemptions include: household furnishings, clothing and jewelry to a value of $3,000; motor vehicle to a value of $2,500; other property to a value of $1,000; personal injury recoveries to a value of $7,500. Exemptions may be claimed for: a mechanic's or artisan's tools to a value of $300; a farmer's tools, equipment and livestock to a value of $3,000; various professionals' libraries, instruments and office equipment to a value of $1,000. Seventy-five percent of earned but unpaid wages is exempt (may be higher for low-income debtors). (Kentucky Revised Statutes Sec. 427.010; Sec. 427.030; Sec. 427.040; Sec. 427.060; Sec. 427.150; Sec. 427.160.)

Louisiana

The homestead limitation of value is $15,000.

Personal property exemptions include clothing, wedding and engagement rings, various household furnishings and equipment, family portraits, some military equipment, musical instruments, certain livestock and income from a dowry to a value of $5,000. Trade or professional tools, instruments, books, truck or non-luxury automobile and utility trailer are exempt. Seventy-five percent of earned but unpaid wages is exempt (may be higher for low-income debtors).

(Louisiana Revised Statutes Sec. 13:3881; Sec. 20:1.)

Maine

The homestead limitation of value is $7,500.

Personal property exemptions include: a motor vehicle to a value of $1,200; various household furnishings and equipment, wearing apparel, books, musical instruments, crops and animals to a value of $200 per item; jewelry to a value of $500; food for six months; stoves, furnaces and certain quantities of fuel; materials needed to raise and harvest food through one growing season; equipment and tools for raising and harvesting food; wrongful death recoveries and life insurance proceeds (if necessary for support) and personal injury recoveries to a value of $7,500; other property to a value of $400 ($4,900 of additional personal property or tools of trade if the homestead exemption is not claimed). Exemptions may be claimed for: professional books, tools and materials to a value of $1,000; one of every type farm implement for commercial raising and harvesting; one commercial fishing boat.

(Maine Revised Statutes Annotated Title 14 Sec. 4422.)

Maryland

Personal property exemptions include household goods and furnishings, wearing apparel, books, pets, and other personal or household items to a value of $500 and other property to a value of $5,500. Exemptions may be taken for books, tools, appliances and wearing apparel necessary for a trade or profession. Seventy-five percent of earned but unpaid wages is exempt (may be higher for low-income debtors).

(Maryland Annotated Code of Commercial Law Sec. 15-601.1; Maryland Annotated Code of Cts. and Jud. Proc. Sec. 11-504.)

Massachusetts

The homestead limitation of value is $100,000.

Personal property exemptions include: necessary wearing apparel, beds and bedding; one heating unit and up to $75 for fuel, heat, water and light; other household furniture to a value of $3,000; sewing machine to a value of $200; school books and bibles to a value of $200; certain farm animals and 4 tons of hay; provisions or cash to a value of $300; a church pew and burial plot; shares in a cooperative association to a value of $100; an automobile to a value of $700; $500 in a bank or credit union; cash not exceeding $200 for rent if the homestead exemption is not claimed; cash or bank deposits of $125 if the wages exemption is not claimed. Exemptions may be taken for: tools and implements, to a value of $500, and materials and stock, to a value of $500, necessary for debtor's business or trade; fisherman's boats and equipment to a value of $500; uniform and arms required by a member of the militia; also $125 of earned but unpaid wages is exempt.

(Massachusetts General Laws Annotated Chap. 188 Sec. 1; Chap. 235 Sec. 34; Chap. 246 Sec. 28A.)

Michigan

The homestead limitations are: value, $3,500; area, one lot in a town or city or 40 acres elsewhere.

Personal property exemptions include: all family pictures, arms, all wearing apparel of every person or family, and provisions and fuel for comfortable subsistence of each householder and his or her family for 6 months; all household goods, furniture, utensils, books and appliances to a value of $1,000; a church pew; a burial plot. Householders may also exempt: family provisions and fuel for six months, various farm animals and six months' feed; $1,000 par value of building and loan association shares if the homestead exemption has not been claimed. Certain tools, materials, vehicle and other things necessary for the debtor's profession or business are exempt to a value of $1,000.

(Michigan Compiled Laws Annotated Sec. 600.6023.)

Minnesota

The homestead exemption is real property limited to 1/2 acre in a city or 80 acres elsewhere, or a mobile home.

Personal property exemptions include: bible, library, musical instruments, church pew and burial plot; wearing apparel, watch, household furniture and various electrical appliances, and food to a value of $4,500;

motor vehicle to a value of $2,000; personal injury recoveries. Also exempt are: farm implements and machines, livestock and crops to a value of $10,000; tools of trade, furniture, stock and library necessary for debtor's trade or profession to a value of $5,000. Seventy-five percent of earned but unpaid wages is exempt (may be higher for low-income debtors and relief recipients).

(Minnesota Statutes Annotated Sec. 550.37.)

Mississippi

The homestead exemption limitations are 160 acres in size and $75,000 in value.

Personal property exemptions include: wearing apparel, sewing machine, family portraits; library, pictures and paintings to a value of $9,000; household furniture to a value of $5,000; various farm produce, animals and feed, and farm equipment. Other exemptions are: mechanic's tools of trade; farmer's agricultural equipment; student's textbooks; militia member's arms and equipment; teacher's educational materials; surgeon's or dentist's professional instruments to a value of $5,000. Personal injury settlements are exempt to a value of $10,000. Seventy-five percent of earned but unpaid wages is exempt (may be higher for low-income debtors). In lieu of tools of trade and personal property exemptions, tangible property of any kind may be exempted to a value of $6,500.

(Mississippi Code Sec. 85-3-1; Sec. 85-3-4; Sec. 85-3-17; Sec. 85-3-21.)

Missouri

The homestead exemption is real property to a value of $8,000 or a mobile home to a value of $1,000.

Personal property exemptions include: wearing apparel, household furnishings and goods, appliances, books, musical instruments, animals and crops to a value of $1,000; jewelry to a value of $500; motor vehicle to a value of $500; wrongful death recoveries; other property to a value of $400 or, for a head of family, other property to a value of $850 plus $250 for each minor child. Tools of trade and professional books are exempt to a value of $2,000. Seventy-five percent of earned but unpaid wages is exempt (may be higher for low-income debtors).

(Annotated Missouri Statutes Sec. 513.430; Sec. 513.440; Sec. 513.475; Sec. 525.030.)

Montana

Homestead exemption limitations are: value, $40,000; area, 1/4 acre in city or town and one acre elsewhere (320 acres if used for agriculture).

Personal property exemptions for head of family or person over 60 include: wearing apparel; desks, tables, chairs and books to a value of $200; specified household furniture and equipment; family pictures; clock; gun; fuel and provisions for three months; horse, saddle and bridle, various farm animals and feed for three months; truck or automobile to a value of $1,000. All other debtors may exempt only wearing apparel. Tools of trade exemptions for heads of families or persons over 60 are diverse and specific to categories of professions or occupations; all other debtors may exempt only arms and uniforms required by law. One hundred percent of earned but unpaid wages is exempt if needed for support of debtor's family.

(Montana Code Annotated Sec. 25-13-611; Sec. 25-13-612; Sec. 25-13-613; Sec. 25-13-614; Sec. 25-13-617; Sec. 70-32-104.)

Nebraska

The homestead exemption for a head of family is limited to: area, two lots within a village or city and 160 acres elsewhere; value, $6,500.

Personal property exemptions include: wearing apparel and immediate personal possessions; household furniture and kitchen utensils to a value of $1,500; fuel and provisions for six months; burial plot; in lieu of homestead exemption, personal property other than wages to a value of $2,500. A head of family may exempt equipment and tools of trade used for family support to a value of $1,500. Eighty-five percent of earned but unpaid wages is exempt for a head of family; 75 percent is exempt for other debtors; the exemption may be higher for low-income debtors.

(Revised Statutes of Nebraska Sec. 12-517; Sec. 25-1552; Sec. 25-1556; Sec. 25-1558; Sec. 40-101.)

Nevada

The homestead exemption is real property or a mobile home limited in value to $90,000.

Personal property exemptions include: household goods and furniture, appliances and equipment to a value of $3,000; vehicle to a value of $1,000; library to a value of $1,500; family pictures, keepsakes and gun. Exemptions may be claimed for: farm trucks, tools, supplies, seed and stock to a value of $4,500; professional library, office equipment and supplies, tools and materials needed for debtor's trade to a value of $4,500; various miner's or prospector's equipment and cabin for operations on a claim worked by debtor to a value of $4,500; uniforms and arms required by law of debtor. Seventy-five percent of earned but unpaid wages is exempt (may be higher for low-income debtor).

(Nevada Revised Statutes Sec. 21.090; Sec. 115.010.)

New Hampshire

The homestead exemption is real property or manufactured housing to a value of $30,000.

Personal property exemptions include: wearing apparel, beds and bedding, cooking stove and utensils, refrigerator, sewing machine, church pew and burial plot; jewelry to a value of $500; automobile to a value of $1,000; household furniture to a value of $2,000; library, bibles and school books to a value of $800; fuel and provisions to a value of $400; certain farm animals to a value of $300 and four tons of hay. Exemptions may be claimed for tools of trade to a value of $2,000 and for uniforms and equipment for a militia member. Earned but unpaid wages are exempt under a formula based on the federal minimum wage.

(New Hampshire Revised Statutes Annotated Sec. 480:1; Sec. 511:2; Sec. 512:21.)

New Jersey

Personal property exemptions include: wearing apparel; household goods and furniture to a value of $1,000; interests in a corporation or shares of stock, goods and chattels, and any personal property (not including wearing apparel) to a value of $1,000. Ninety percent of earned but unpaid wages is exempt unless the debtor's income exceeds $7,500 per year.

(New Jersey Statutes Annotated Sec. 2A:17-19; Sec. 2A:17-56; Sec. 2A:26-4.)

New Mexico

The homestead exemption for a debtor who is married, widowed or supporting another person has a value limitation of $20,000. If the homestead is jointly owned by two persons, each joint owner is entitled to an exemption of $20,000.

Personal property exemptions include: clothing, furniture and books; jewelry to a value of $2,500; motor vehicle to a value of $4,000; other personal property to a value of $500 (this may not be applied to money by debtors supporting only themselves). If the homestead exemption is not claimed, an additional $2,000 of personal or real property is exempt. Tools of trade to a value of $1,500 are exempt.

(New Mexico Statutes Annotated Sec. 42-10-1; Sec. 42-10-2; Sec. 42-10-9; Sec. 42-10-10.)

New York

The homestead exemption is real property, a mobile home or an interest in a condominium or cooperative apartment to a value of $10,000.

Personal property exemptions include: wearing apparel; household furniture and various appliances, stoves and fuel for 60 days; church pew; motor vehicle not exceeding $2,400 above liens and encumbrances of debtor; wedding ring and watch to a value of $35; school books, family pictures and bible, other books to a value of $50; family food for 60 days; domestic animals and 60 days' food to a value of $450; security deposits to utilities and landlord; principal of a trust fund and 90 percent of the income or other payments; personal injury recoveries to a value of $7,500 and wrongful death recoveries. Total personal property exemptions are limited to a value of $5,000; to the extent that this limit is not exceeded, the debtor may exempt up to $2,500 in cash in lieu of the homestead exemption. Various tools of trade, professional library and furniture are exempt to a value of $600. Ninety percent of earned but unpaid wages are exempt (100 percent for some military members).

(New York Civil Practice Law and Rules Sec. 5205; Sec. 5206. New York Debtor and Creditor Law Sec. 282-284.)

North Carolina

A debtor may choose either of the two state systems.

Exemption System #1

The homestead exemption on real property for a head of family is limited in value to $1,000.

Personal property may be exempted to a value of $500. One hundred percent of earned but unpaid wages is exempt if needed for family support.

(North Carolina Constitution Article X, Sec. 1 & 2. General Statutes of North Carolina Sec. 1-362.)

Exemption System #2

The homestead exemption value limitation on real or personal property used as a residence is $7,500.

Personal property exemptions include: wearing apparel, household furniture and goods, appliances, musical instruments, books, animals and crops to a value of $2,500 (plus $500 per dependent to an additional value of $2,000); a motor vehicle to a value of $1,000; personal injury and wrongful death recoveries; other property to a value of $2,500 in lieu of the homestead exemption. Professional books and tools of trade are exempt to a value of $500.

(General Statutes of North Carolina Sec. 1C-1601.)

North Dakota

The homestead exemption is real property to a value of $20,000. If the homestead is owned jointly by two persons, each joint owner is entitled to an exemption of $20,000.

Personal property exemptions include: personal property of $500; tools of the trade in the amount of $1,500; one motor vehicle in the amount of $4,000; jewelry in the amount of $2,500; clothing; furniture; books; medical-health equipment being used for the health of the person and not for his profession. Any resident of the state who does not own a homestead shall in addition to other exemptions hold exempt real or personal property in the amount of $2,000 in lieu of the homestead exemption.

(North Dakota Century Code Sec. 28-22-02; Sec. 28-22-03.1; Sec. 28-22-04; Sec. 28-22-05; Sec. 32-09.1-.03; Sec. 47-18-01.)

Ohio

The homestead exemption limitation of value is $5,000 of real or personal property used as a residence.

Personal property exemptions include: wearing apparel, household goods and furnishings, appliances, books, musical instruments, firearms, fishing and hunting equipment, crops and animals to a value of $200 per item; refrigerator and stove to a value of $300 each; jewelry to a value of $400 (one item) and $200 (all other items); motor vehicle to a value of $1,000; burial plot; wrongful death recoveries; personal injury recoveries to a value of $5,000; cash, tax refunds, money payable, money on deposit with public utilities, landlord and various savings institutions to a value of $400; any other property to a value of $400. The total exemption for jewelry and household furnishings, etc., is $1,500; if the homestead exemption is not claimed, the total is $2,000. Professional books and tools of trade are exempt to a value of $750. Seventy-five percent of earned but unpaid wages is exempt (may be higher for low-income debtors).

(Ohio Revised Code Sec. 2329.66.)

Oklahoma

The homestead exemption is real property limited in value to $5,000 and in area to one acre in town or city and 160 acres elsewhere or, without a value limit, either 1/4 acre or a manufactured home.

Personal property exemptions include: wearing apparel, household furniture, pictures and books, gun; burial plot; motor vehicle to a value of $1,500; family provisions for one year; various farm animals and forage for one year; workers compensation, personal injury and wrongful death recoveries to a value of $50,000. Professional books, tools of trade and husbandry implements used on homestead are exempt. Seventy-five percent of earned but unpaid wages is exempt (may be higher for low-income debtors).

(Oklahoma Statutes Annotated Title 31 Sec. 1 & 2.)

Oregon

The homestead exemption value limitation for real property or a mobile home is $15,000 ($20,000 total for family), and the area limitation is one block within a city or town and 160 acres elsewhere.

Personal property exemptions include: wearing apparel, jewelry and other personal items to a value of $900; household goods and furniture and certain appliances to a value of $1,450; musical instruments, books and pictures to a value of $300; vehicle to a value of $1,200; shotgun or rifle and pistol; animals kept for family use to a value of $1,000 and feed for 60 days; personal injury recoveries to a value of $7,500; additional personal property to a value of $400. A householder may also exempt fuel and provisions for

60 days. Professional library and tools of trade are exempt to a value of $750. Seventy-five percent of earned but unpaid wages is exempt (may be higher for low-income debtors).

(Oregon Revised Statutes Sec. 23.160; Sec. 23.164; Sec. 23.185; Sec. 23.200; Sec. 23.240.)

Pennsylvania

Personal property exemptions include: wearing apparel, sewing machine, bibles, school books, uniforms; other real or personal property to a value of $300. One hundred percent of earned but unpaid wages is exempt.

(Pennsylvania Consolidated Statutes Annotated Title 42 Sec. 8123, 8124 & 8127.)

Rhode Island

Personal property exemptions include: wearing apparel; arms and ammunition; church pew and burial plot; school books, bibles and other books to a value of $300; debts secured by a promissory note. A housekeeper may also exempt: family stores and household furniture to a value of $1,000; certain animals and 1 ton of hay. Exemptions may be claimed for: professional library; uniform, arms and equipment for militia member; tools of trade to a value of $500. One hundred percent of earned but unpaid wages due a seaman or any other debtor who received relief within the year is exempt; 50 percent is exempt for other debtors.

(General Laws of Rhode Island Sec. 9-26-4.)

South Carolina

The homestead exemption is real or personal property to a value of $5,000 (total for family, $10,000).

Personal property exemptions include: wearing apparel, household goods and furniture, appliances, musical instruments, books, crops and animals to a value of $2,500; jewelry to a value of $500; motor vehicle to a value of $1,200; wrongful death and personal injury recoveries; cash and other liquid assets to a value of $1,000 in lieu of the homestead exemption. Professional books and tools of trade are exempt to a value of $750.

(Code of Laws of South Carolina Sec. 15-41-200.)

South Dakota

The homestead exemption may be either a mobile home or real property limited in size to one acre in town or 160 acres elsewhere.

Personal property exemptions include: wearing apparel; fuel and provisions for one year; church pew, burial plot, family pictures, family bible, school books, and library to a value of $200. A head of family may also exempt additional personal property to a value of $1,500; other debtors, to a value of $600. Instead of the previous exemption, a head of family may exempt: household furniture; musical instruments and books to a value of $200; certain animals and sufficient feed for one year; specific farm equipment to a value of $1,250; professional library and instruments to a value of $300; mechanic's tools and stock to a value of $200. One hundred percent of earned but unpaid wages is exempt if needed by the family.

(South Dakota Codified Laws Sec. 15-20-12; Sec. 43-31-4; Sec. 43-45-2; Sec. 43-45-4.)

Tennessee

The homestead exemption value limitation is $5,000 ($7,500 for a married couple).

Personal property exemptions include: wearing apparel, family bible, family pictures, school books; burial plot; wrongful death recoveries to a value of $10,000; personal injury recoveries to a value of $7,500; other personal property to a value of $4,000. Professional books and tools of trade are exempt to a value of $750. Seventy-five percent of earned but unpaid wages is exempt (may be higher for low-income debtors).

(Tennessee Code Annotated Sec. 26-2-102; Sec. 26-2-103; Sec. 26-2-106; Sec. 26-2-111; Sec. 26-2-301; Sec. 26-2-305.)

Texas

The homestead exemption is limited in area to one acre within a town or city or to 200 acres elsewhere (100 acres if debtor is single).

Personal property exemptions include: wearing apparel, household furnishings, family heirlooms, sporting and athletic equipment, two firearms, pets, provisions; specified livestock and their feed; cars and light trucks not used for income production and choice of two other animals or vehicles. Books, equipment and tools of trade and implements for ranching or farming are exempt. The total value of these exemptions and certain insurance exemptions may not exceed $60,000 for a married couple ($30,000 for a single debtor). One hundred percent of earned but unpaid wages is exempt. (Texas Property Code Annotated Sec. 41.001; Sec. 42.002.)

Utah

The homestead exemption for real property or a mobile home is limited in value to $8,000 plus $2,000 for a spouse and $500 for each additional dependent.

Personal property exemptions include: wearing apparel, various household appliances and furnishings, provisions for three months; other appliances and furnishings to a value of $500; musical instruments, books and animals to a value of $500; one heirloom or item of sentimental value; art works of or by debtor or family; wrongful death and personal injury recoveries. Exemptions may be claimed for a motor vehicle (used in business) to a value of $1,500 and professional books and tools of trade to a value of $1,500.

(Utah Code Sec. 78-23-3; Sec. 78-23-5; Sec. 78-23-8.)

Vermont

The homestead exemption value limitation is $30,000.

Personal property exemptions include: wearing apparel, articles of household furnishings, sewing machine, arms, tools, bibles and other books, church pew; sidearms and equipment, held by a soldier or his heirs; five tons of coal or 10 cords of wood; specified amounts of crops and numbers and value limitations of animals, equipment and feed. Exemptions may be claimed for: professional books of clergy and attorneys to a value of $200; professional books and instruments of doctors and dentists to a value of $200; mechanic's tools.

(Vermont Statutes Annotated Title 12 Sec. 2740; Title 27 Sec. 101.)

Virginia

Personal property exemptions for a householder include: wearing apparel, bible, school books, library, family pictures, engagement and wedding rings; pets; burial plot; specified household furnishings, appliances and tools (some with value limitations); specified provisions and animals (some with value limitations); other real and personal property to a value of $5,000 (disabled veterans may claim an additional $2,000). Written declaration of intent to claim real property exemption must be recorded prior to bankruptcy. Other exemptions may be claimed by: mechanics, tools of trade; fishermen and oystermen, boat and tackle to a value of $1,500; debtors in agriculture, various animals, equipment and fertilizer (some with value limitations). Seventy-five percent of earned but unpaid wages is exempt (may be higher for low-income debtors).

(Code of Virginia Sec. 34-4; Sec. 34-4.1; Sec. 34-6; Sec. 34-26; Sec. 34-27; Sec. 34-29.)

Washington

The homestead limitation of value is $25,000.

Personal property exemptions include: wearing apparel, not exceeding a value of $750 in jewelry and furs per person; household goods, furniture and appliances and yard and home equipment to a value of $1,500; family pictures and keepsakes; libraries to a value of $1,000; motor vehicle to a value of $1,200; fuel and provisions for three months; other property to a value of $500 (not more than $100 in cash, bank or savings and loan accounts, stocks, bonds or securities). Other exemptions may be claimed by: farmers, farm equipment and supplies to a value of $3,000; professionals, library and office equipment and supplies to a value of $3,000; other debtors, supplies and tools of trade to a value of $3,000. Seventy-five percent of earned but unpaid wages is exempt (may be higher for low-income debtors).

(Revised Code of Washington Annotated Sec. 6.12.050; Sec. 6.16.020; Sec. 7.33.280.)

West Virginia

The homestead exemption has a value limitation of $25,000.

Personal property exemptions include: wearing apparel, household goods and furnishings, appliances, books, musical instruments, animals and crops to a total value of $1,000 (limit of $200 per item); jewelry to a value of $500; motor vehicle to a value of $1,200; wrongful death recoveries; personal injury recoveries to a value of $7,500; other property to a value of

$400 ($7,900 in lieu of homestead exemption). Professional books and tools of trade are exempt to a value of $750.

(West Virginia Code Sec. 38-10-4.)

Wisconsin

The homestead exemption limit of value is $25,000.

Personal property exemptions include: wearing apparel, bible, library, school books, family pictures, sewing machine; jewelry to a value of $400; specified household furnishings and appliances; other household furniture and utensils to a value of $200; firearm to a value of $50; fuel and provisions for one year; patents; church pew and burial plot; U.S. Savings Bonds to a value of $200; bank or savings deposits to a value of $1,000 in lieu of homestead exemption; certain farm animals and feed for one year; specified farm equipment (some value limitations). In addition to books, maps, plats and other papers for making land abstracts, exemptions that may be claimed are: by printers and publishers, printing presses and materials to a value of $1,500; by national guard members, uniform and arms; by mechanics and others, tools of trade and stock to a limit of $200. Sixty percent of earned but unpaid wages (not less than $75 nor more than $100) may be exempted by debtors with no dependents; a debtor with dependents may exempt $120 plus $20 per dependent (not exceeding 75 percent of wages).

(Wisconsin Statutes Annotated Sec. 815.18; Sec. 815.20.)

Wyoming

The homestead exemption is real property or a mobile home limited to a value of $10,000.

Personal property exemptions include: wearing apparel to a value of $1,000; household furnishings and provisions to a value of $2,000; bible, school books, pictures, burial plot. Also exempt are tools of trade, motor vehicle and stock to a value of $2,000 or professional library and instruments to a value of $2,000. Fifty percent of earned but unpaid wages are exempt if needed by debtor's family.

(Wyoming Statutes Annotated Sec. 1-17-411; Sec. 1-20-101; Sec. 1-20-105; Sec. 1-20-106.)

Appendix E
Common Motions, Adversaries, Objections and Applications

When there is a dispute in the bankruptcy process between the debtor and either the trustee or a creditor and a bankruptcy judge has been asked to decide the issue, someone filed a motion, adversary or objection. If the debtor wants permission to do something and the judge must give that permission, a request or application is prepared by the debtor's attorney and filed with the court.

The following represent the most common motions, adversaries, objections and applications consumer debtors may experience in bankruptcy. Each has an explanation of the circumstances that must exist for it to be filed.

Motion to lift automatic stay. This is the most common motion filed in bankruptcy court. It is usually filed by a secured creditor who has not been paid for a long time. When the creditor files the motion, the bankruptcy judge is being asked either to let the creditor have its collateral, for instance your car, or to require you to start making payments. These payments are intended to adequately protect the creditor's interest in the property while you have it.

Motion to dismiss. This motion is filed by either a creditor or the trustee when he or she believes a debtor does not belong in bankruptcy. For example, if you are in a Chapter 13 adjustment of debt bankruptcy and miss payments on your plan, the trustee will file a motion to dismiss your case for failure to pay.

Motion to redeem. This motion is filed by the debtor in a Chapter 7 bankruptcy when the debtor cannot get a creditor to agree on the value to be paid on the collateral to redeem it. The debtor asks the judge to decide on the value of the collateral. Once the value is determined, the debtor can pay this amount and be allowed to keep the collateral free of any lien. The balance of the debt is wiped out by the bankruptcy.

Objection to discharge. This adversary is filed against a debtor if someone believes the debtor has broken bankruptcy rules or has tried to defraud the court. If successful, the debtor would not be allowed a discharge of any debts.

Objection to dischargeability. This adversary, filed by a creditor against a debtor, says that the debtor did something to allow the creditor's debt to survive the bankruptcy and still be collected. Usually the creditor alleges the debtor committed some kind of fraud, such as lying on a financial statement, in obtaining the loan.

Objection to Chapter 13 plan. This objection is filed by either the trustee or a creditor when it is believed that the debtor's proposed plan does not fulfill the requirements of confirmation or when a creditor believes its claim is not being treated fairly.

Objection to exemptions. This adversary is filed against the debtor when someone believes that property the debtor is claiming as exempt and wants to retain is really nonexempt and should be sold to satisfy debts. This objection must be filed within 30 days of the creditors' meeting.

Motion for evaluation. On certain types of collateral a debtor can pay the value rather than what is owed. If the debtor and creditor cannot agree on the value, this motion is filed so the judge can decide.

Motion to determine tax liability. When a debtor is not sure what is owed to the Internal Revenue Service, this motion is filed. If you are trying to pay the Internal Revenue Service in a Chapter 13 plan, you want to know exactly how much is owed and whether any of the taxes can be treated as a general unsecured claim and be paid off at less than 100 percent. This motion will get that information for the debtor.

Modification of Chapter 13 plan. This is filed by the debtor when the Chapter 13 plan that was approved by the court needs changing. The usual situation is that the debtor's circumstances have changed and the plan payment needs to be lowered in order for the debtor to continue under a Chapter 13 plan.

Motion to avoid lien. In some states a debtor is allowed to take a lien off of household goods and other property if the property was put up for collateral on a loan. This type of loan is called a non–purchase-money, non-possessory loan. This motion is filed to take the lien off so that the debtor will be able to keep the collateral. The debt is wiped out. This motion also can be used to remove judgment liens from exempt property.

Application to reaffirm a debt. This is filed when a debtor wants the court to approve an agreement to pay a creditor, even though the debt would have been wiped out by the bankruptcy. This is not recommended.

Appendix F
Resources

The information in this section provides the names, addresses and phone numbers of organizations and publications that can help you manage your money responsibly, deal with money troubles and understand the bankruptcy process.

How To Deal with Spending and Debt

Organizations That Can Help You

Credit Consumer Counseling Service (CCC). This is a national, nonprofit organization with local offices around the country. It provides low-cost/no-cost financial counseling to consumers as well as classes on money management. CCC will also help a consumer try to avoid bankruptcy by negotiating lower debt payments with creditors. To get the phone number and location of the CCC office closest to you, look in your local phone book or call 800-388-2227.

Debtors Anonymous. A national organization with local chapters dedicated to helping people overcome problems with overspending and debt through the techniques and principles of Alcoholics Anonymous. To find the chapter nearest you, look in your local phone book or call 212-642-8220.

Books About Dealing with Debt and Bankruptcy

Big Debt Survival Guide by Samuel McKinney III and Rozanne Moore McKinney, Marshall Publishing Company, 1991.

Chapter 13 Bankruptcy by Robin Leonard, Nolo Press, 1995.

Conquer Your Debt by William Kent Brunette, Prentice Hall Press, 1990.

The Credit Repair Kit by John Ventura, Dearborn Financial Publishing, Inc., 1993.

Fresh Start! Surviving Money Troubles, Rebuilding Your Credit, Recovering Before or After Bankruptcy by John Ventura, Dearborn Financial Publishing, Inc., 1992.

How Anyone Can Negotiate With the IRS—and Win! by Daniel J. Pila, Winnows Publications, 1988.

How to File for Bankruptcy by Stephen Elias, Albin Renauer and Robin Leonard, Nolo Press, 1995.

How To Get Out of Debt, Stay Out of Debt & Live Prosperously by Jerold Mundis, Bantam Books, 1988.

Money Troubles: Legal Strategies to Cope With Your Debt by Robin Leonard, Nolo Press, 1991.

Out of Debt: How to Clean Up Your Credit and Balance Your Budget by Robin Leonard, Nolo Press, 1991.

Surviving Bankruptcy: A Personal and Small Business Guide by Dan Gross Anderson and M. J. Wardell, Prentice Hall, 1992.

Books and Newsletters about Responsible Money Management

The Budget Kit: The Common Cent$ Money Management Workbook by Judy Lawrence, Dearborn Financial Publishing, Inc., 1993.

The Easy Family Budget by Jerald W. Mason, Houghton Mifflin, 1990.

How to Borrow Money and Use Credit by Martin Weiss, Houghton Mifflin, 1990.

How to Live Within Your Means and Still Finance Your Dreams by Robert A. Ortaldo, Fireside Books, 1994

How to Pinch a Penny Till it Screams by Rochelle McDonald, Avery Publishing Group, 1994.

Living Well or Even Better on Less by Ellen Kunes, Perigee Books, 1991.

Making the Most of Your Money: Smart Ways to Create Wealth and Plan Your Finances in the '90s by Jane Bryant Quinn, Simon & Schuster, 1991.

Penny Pinching: How to Lower Your Everyday Expenses Without Lowering Your Standard of Living by Lee and Barbara Simmons, Bantam Books, 1991.

Personal Finance for Dummies by Eric Tyson, IDG Books, 1994,

Bottom Line/Personal. Published twice monthly, this newsletter is devoted to helping people manage their lives more effectively. It provides information on money management and investments, careers, and health as well as money saving tips. To subscribe, write to *Bottom Line/Personal,* P.O. Box 58446, Boulder, CO 80322. Subscription is $49/year.

The Tightwad Gazette. A monthly newsletter that provides information and ideas for people who live on a tight budget. To subscribe, write to Tightwad Gazette, RR1, Box 3570, Leeds, ME 04263. Subscription is $12/year.

How To Locate Trustees

In the event you need to contact the trustee involved in your bankruptcy case, this section provides the names, addresses and phone numbers of the Chapter 7 and Chapter 13 Panel and Standing Trustees throughout the United States as well as in St. Thomas, Virgin Islands, and Christiansted, Saint Croix, Virgin Islands. Also included are the names, addresses and phone numbers of the U.S. Trustees Regional Management officials. They oversee the work of the trustees in each region and monitor individual bankrutpcy cases.

Chapter 7 Trustees

Name	Address	City	State	Zip	Telephone
REGION 1					
Maine					
Martha Ann Grant	128 Main Street	Fort Fairfield	ME	04742	207-472-3321
Gary Michael Growe	50 Columbia St. #79	Bangor	ME	04401	207-945-5608
William H. Howison	P.O. Box 585 DTS	Portland	ME	04114	207-775-6371
Joseph O'Donnell	465 Congress Street	Portland	ME	04112	207-772-4808
Pasquale J. Perrino, Jr.	124 State Street	Augusta	ME	04330	207-622-1918
Massachusetts					
John James Aquino, III	One Beacon Street	Boston	MA	02108	617-573-0191
Jillian Kindlund Aylward	114 State Street	Boston	MA	02109	617-227-6500
William G. Billingham	1025 Plain Street	Marshfield	MA	02050	617-837-5252
Joseph Braunstein	3 Center Plaza	Boston	MA	02108	617-523-9000
John Alfred Burdick, Jr.	340 Main Street, Suite 800	Worcester	MA	01608	508-752-4633
Joseph B. Collins	101 State Street	Springfield	MA	01103	413-734-6411
Gary W. Cruickshank	One International Place, Ste. 701	Boston	MA	02110	617-951-9980
Mark Guy DeGiacomo	One Post Office Square	Boston	MA	02109	617-451-9300
John O. Desmond	24 Union Avenue	Framingham	MA	01701	508-879-9638
Kathleen P. Dwyer	One Corp. Place, 55 Ferncroft Rd.	Danvers	MA	01923	508-774-7123
Henry C. Ellis	79 Church Green	Taunton	MA	02780	508-824-7597
Michael B. Feinman	23 Main Street	Andover	MA	01810	508-475-0080
Stephen Gray	270 Congress Street	Boston	MA	02210	617-482-4242
Paul J. Grella	One Financial Place	Boston	MA	02111	617-348-8330
Stewart F. Grossman	101 Arch Street	Boston	MA	02110	617-951-2800
Jack E. Houghton, Jr.	78 Bartlett Avenue	Pittsfield	MA	01201	413-447-7385
Michael B. Katz	33 State Street	Springfield	MA	01103	413-781-0560
Susan Nicole Kenneally-Walton	Three Center Plaza	Boston	MA	02108	617-523-9000
Donald R. Lassman	101 Arch Street	Boston	MA	02110	617-439-3800
Harold B. Murphy	1 Federal Street, 13th Floor	Boston	MA	02110-2007	617-423-0400
David M. Nickless	495 Main Street	Fitchburg	MA	01420	508-342-4590
David J. Noonan	One Monarch Place	Springfield	MA	01144	413-781-0472
Terrence Leroy Parker	85 Devonshire Street, Suite 1000	Boston	MA	02109	617-367-8867
L. George Reder	74 North Street	Pittsfield	MA	01201	413-442-2731
Lynne Furey Riley	101 Tremont Street	Boston	MA	02108	617-482-2111
Matthew D. Rockman	292 Main Street, Suite M	Northborough	MA	01532	508-393-6278
Stephan M. Rodolakis	1 Exchange Place	Worcester	MA	01608	508-756-6940
Richard P. Salem	1832 West Main Street	Leicester	MA	01524	508-892-1101
Stephen E. Shamban	P.O. Box 850973	Braintree	MA	02185-0973	508-849-1136
Steven Weiss	1441 Main Street	Springfield	MA	01103	413-737-1131
Jonathan David Yellin	100 Federal Street	Boston	MA	02110	617-482-6800
New Hampshire					
Victor W. Dahar	20 Merrimack Street	Manchester	NH	03101	603-622-6595
Richard R. Erricola	Sutton Square, Suite 30, P.O. Box 551	Sutton	MA	01590	508-856-3030
Steven M. Notinger	146 Main Street	Nashua	NH	03060	603-699-2212
Jennifer Rood	116 Lowell Street, Box 516	Manchester	NH	03105	603-668-7272
Jeffery A. Schreiber	99 Rosewood Drive	Danvers	MA	01923	508-744-9601
Rhode Island					
Arnold L. Blasbalg	128 Dorrance St., Rm. 350	Providence	RI	02903	401-421-1626
Louis A. Geremia	189 Canal Street	Providence	RI	02903	401-751-4700
Matthew J. McGowan	321 South Main Street	Providence	RI	02903	401-274-0300
Jason D. Monzack	888 Reservoir Avenue	Cranston	RI	02910	401-946-3200
Andrew S. Richardson	182 Waterman Street	Providence	RI	02906	401-273-9600
Marc D. Wallick	51 Jefferson Blvd.	Warwick	RI	02888	401-461-0100

Name	Address	City	State	Zip	Telephone

REGION 2

Connecticut

Name	Address	City	State	Zip	Telephone
Richard L. Belford	9 Trumbull Street	New Haven	CT	06511	203-865-0867
Richard M. Coan	495 Orange Street	New Haven	CT	06511	203-624-4756
Michael John Daly	255 Main Street	Hartford	CT	06106	203-527-3271
Barbara L. Hankin	16 Moss Ledge Road	Westport	CT	06880	203-259-1228
Martin W. Hoffman	50 Columbus Blvd.	Hartford	CT	06103	203-525-4287
Barbara H. Katz	234 Church Street, 12th Floor	New Haven	CT	06510	203-772-4828
Anthony S. Novak	81 Wolcott Hill Road	Wethersfield	CT	06109	203-257-1980
John J. O'Neil	255 Main Street	Hartford	CT	06106	203-527-3171
Neil Ossen	21 Oak Street	Hartford	CT	06106	203-728-6635
Alan D. Sibarium	24 Farm Drive	Farmington	CT	06032	203-674-1839
Byron P. Yost	Two Whitney Avenue	New Haven	CT	06510	203-789-1250

New York - Eastern

Name	Address	City	State	Zip	Telephone
Neil H. Ackerman	EAB Plaza	Uniondale	NY	11556	516-357-3130
Robert Kenneth Barnard	11 Stewart Avenue	Huntington	NY	11743	516-423-8525
Gary S. Basso	1937 Williamsbridge Road	Bronx	NY	10461	212-931-1220
Bonita Rae Bequet	600 Old Country Road, Suite 241	Garden City	NY	11566	516-228-9595
David J. Doyaga	16 Court Street, Suite 2300	Brooklyn	NY	11241	718-488-7500
Marilyn A. Frier	557 Church Avenue	Woodmere	NY	11598	516-295-4218
Kenneth I. Kirschenbaum	200 Garden City Plaza	Garden City	NY	11530	516-747-6700
Paul I. Krohn	40 Clinton St., Suite 1G	Brooklyn	NY	11201	718-875-7431
Richard J. McCord	1045 Oyster Bay Road	East Norwich	NY	11732	516-922-0583
Allan B. Mendelsohn	33 Queens Street P.O. Box 510	Syosset	NY	11791-0510	516-921-1670
Robert J. Musso	78 Livingston Street	Brooklyn	NY	11201	718-237-9059
Martin P. Ochs	501 Fifth Avenue	New York	NY	10017	212-986-5275
Marc A. Pergament	585 Stewart Avenue	Garden City	NY	11530	516-222-2323
Robert L. Pryor	114 Old Country Road	Mineola	NY	11501	516-294-5778
Richard L. Stern	164 Main Street	Huntington	NY	11743	516-549-7900
Andrew M. Thaler	390 Old Country Road	Garden City	NY	11530	516-742-5885
Edward Zinker	12 Bank Avenue P.O. Box 866	Smithtown	NY	11787	516-265-2133

New York - Northern

Name	Address	City	State	Zip	Telephone
Michael J. Balanoff	247-259 West Fayette Street	Syracuse	NY	13202	315-472-7832
Allan J. Bentkofsky	2 Fort Street	Auburn	NY	13021	315-255-3414
James C. Collins	19 Chenango Street 1201 Press Bldg.	Binghamton	NY	13901	607-722-5339
Carolyn J. Cooley	405 Mayro Building	Utica	NY	13501	315-724-3749
Philip J. Danaher	11 North Pearl Street	Albany	NY	12207	518-449-5026
Marc S. Ehrlich	64 Second Street	Troy	NY	12180	518-272-2110
Paul M. Fischer	36 Park Street	Canton	NY	13617	315-379-9428
Thomas Genova	302 North Street	Newburgh	NY	12550	914-561-2500
Nathan M. Goldberg	296 Washington Ave. Ext.	Albany	NY	12203	518-456-9616
Gregory G. Harris	11 North Pearl Street, Suite 100	Albany	NY	12207	518-436-1661
David G. Klim	206 North Townsend Street	Syracuse	NY	13203	315-472-0161
Mary Elizabeth Leonard	12 Groton Avenue, P.O. Box 762	Cortland	NY	13045	607-753-3551
William M. McCarthy	60 South Swan Street	Albany	NY	12210	518-434-6141
Michael Jude O'Connor	20 Corporate Woods Blvd.	Albany	NY	12211	518-465-3484
Michael O'Leary	P.O. Box 292	Middletown	NY	10940	914-343-6227
Randy J. Schaal	100 West Seneca Street	Sherrill	NY	13461	315-363-6888
John T. Snell	West Bay Plaza, Suite 201	Plattsburgh	NY	12901	518-561-7190
Richard H. Weiner	39 North Pearl Street	Albany	NY	12207	518-449-3100
Lee E. Woodard	One Lincoln Center, Suite 300	Syracuse	NY	13202	315-478-2222
L. David Zube	P.O. Box 2043	Binghamton	NY	13902	607-722-8823

New York - Northern & Southern

Name	Address	City	State	Zip	Telephone
Paul L. Banner	P.O. Box 70	Poughkeepsie	NY	12601	914-454-3210
Eric C. Kurtzman	9 Pearlman Drive	Spring Valley	NY	10977	914-352-8800

Name	Address	City	State	Zip	Telephone
New York - Southern					
Robert M. Fisher	200 Park Avenue South	New York	NY	10003	212-777-5222
Yann Geron	711 Third Avenue, 15th Floor	New York	NY	10017	212-682-7575
Lynn P. Harrison, III	101 Park Avenue	New York	NY	10178-0061	212-696-6199
Hal M. Hirsch	2700 Westchester Avenue	Purchase Park	NY	10577-2560	914-251-1030
David Roy Kittay	81 Main Street	White Plains	NY	10601	914-686-1900
Sarah C. Lichtenstein	1251 Avenue of Americas	New York	NY	10020-1193	212-827-3452
Jeffrey L. Sapir	399 Knollwood Road	White Plains	NY	10603	914-328-7272
Alexander Schachter	220 E. 54th St., Suite 1C	New York	NY	10022	212-755-7300
Bruce D. Scherling	6 East 45th Street, Suite 305	New York	NY	10017	212-972-8100
Barbara Balaber Strauss	81 Main Street	White Plains	NY	10601-1711	914-949-9822
Albert Togut	One Penn Plaza, Suite 1714	New York	NY	10119	212-594-5000
Mark S. Tulis	245 Saw Mill River Road	Hawthorne	NY	10532	914-741-0900
New York - Southern & Eastern					
Roy Babitt	666 Third Avenue	New York	NY	10017	212-850-0874
John Paul Campo	125 W. 55th Street	New York	NY	10019	212-424-8000
Ian J. Gazes	110 East 59th Street	New York	NY	10022	212-755-4450
Robert L. Geltzer	919-3rd Avenue	New York	NY	10022-3897	212-735-7860
Gregory Messer	423 Fulton Street	Brooklyn	NY	11201	718-858-1474
Alan Nisselson	61 Broadway	New York	NY	10006	212-797-9100
Richard E. O'Connell	161-24 Northern Boulevard	Flushing	NY	11358	718-358-5520
John S. Pereira	150 East 58th Street	New York	NY	10155	212-758-5777
Kenneth P. Silverman	300 Garden City Plaza	Garden City	NY	11530-3302	516-746-8000
Angela G. Tese-Milner	410 Park Avenue	New York	NY	10022	212-326-0877
New York - Western					
John A. Belluscio	400 Wilder Building	Rochester	NY	14614	716-454-4635
Daniel Evans Brick	91 Tremont Street	No. Tonawanda	NY	14120	716-693-2335
Harold P. Bulan	1440 Band Building	Buffalo	NY	14203	716-854-1332
Robert S. Cooper	2425 Clover Street	Rochester	NY	14618	716-442-2270
Thomas A. Dorey	P.O. Box 247	Lakewood	NY	14750	716-484-1021
Thomas J. Gaffney	300 Delaware Avenue	Buffalo	NY	14202	716-852-1800
Warren H. Heilbronner	600 First Federal Plaza	Rochester	NY	14614	716-325-2500
John H. Heyer	604 Exchange Nat'l Bank Bldg.	Olean	NY	14760	716-372-0395
Morris L. Horwitz	2696 Sheridan Drive	Tonawanda	NY	14150-9414	716-693-4529
Edwin R. Ilardo	20 Buffalo Street	Hamburg	NY	14075	716-649-0161
C. Bruce Lawrence	700 First Federal Plaza	Rochester	NY	14614	716-325-6446
William E. Lawson	500 Convention Tower	Buffalo	NY	14202	716-854-3015
Douglas J. Lustig	Two State Street, Suite 427	Rochester	NY	14614	716-232-6700
Douglas Warren Marky	471 Main Street	East Aurora	NY	14052	716-652-0828
Lucien A. Morin, II	25 East Main Street	Rochester	NY	14614-1874	716-546-2500
John Henry Ring, III	620 Liberty Bldg.	Buffalo	NY	14202	716-842-4123
Mark J. Schlant	404 Cathedral Place, 298 Main Street	Buffalo	NY	14202	716-855-3200
Peter R. Scribner	1100 University Avenue	Rochester	NY	14607	716-256-6461
Richard P. Vullo	2 State Street, Suite 950	Rochester	NY	14614	716-325-3175
Mark S. Wallach	169 Delaware Avenue	Buffalo	NY	14202	716-852-1835
Paul Robert Warren	900 Midtown Tower	Rochester	NY	14604	716-232-5300
New York & Vermont - Northern					
Douglas J. Wolinsky	200 Main Street, P.O. Box 1505	Burlington	VT	05402	802-658-2826
Vermont					
John R. Canney	South Main Street, P.O. Box 6626	Rutland	VT	05702-6626	802-773-0416
Gleb G. Glinka	P.O. Box 7	Cadot	VT	05647	802-626-9333
Raymond J. Obuchowski	Box 60	Bethel	VT	05302	802-234-6245

Name	Address	City	State	Zip	Telephone

REGION 3

Delaware

Name	Address	City	State	Zip	Telephone
Jeoffrey L. Burtch	824 Market Street Mall	Wilmington	DE	19899	302-984-3810
Michael B. Joseph	824 Market St., Suite 601	Wilmington	DE	19899	302-575-1555
Norman L. Pernick	1310 King Street	Wilmington	DE	19899	302-888-6526

Delaware & Pennsylvania - Eastern

Name	Address	City	State	Zip	Telephone
Michael H. Kaliner	312 Oxford Valley Road	Fairless Hills	PA	19030	215-946-4342
Arthur P. Liebersohn	924 Cherry Street	Philadelphia	PA	19107	215-922-7990

New Jersey

Name	Address	City	State	Zip	Telephone
Bunce D. Atkinson	P.O. Box 8415	Red Bank	NJ	07701	908-530-5300
Karen E. Bezner	567 Park Avenue, Suite 103	Scotch Plains	NJ	08876	908-322-8484
John F. Bracaglia, Jr.	362 E. Main Street	Somerville	NJ	08876	908-526-1131
James J. Cain	2312 Laurel Drive	Cinnaminson	NJ	08077-3851	609-786-0441
John A. Casarow	32 North Pearl Street	Bridgeton	NJ	08302	609-455-0566
Michael L. Detzky	45 Court Street	Freehold Boro	NJ	07728	908-780-3090
Barbara A. Edwards	100 28th Street, P.O. Box 2770	Fair Lawn	NJ	07410	201-796-3100
Charles M. Forman	60 Park Place, Suite 1400	Newark	NJ	07102	201-824-7222
Barry W. Frost	691 Route #33	Trenton	NJ	08619	609-890-1500
John W. Hargrave	216 Haddon Ave., Suite 510	Westmont	NJ	08108	609-854-3410
William J. Hunt	744 Broad St., Suite 1400	Newark	NJ	07102	201-623-1699
Steven P. Kartzman	101 Gibraltar Drive	Morris Plains	NJ	07950	201-267-3300
Jonathan Kohn	50 Park Place	Newark	NJ	07102	201-622-7713
David E. Krell	56 Fayette Street	Bridgeton	NJ	08302	609-455-6000
Jeffrey A. Lester	374 Main Street	Hackensack	NJ	07601	201-487-5544
Bruce H. Levitt	One Upper Pond Road, Bldg. D	Parsippany	NJ	07054	201-335-0004
Theodore Liscinski, Jr.	265 Davidson Ave., Suite 205	Somerset	NJ	08873	908-469-8020
Carmen J. Maggio	1065 Bloomfield Avenue	Clifton	NJ	07012	201-472-8170
Joseph D. Marchand	117-119 West Broad St. P.O. Box 298	Bridgeton	NJ	08302	609-451-7600
Steven B. Neuner	108 Center Blvd., Suite #1	Marlton	NJ	08053	609-596-2828
Robert H. Obringer	P.O. Box 269	Marlton	NJ	08053	609-983-1600
Thomas J. Orr	331 High St., 2nd Floor	Burlington	NJ	08016	609-386-8700
Russell J. Passamano	131 Madison Avenue	Morristown	NJ	07962	201-285-1000
Andrew I. Radmin	598-600 Somerset Street	No. Plainfield	NJ	07060	908-754-8600
Albert Russo	111 Dunnell Road	Maplewood	NJ	07040	201-762-3393
Peggy E. Stalford	100 Main Street	Allenhurst	NJ	07711	908-517-8555
Douglas S. Stanger	3201 Atlantic Avenue	Atlantic City	NJ	08401	609-344-5942
Daniel E. Straffi	1415 Hooper Avenue	Toms River	NJ	08753	201-341-3800
Thomas J. Subranni	1624 Pacific Avenue	Atlantic City	NJ	08404	609-347-7000
Katherine A. Suplee	2333 Morris Avenue, Ste. C2	Union	NJ	07083	201-687-7080
John W. Sywilok	51 Main Street	Hackensack	NJ	07601	201-487-9390
Brian S. Thomas	600 Fire Road	Pleasantville	NJ	08232	609-645-2201
Stephen Tsai	33 Wood Avenue South, 5th Floor	Iselin	NJ	08830	908-906-8666
Robert Barry Wasserman	225 Millburn Avenue	Millburn	NJ	07041	201-467-2700

Pennsylvania - Eastern

Name	Address	City	State	Zip	Telephone
John T. Carroll, III	1700 Land Title Bldg., 100 S. Broad St.	Philadelphia	PA	19110	215-564-5190
David Alan Eisenberg	1132 Hamilton Street, Ste. 204	Allentown	PA	18101	215-437-1410
Robert H. Holber	334 W. Front Street	Media	PA	19063	215-565-5463
Mitchell W. Miller	1640 PSFS Building	Philadelphia	PA	19107	215-922-1988
Gloria Satriale	319 North Woodmont Drive	Downingtown	PA	19335	215-873-9499
Andrew N. Schwartz	1411 Walnut Street, Suite 1015	Philadelphia	PA	19102	215-972-0020
Christine C. Shubert	7 Fox Sparrow Turn	Tabernacle	NJ	08088	609-858-0100
Barry A. Solodky	28 Penn Square	Lancaster	PA	17603	717-299-1100

Pennsylvania - Middle

Name	Address	City	State	Zip	Telephone
Steven M. Carr	11 East Market Street	York	PA	17401	717-846-6566

Name	Address	City	State	Zip	Telephone
Mark J. Conway	600 Penn Security Bank Bldg.	Scranton	PA	18503	717-346-7569
Lawrence G. Frank	2023 North Second Street	Harrisburg	PA	17102	717-234-7455
David A. Gniewek	115 E. Harford Street	Milford	PA	18337	717-296-5860
Leon P. Haller	1719 North Front Street	Harrisburg	PA	17102	717-234-4178
John J. Martin	1022 Court Street	Honesdale	PA	18431	717-253-6899
Benjamin Novak	412 S. Allen Street P.O. Box 828	State College	PA	16804	814-237-5863
William G. Schwab	811 Blakeslee Blvd., P.O. Box 56	Lehighton	PA	18235	215-377-5200
Robert P. Sheils, Jr.	108 N. Washington Ave., Suite 603	Scranton	PA	18503	717-341-3240
Charles A. Szybist	423 Mulberry Street	Williamsport	PA	17701	717-326-0559
Lawrence V. Young	29 North Duke Street	York	PA	17401	717-848-4900

Pennsylvania - Western

Name	Address	City	State	Zip	Telephone
Thomas P. Agresti	319 West Tenth Street	Erie	PA	16502	814-454-5868
Joseph J. Bernstein	1133 Penn Avenue	Pittsburgh	PA	15222	412-471-1270
Carlota M. Bohm	2 Chatham Center, 12th Floor	Pittsburgh	PA	15219	412-281-5060
Claude C. Council, Jr.	307 Fourth Ave., Suite 1201	Pittsburgh	PA	15222	412-391-7412
Robert G. Dwyer	120 West 10th Street	Erie	PA	16501	814-459-2800
Burton Leroy Fish	5218 Buffalo Road	Erie	PA	16510	814-899-3572
Mark Louis Glosser	1331 Gulf Tower	Pittsburgh	PA	15219	412-281-6555
Carl P. Izzo, Jr.	101 N. Main Street	Greensburg	PA	15601	412-836-0224
K. Lawrence Kemp	953 Fifth Avenue	New Kensington	PA	15068	412-339-4363
Stanley G. Makoroff	7th Floor, Frick Building	Pittsburgh	PA	15219	412-471-4996
James K. McNamara	2222 W. Grandview Blvd.	Erie	PA	16506	814-833-2222
William F.E. Pineo	791 North Main Street	Meadville	PA	16335	814-724-4244
Henry Ray Pope, III	10 Grant Street	Clarion	PA	16214	814-226-5700
James A. Prostko	801 Lawyers Building	Pittsburgh	PA	15219	412-281-1977
Mary H. Reitmeyer	Allegeny Building, Suite 1310	Pittsburgh	PA	15219	412-288-0800
Mark M. Ristau	410-411 Marine Bank Building	Warren	PA	16365	814-723-1655
Richard W. Roeder	101 West Main Street, P.O. Box 325	Titusville	PA	16354	814-827-1844
Gary V. Skiba	345 West 6th Street	Erie	PA	16507	814-454-6345
Robert Henry Slone	223 South Maple Avenue	Greensburg	PA	15601	412-834-2990
Gary L. Smith	6 Cannon Street	Pittsburgh	PA	15205	412-921-6798

REGION 4

District of Columbia

Name	Address	City	State	Zip	Telephone
Marc E. Albert	300 N. Washington Street, #500	Alexandria	VA	22314	703-549-5000
Kevin R. McCarthy	1146 19th Street, N.W., 3rd Fl.	Washington	DC	20036	202-857-0242
Wendell W. Webster	1819 H Street, N.W., Suite 300	Washington	DC	20006	202-659-8510
William Douglas White	1146 19th Street, N.W., 3rd Fl.	Washington	DC	20037	202-857-0242

Maryland

Name	Address	City	State	Zip	Telephone
Marc H. Baer	3545 Chestnut Avenue	Baltimore	MD	21211	410-235-4150
Merrill Cohen	11820 Parklawn Dr., Suite 500	Rockville	MD	20852	301-654-6400
Kenneth F. Davies	250 W. Pratt Street, 13th Floor	Baltimore	MD	21201	301-659-1303
Deborah H. Devan	100 South Charles Street	Baltimore	MD	21201	410-332-8834
Scott D. Field	11300 Rockville Pike, Suite 1202	Gaithersburg	MD	20852	301-977-5846
Mark J. Friedman	36 South Charles Street	Baltimore	MD	21201	410-539-2530
Brian A. Goldman	36 S. Charles Street	Baltimore	MD	21201	301-547-1400
Alexander Gordon, IV	112 N. West Street	Easton	MD	21601	410-822-3702
Steven H. Greenfeld	2021 L. Street, NW, Suite 200	Washington	DC	20036	202-785-9123
Zvi Guttman	100 Light Street	Baltimore	MD	21201	410-727-1164
Robert D. Harwick, Jr.	444 World Trade Center, 4th Fl.	Baltimore	MD	21202	410-837-1140
Gregory Paul Johnson	206 North Adams Street	Rockville	MD	20850	301-762-1400
Edward Bernard Justis	250 West Pratt Street	Baltimore	MD	21201	410-539-5040
Marc Robert Kivitz	201 N. Charles Street, #1300	Baltimore	MD	21201	410-625-2300
Richard M. Kremen	36 S. Charles Street	Baltimore	MD	21201	410-539-2530
George W. Liebmann	8 West Hamilton Street	Baltimore	MD	21201	410-752-5887
Sarah Elizabeth Longson	2 Hopkins Plaza, Suite 600	Baltimore	MD	21201	410-539-5195
Terry Lee Musika	2 N. Charles Street, Suite 210	Baltimore	MD	21201	410-727-5341

Name	Address	City	State	Zip	Telephone
Michael G. Rinn	30 East Padonia Road, Ste. 404	Timonium	MD	21093	410-561-3161
Cheryl E. Rose	One Metro Sq., 51 Monroe Street, #1800	Rockville	MD	20850	301-340-8200
Gary A. Rosen	One Church Street, Suite 802	Rockville	MD	20850	301-913-5400
Joel I. Sher	36 South Charles St., Ste. 2000	Baltimore	MD	21201	301-385-0202
Michael G. Wolff	19510 Club House Road	Gaithersburg	MD	20879	301-670-9168
James R. Wooten	2 Hopkins Plaza, 9th Floor	Baltimore	MD	21202	410-752-1112

Maryland & DC

Name	Address	City	State	Zip	Telephone
Roger Schlossberg	134 West Washington Street	Hagerstown	MD	21740	301-739-8610

South Carolina

Name	Address	City	State	Zip	Telephone
Robert F. Anderson	P.O. Box 76	Columbia	SC	29202	803-252-8600
Kevin Campbell	890 Highway 17 Bypass, P.O. Box 684	Mt. Pleasant	SC	29465	803-884-6874
John K. Fort	195 North Fairview Avenue	Spartenburg	SC	29302	803-573-5311
W. Ryan Hovis	P.O. Box 10269	Rock Hill	SC	29731	803-324-1122
Lewis Winston Lee	10 Brookside Circle	Greenville	SC	29609	803-242-6032
Cynthia J. Lowery	200 Meeting Street, Suite 202	Charleston	SC	29401	803-723-2000
Ralph C. McCullough, II	P.O. Box 1799	Columbia	SC	29202	803-765-2935

Virginia - Eastern

Name	Address	City	State	Zip	Telephone
H. Lee Addison, III	160 Newtown Road, Suite 311	Virginia Beach	VA	23462	804-490-2900
Richard A. Bartl	300 N. Washington Street, #500	Alexandria	VA	22314	703-549-5000
James S. Buis	700 E. Main Street Suite 1104	Richmond	VA	23202	804-649-9251
Ruth Ann Gibson	3402 Acorn St., #102	Norge	VA	23127	804-564-0883
H. Jason Gold	1800 Diagonal Road, 3rd Floor	Alexandria	VA	22314	703-836-7004
Edward G. Grant	1791 Tait Terrace	Norfolk	VA	23509	804-627-4116
Donna Marie Joyce Hall	150 Boush Street, 8th Floor	Norfolk	VA	23510	804-627-5500
Richard W. Hudgins	10352 Warwick Boulevard	Newport News	VA	23601	804-595-2239
Kevin R. Huennekens	801 East Main Street	Richmond	VA	23219	804-644-0313
Donald F. King	9302 Lee Highway, Suite 1100	Fairfax	VA	22031	703-218-2116
Sherman B. Lubman	8100 Three Chopt Rd., Ste. 102	Richmond	VA	23288	804-283-5100
Jack D. Maness	702 Plaza One Building	Norfolk	VA	23510	804-622-6787
Charles L. Marcus	P.O. Box 69	Portsmouth	VA	23705	804-393-2555
Bruce H. Matson	411 E. Franklin Street, Suite 600	Richmond	VA	23219	804-344-3400
Robert G. Mayer	9677 Main Street, Suite B	Fairfax	VA	22031	703-425-2700
Erwin B. Nachman	708-C Thimble Shoals Boulevard	Newport News	VA	23606	804-873-1840
George W. Neal	P.O. Box 431	White Marsh	VA	23183	804-693-6643
Gordon P. Peyton	1216 King St., #201	Alexandria	VA	22314-2927	703-549-0200
Keith L. Phillips	4825 Radford Ave., Suite 201	Richmond	VA	23219-0560	804-358-8000
Harry B. Price, III	1113 Lee Road	Virginia Beach	VA	23451	804-428-1495
Harry Shaia, Jr.	8550 Maryland Drive	Richmond	VA	23229	804-747-0920
Alexander P. Smith	P.O. Box 3368	Norfolk	VA	23514-3368	804-622-1621
Tom C. Smith	2604 Pacific Avenue	Virginia Beach	VA	23451	804-428-3481
R. Clinton Stackhouse, Jr.	P.O. Box 3640	Norfolk	VA	23510	804-623-3555
Dean W. Sword, Jr.	P.O. Box 7221	Portsmouth	VA	23707	804-399-2421
Robert O. Tyler	300 N. Washington Street, #500	Alexandria	VA	22314	703-549-5000

Virginia - Western

Name	Address	City	State	Zip	Telephone
Charles R. Allen, Jr.	120 Church Ave., SW., Ste. 200	Roanoke	VA	24011	703-342-1731
Henry G. Bennett, Jr.	231 Magnolia Drive	Danville	VA	24541	804-793-7244
Roy V. Creasy, Jr.	915 Dominion Bank Building	Roanoke	VA	24011	703-342-0729
Evelyn K. Krippendorf	P.O. Box 21823	Roanoke	VA	24018	703-772-2500
John G. Leake	1000 South High Street	Harrisonburg	VA	22801	703-434-7425
Archibald Carter Magee, Jr.	P.O. Box 404	Roanoke	VA	24003	703-343-5194
George A. McLean, Jr.	P.O. Box 1284	Roanoke	VA	24006	703-982-8430
Richard A. Money	P.O. Box 345	Marion	VA	24354	703-783-7174
W. Stephen Scott	P.O. Box 2737	Charlottesville	VA	22902	804-296-2161
W. Alan Smith, Jr.	Sovran Bank Building, Ste. 721	Lynchburg	VA	24505	804-528-1058
George I. Vogel, II	P.O. Box 2420	Roanoke	VA	24010	703-982-1220
Robert E. Wick, Jr.	P.O. Drawer 8	Bristol	VA	24203-0008	703-466-4488

Name	Address	City	State	Zip	Telephone
Roy V. Wolfe, III	9 North Court Square P.O. Box 671	Harrisonburg	VA	22801	703-434-7382

West Virginia - Northern

Name	Address	City	State	Zip	Telephone
Thomas H. Fluharty	211 Goff Building	Clarksburg	WV	26301	304-624-7832
Charles K. Grant	310 West King Street	Martinsburg	WV	25401	304-267-0904
Martin P. Sheehan	1233 Main Street	Wheeling	WV	26003	304-233-1212
Robert W. Trumble	1446-3 Eswin Miller Drive	Martinsburg	WV	25401	304-264-4621

West Virginia - Southern

Name	Address	City	State	Zip	Telephone
Herbert Lynden Graham, Jr.	1604 Jefferson Street	Bluefield	WV	24701	304-327-8908
Helen M. Morris	731 5th Avenue	Huntington	WV	25701	304-523-8451
Arthur Mathew Standish	P.O. Box 1588	Charleston	WV	25326	304-345-7407

REGION 5

Louisiana - Eastern

Name	Address	City	State	Zip	Telephone
Wilbur J. Babin, Jr.	424 Gravier Street	New Orleans	LA	70130	504-586-9120
Aaron E.L. Caillouet	107 Menard Place	Thibodaux	LA	70301	504-447-1284
Carroll M. Chiasson	P.O. Box 1672	Gretna	LA	70056-1672	504-391-1290
Robert L. Marrero	401 Whitney, #303	Gretna	LA	70053	504-366-8025
John T. Pender	228 St. Charles Ave., #1435	New Orleans	LA	70130	504-581-2024
Claude R. Smith	P.O. Box 1062	Metairie	LA	70004	504-455-4283
Cynthia Lee Traina	3500 N. Causeway, #450	Metairie	LA	70002	504-835-4344

Louisiana - Middle

Name	Address	City	State	Zip	Telephone
Samera L. Abide	7940 Jefferson Hwy., Suite 200	Baton Rouge	LA	70809	504-923-1404
Dwayne M. Murray	1606 Scenic Hwy., Ste. B	Baton Rouge	LA	70802	504-383-3675
Martin A. Schott	7906 Wrenwood Blvd. Suite A	Baton Rouge	LA	70809	504-928-9520

Louisiana - Western

Name	Address	City	State	Zip	Telephone
J. Elizabeth Andrus	345 Doucet Road, Suite 233	Lafayette	LA	70503	318-981-3858
Randall B. Boughton	P.O. Box 396	Jonesville	LA	71343	318-339-9008
Ted Brett Brunson	P.O. Box 1209	Natchitoches	LA	70458	318-352-3602
Wesley D. Burdine	P.O. Box 279	Benton	LA	71006	318-965-9733
John Clifton Conine	P.O. Box 1209	Natchitoches	LA	71458	318-352-3602
Paul N. DeBaillon	P.O. Box 2069	Lafayette	LA	70502	318-237-0598
Ellen Rose Eade	P.O. Box 2270	Monroe	LA	71207-2270	318-325-7000
Bryan F. Gill, Jr.	625 Kirby Street	Lake Charles	LA	70601	318-433-8116
Barry Kuperman	4613 Fern Avenue	Shreveport	LA	71105	318-869-4400
John W. Luster	P.O. Box 1209	Natchitoches	LA	71458-1209	318-352-3602
Thomas C. McBride	30 Jackson Street, Suite 301	Alexandria	LA	71309	318-445-8800
Max M. Morris	1322 Ryan Street	Lake Charles	LA	70601	318-436-6188
W. Simmons Sandoz	P.O. Drawer 471	Opelousas	LA	70571-7279	318-942-8956
Mark K. Sutton	P.O. Box 2239	Natchitoches	LA	71457	318-352-6267
Billy R. Vining	P.O. Box 206	Pioneer	LA	71266	318-322-3778
Thomas R. Willson	P.O. Box 1630	Alexandria	LA	71309	318-442-8658
Rudolph Odo Young	P.O. Box 3008	Lake Charles	LA	70602	318-436-5842

Mississippi - Northern

Name	Address	City	State	Zip	Telephone
Alexander Brown Gates	P.O. Box 216	Sumner	MS	38957	601-375-8728
Jeffrey A. Levingston	P.O. Box 1327	Cleveland	MS	38732	601-843-2791
Stephen P. Livingston, Sr.	P.O. Drawer 729	New Albany	MS	38652	601-534-9581
Jacob C. Pongetti	P.O. Box 947	Columbus	MS	39703	601-328-5400

Mississippi - Southern

Name	Address	City	State	Zip	Telephone
Charles Thomas Anderson	918 1/2 Washington Ave. P.O. Box 566	Ocean Springs	MS	39564	601-875-0176
Eileen Shaffer Bailey	401 E. Capital, Suite 302, P.O. Box 1177	Jackson	MS	39215-1176	601-969-3006
Jefferson C. Bell	216 W. Pine Street, P.O. Box 566	Hattiesburg	MS	39403	601-582-5011

Name	Address	City	State	Zip	Telephone
Derek A. Henderson	188 East Capitol, Suite 901	Jackson	MS	39201	601-354-3166
Robert G. Nichols, Jr.	P.O. Box 1526	Jackson	MS	39205	601-353-9522
Harvey Samuel Stanley, Jr.	4812 Jefferson Avenue	Gulfport	MS	39501	601-864-1100
Frank M. Youngblood	P.O. Box 22686	Jackson	MS	39205-2686	601-354-0071

REGION 6

Texas - Eastern

Robert A. Anderson	P.O. Box 3343	Longview	TX	75606-3343	214-757-2868
Jim Echols	P.O. Box 240	Tyler	TX	75710	214-595-3791
Linda S. Payne	First National Bank Bldg., Suite 300	Paris	TX	75460	903-784-4393
Jason R. Searcy	P.O. Box 3929	Longview	TX	75606	903-757-3399
Mark A. Weisbart	4100 First City Center	Dallas	TX	75201-4618	214-969-2883
Wm. Randy Wright	P.O. Box 1317	Hope	AR	71801	501-777-5483
Stephen Joseph Zayler	102 S. Second Street	Lufkin	TX	75901	409-634-1020

Texas - Eastern & Northern

J. James Jenkins	600 N. Pearl, Ste. 2400	Dallas	TX	75201-2828	214-220-3131
Dale L. McCullough	5412 Vista Meadow Drive	Dallas	TX	75248	214-661-1937

Texas - Northern

Pam Bassel	3200 Team Bank Bldg.	Ft. Worth	TX	76102	817-878-6347
O. M. Calhoun	1700 Texas American Bank Bldg.	Amarillo	TX	79101	806-372-5569
James W. Cunningham	6412 Sondra Drive	Dallas	TX	75214	214-827-9112
Harry L. Cure, Jr.	1201 East Belknap Street	Fort Worth	TX	76102	817-332-1172
Carey D. Ebert	1236 Southridge Court	Hurst	TX	76053	817-268-2486
Floyd D. Holder, Jr.	1001 Main Street, Suite 801	Lubbock	TX	79401	806-763-9296
John H. Litzler	750 N. St. Paul, Ste. 1600	Dallas	TX	75201	214-559-4474
Myrtle L. McDonald	1600 Civic Center Plaza	Lubbock	TX	79408	806-765-8851
Robert Milbank, Jr.	600 N. Pearl, Suite 500	Dallas	TX	75201	214-953-3090
Jeffrey H. Mims	3102 Oaklawn, Suite 700	Dallas	TX	75219	214-522-1678
Harvey L. Morton	P.O. Box 10305	Lubbock	TX	79408	806-762-0570
Robert F. Newhouse	P.O. Box 820924	Dallas	TX	75382	214-343-3007
Deborah J. Penner	P.O. Box 65166	Lubbock	TX	79464	214-793-0776
Joseph F. Postnikoff	P.O. Box 2547	Lubbock	TX	79408	806-762-0214
Thomas D. Powers	777 Main Street, Suite 3100	Fort Worth	TX	76102	817-335-5050
J. Gregg Pritchard	14850 Quorum Dr., Ste 200	Dallas	TX	75240	214-663-0300
Diane G. Reed	5944 Luther Lane, Suite 750	Dallas	TX	75225	214-373-7333
Henry C. Seals	3417 Hulen St.	Fort Worth	TX	76107	817-731-4733
Scott M. Seidel	2500 Renaissance Tower	Dallas	TX	75270	214-742-2121
Daniel J. Sherman	509 N. Montclair Avenue	Dallas	TX	75208	214-942-5502
John Dee Spicer	7001 Grapevine Hwy., Suite 510	Fort Worth	TX	76180	817-589-0270
Max R. Tarbox	3223 South Loop 289, Ste 315	Lubbock	TX	79423	806-762-0214
Thomas M. Wheeler	402 Cypress, Suite 130	Abilene	TX	79601	915-677-3386
Robert Yaquinto, Jr.	509 N. Montclair Avenue	Dallas	TX	75208	214-942-5502

REGION 7

Texas - Southern

David Askanase	1415 Louisiana 37th Floor	Houston	TX	77002	713-759-0818
D. Michael Boudloche	1508 American Bank Plaza	Corpus Christi	TX	78475	512-883-5786
Lowell T. Cage	5851 San Felipe, #950	Houston	TX	77057	713-789-0500
Ben B. Floyd	910 Louisiana, Suite 400	Houston	TX	77002-4906	713-227-2525
Kenneth Reagan Havis	211 E. Washington	Navasota	TX	77868	409-825-7982
Joseph M. Hill	5851 San Felipe, Suite 950	Houston	TX	77057	713-789-0500
Pamela Gale Johnson	1100 Louisiana, Suite 4800	Houston	TX	77002	713-654-1100
Anthony Juarez, III	2315 Civitan Drive	Corpus Christi	TX	78417	512-854-0887
Lisa J. Nichols	3649 Leopard, Suite 404	Corpus Christi	TX	78408	512-882-2073
Jeffrey A. Shadwick	910 Travis Building Suite 1600	Houston	TX	77002-5895	713-650-2761
Wayne Stevens Smith	910 Louisiana, Suite 400	Houston	TX	77002	713-227-2525

Name	Address	City	State	Zip	Telephone
Ronald J. Sommers	2700 Post Oak Blvd., Ste. 2500	Houston	TX	77056	713-960-0303
Rodney Dwayne Tow	709 N. San Jacinto	Conroe	TX	77301	409-539-5969
Robbye R. Waldron	1212 Bay Area Blvd., #101	Houston	TX	77058	713-488-4438
Randy W. Williams	1111 Bagby Suite 2200	Houston	TX	77002	713-650-0022

Texas - Western

Name	Address	City	State	Zip	Telephone
Dennis Lee Elam	4526 E. University #5F	Odessa	TX	79762	915-368-9999
Marsha G. Kocurek	904 West Avenue, Suite A	Austin	TX	78701	512-482-9114
Andrew B. Krafsur	5th Floor First City Bank Bldg.	El Paso	TX	79901-1369	915-533-2468
Lynda L. Lankford	600 Congress Ave., Suite 2200	Austin	TX	78701	512-499-3800
Donald S. Leslie	725 First City National Bank	El Paso	TX	79901	915-861-8833
John P. Lowe	318 East Nopal Street	Uvalde	TX	78801	512-278-4471
Randolph N. Osherow	342 W. Woodlawn, Suite 300	San Antonio	TX	78212	210-828-2001
Stephen A. Sallot, III	4226 Hidden Canyon Cove	Austin	TX	78746	512-328-5090
Henry C. Seals	3417 Hulen St.	Fort Worth	TX	76107	817-731-4733
Johnny W. Thomas, Jr.	1153 E. Commerce	San Antonio	TX	78205	210-226-5888
Gaines Franklin West, II	3000 Briarcrest Drive, 5th Floor	Bryan	TX	77802	409-776-2282

REGION 8

Kentucky - Eastern

Name	Address	City	State	Zip	Telephone
Michael L. Baker	517 Madison Ave., P.O. Box 1028	Covington	KY	41012-2038	606-491-1700
Robert J. Brown	600 Lexington Bldg., 201 W. Short St.	Lexington	KY	40507-1334	606-252-2697
Donald L. Frailie, II	820 First American Bldg. 1544 Winchester	Ashland	KY	41101	606-324-8934
Charles L.J. Freihofer	2493 Dixie Highway	Ft. Mitchell	KY	41017	606-341-4454
Lucinda M. Hall	249 E. Main St., Suite 300	Lexington	KY	40507	606-233-3441
Maxie E. Higgason	109 West First Street	Corbin	KY	40701	606-528-4140
Bruce A. Levy	606 Hambley Blvd., P.O. Box 1348	Pikeville	KY	41502	606-432-1631
James D. Lyon	171 N. Upper Street	Lexington	KY	40507	606-254-3302
Mark T. Miller	100 South Main Street	Nicholasville	KY	40356	606-887-1087
James A. Nolan	27 E. 4th Street	Covington	KY	41011	606-431-3377
Stephen Palmer	804 Security Trust Bldg., 271 W. Short St.	Lexington	KY	40507	606-233-0551
J. James Rogan	345 South Fourth Street	Danville	KY	40422	606-236-8121
Phaedra Spradlin	6325 Old Richmond Road	Lexington	KY	40515	606-263-3210
James R. Westenhoefer	212 South Third St., P.O. Box 146	Richmond	KY	40476-0146	606-624-0145
Castil Williams, Jr.	333 West Vine Street, #1610	Lexington	KY	40507	606-253-0131

Kentucky - Western

Name	Address	City	State	Zip	Telephone
Scott A. Bachert	P.O. Box 1270, 324 E. 10th Ave.	Bowling Green	KY	42102-1270	502-782-3938
Joseph W. Castlen, III	121 W. Second Street	Owensboro	KY	42303	502-685-6000
Kyle Allan Cooper	2210 GreenWay	Louisville	KY	40220	502-495-6500
Mark H. Flener	1032 College St. P.O. Box 2130	Bowling Green	KY	42102-2130	502-781-9870
Thomas W. Frentz	2500 Brown & Williamson Tower Bldg.	Louisville	KY	40202	502-584-1135
Charles A. Goodman, III	139 North Public Square, P.O. Box 663	Glasglow	KY	42142-0663	502-651-8812
William W. Lawrence	200 South Seventh Street, #310	Louisville	KY	40202	502-581-9042
Harry L. Mathison, Jr.	140 N. Main St., 4th Fl., P.O. Box 43	Henderson	KY	42420	502-827-1852
Charles E. Peyton	213 Bellemeade Road	Louisville	KY	40222	502-426-1728
Cathy S. Pike	2800 First National Tower	Louisville	KY	40202	502-589-4440
W. Stephen Reisz	6303 Lime Road	Louisville	KY	40222	502-429-8947
Joseph E. Rose	710 W. Main Street #110LL	Louisville	KY	40202	502-585-5169
J. Baxter Schilling	1513 S. Fourth Street	Louisville	KY	40208	502-636-2031
Alan C. Stout	111 W. Bellville Street, P.O. Box 81	Marion	KY	42064	502-965-4600
Russel L. Wilkey	121 West Second Street	Owensboro	KY	42303	502-926-1385
John R. Wilson	2350 Meidinger Tower	Louisville	KY	40202	502-583-2250

Tennessee - Eastern

Name	Address	City	State	Zip	Telephone
Scott N. Brown, Jr.	713 Cherry Street	Chattanooga	TN	37402	615-266-2121
Robert B. Carter	Hamilton Bank Bldg., Suite 403	Johnson City	TN	37601	615-926-1541

Name	Address	City	State	Zip	Telephone
Jerry D. Farinash	320 N. Holtzclaw Ave.	Chattanooga	TN	37404	615-622-4535
Dean B. Farmer	617 Main Street, P.O. Box 869	Knoxville	TN	37901-0869	615-546-9611
Michael H. Fitzpatrick	2121 Plaza Tower	Knoxville	TN	37929-2121	615-524-1873
William M. Foster	Pioneer Building, Suite 515	Chattanooga	TN	37402-2621	615-266-1141
Margaret B. Fugate	114 E. Market Street	Johnson City	TN	37604	615-928-6561
Maurice K. Guinn	P.O. Box 1990	Knoxville	TN	37901	615-525-5300
William T. Hendon	11701 N. Monticello Dr., P.O. Box 23228	Knoxville	TN	37901	615-966-7871
Richard P. Jahn, Jr.	620 Lindsay Street	Chattanooga	TN	37402	615-756-8473
Douglas R. Johnson	58 Commons Bldg., #108B, 4355 Hwy. 58	Chattanooga	TN	37416	615-499-4949
Ann Reilly Mostoller	136 South Illinois Ave., Suite 104	Oak Ridge	TN	37830	615-482-4466
John P. Newton, Jr.	P.O. Box 2132	Knoxville	TN	37901	615-531-5905
Michael J. O'Connor	101 Fountain Place, Ste. 2-C	Johnson City	TN	37604	615-926-8191
James R. Paris	404 James Building	Chattanooga	TN	37402	615-265-2367
Thomas E. Ray	17 Cherokee Blvd., Suite 413	Chattanooga	TN	37405	615-265-2641
N. David Roberts, Jr.	550 Main #500, P.O. Box 39	Knoxville	TN	37902	615-546-9321
C. Kenneth Still	302 Park Place Bldg., 1010 Market St.	Chattanooga	TN	37402	615-265-2261
Mary C. Walker	715 First American Ctr., P.O. Box 2774	Knoxville	TN	37901	615-523-0700
L. Kirk Wyss	617 W. Main P.O. Box 1778	Morristown	TN	37816-1778	615-581-3773

Tennessee - Middle

Name	Address	City	State	Zip	Telephone
Samuel K. Crocker	611 Commerce St., Suite 2909	Nashville	TN	37203	615-726-3322
Thomas Larry Edmondson	808 Broadway, 2nd Floor	Nashville	TN	37203	615-254-3765
Michael Gigandet	P.O. Box 3375, 200 4th Ave., North	Nashville	TN	37219-0375	615-256-9999
James Davidson Lane, II	Suite 101, 303 Church St.	Nashville	TN	37201	615-726-1027
Susan R. Limor	611 Commerce St., #2727	Nashville	TN	37203	615-742-1304
John C. McLemore	150 4th Ave., North, P.O. Box 198947	Nashville	TN	37219	615-255-4545
William L. Newport	303 Church St., Suite 100	Nashville	TN	37201	615-726-1766
David G. Rogers	P.O. Box 1588	Brentwood	TN	37024-1588	615-377-7722
Robert H. Waldschmidt	300 James Robertson Pky., Court Sq. Bldg.	Nashville	TN	37201	615-244-3370

Tennessee - Western

Name	Address	City	State	Zip	Telephone
Richard T. Doughtie, III	239 Adams Avenue	Memphis	TN	38103	901-525-0257
George W. Emerson, Jr.	200 Jefferson Ave., Suite 1107	Memphis	TN	38103	901-576-1313
William L. Guy	59 Conrad Dr., P.O. Box 1313	Jackson	TN	38302-1313	901-664-1313
Norman P. Hagemeyer	99 N. Third Street	Memphis	TN	38104	901-523-0416
Ted M. Hunderup	1414 Main Street, P.O. Box 120	Humboldt	TN	38343	901-784-3700
Barbara R. Loevy	1451 Union Avenue, Suite 120	Memphis	TN	38104	901-278-2800
Edward L. Montedonico, Jr.	200 Jefferson Ave., Suite 222	Memphis	TN	38103	901-521-9390
George W. Stevenson	200 Jefferson Ave., Suite 1107	Memphis	TN	38103	901-576-1313
Michael T. Tabor	202 W. Baltimore, P.O. Box 2877	Jackson	TN	38301	901-424-3074
P. Preston Wilson, Jr.	81 Monroe, Suite 600	Memphis	TN	38103	901-525-6781

REGION 9

Michigan - Eastern

Name	Address	City	State	Zip	Telephone
David W. Allard, Jr.	2600 Buhl Bldg., 535 Griswold	Detroit	MI	48226	313-961-6141
Thomas J. Bleau	1001 Center Ave., P.O. Box 250	Bay City	MI	48707	517-894-9001
Paul Borock	1 Woodward, Suite 2400	Detroit	MI	48226	313-961-8380
George P. Dakmak	600 Ford Building	Detroit	MI	48226	313-964-0800
Frederick J. Dery	803 W. Big Beaver, Suite 353	Troy	MI	48084	810-362-3676
Douglas S. Ellmann	206 South Fifth Ave., Suite 200	Ann Arbor	MI	48104	313-668-4800
Randall L. Frank	303 Davidson Building	Bay City	MI	48707	517-893-2461
Lawrence Allen Friedman	24901 Northwestern Hwy., #502	Southfield	MI	48075	810-356-3030
Stuart A. Gold	24901 Northwestern Hwy., Suite 511	Southfield	MI	48075	810-350-8220
G. E. Grogan	3176 Penobscot Building	Detroit	MI	48226	313-963-6240
Daniel C. Himmelspach	2112 Marshall Court	Saginaw	MI	48602	517-790-2102
Kyung-Jin Lim	645 Griswold, Suite 3050	Detroit	MI	48226	313-237-0850
Michael A. Mason	516 W. Court Street	Flint	MI	48503	313-234-4941
Homer W. McClarty	24400 Northwestern Hwy., Suite 204	Southfield	MI	48075	810-352-7686

Name	Address	City	State	Zip	Telephone
Kenneth Andrew Nathan	29100 Northwestern Hwy., 260 Franklin Ctr.	Southfield	MI	48034	810-351-0099
Basil T. Simon	422 W. Congress, Suite 350	Detroit	MI	48226	313-962-6400
Shelia Solomon	6905 Telegraph Road, Suite 311	Bloomfield Hills	MI	48301	810-642-5555
Michael A. Stevenson	140 S. Saiginaw, Suite 700	Pontiac	MI	48342	810-858-5850
Neal R. Sutherland	25 North Saginaw, Suite 908	Pontiac	MI	48342	810-334-8092
Charles Joseph Taunt	700 East Maple-Fourth Floor	Birmingham	MI	48009-6361	810-647-1127

Michigan - Western

Name	Address	City	State	Zip	Telephone
Rose Ellen Bareham	P.O. Box 570	Suttons Bay	MI	49682	616-271-6866
James Wesley Boyd	410 S. Union St., Suite 203	Traverse City	MI	49684	616-941-3446
Thomas Allen Bruinsma	303 N. Rose Street	Kalamazoo	MI	49007	616-373-1331
Elizabeth C. Chalmers	3920 Plainfield N.E., Suite 163	Grand Rapids	MI	49505	616-365-2766
James William Hoerner	One Timber Trail, S.E.	Ada	MI	49301	616-676-0365
James R. Jessup	102 W. Washington St., Suite 213	Marquette	MI	49855	906-228-2205
Marcia R. Meoli	300 South State Street, Suite 9	Zeeland	MI	49464	616-772-9000
John A. Porter	6059 Cannon Highlands Dr., N.E.	Belmont	MI	49417	616-874-4800
Michael William Puerner	313 South Washington Square	Lansing	MI	48933	517-371-8123
Thomas R. Tibble	6100 N. 14th Street	Kalamazoo	MI	49004-9420	616-342-9444

Ohio - Northern

Name	Address	City	State	Zip	Telephone
Brian Alan Bash	26th Floor Erieview Tower	Cleveland	OH	44114	216-696-3311
Richard A. Baumgart	1100 Ohio Savings Plaza	Cleveland	OH	44114	216-696-6000
Kathryn Augusta Belfance	135 Ghent Road	Akron	OH	44333	216-864-9016
Edwin H. Breyfogle	921 Lincoln Way East	Massillon	OH	44646	216-837-9735
Thomas L. Corroto, Jr.	403 Legal Arts Bldg.	Youngstown	OH	44503	216-743-4116
Harold Allen Corzin	234 Portage Trail, P.O. Box 535	Cuyahoga Falls	OH	44222	216-929-0507
Steven Scott Davis	450 Standard Bldg.	Cleveland	OH	44113	216-781-7272
Michael Victor Demczyk	P.O. Box 867	Uniontown	OH	44685	216-699-6703
Saul Eisen	601 Rockwell Ave., Suite 610	Cleveland	OH	44114	216-623-0000
Bruce Comly French	165 Tolowa Trail	Lima	OH	45805	419-222-6360
Marc Preston Gertz	One Cascade Plaza, 12th Floor	Akron	OH	44308	216-376-8336
Richard B. Ginley	1510 Standard Building	Cleveland	OH	44113	216-241-2680
Malcolm L. Goodman	137 1/2 S. Prospect Street	Marion	OH	43302	614-382-4445
John N. Graham	4853 Monroe St., #260	Toledo	OH	43623	419-479-3969
John Joseph Hunter	1700 Cantun Avenue	Toledo	OH	43624	419-255-4300
James Robert Kandel	401 Central Trust Tower	Canton	OH	44702	216-456-8376
Josiah Locke Mason	153 West Main St., P.O. Box 345	Ashland	OH	44805	419-289-1600
Mary Ann Rabin	55 Public Square, #2000	Cleveland	OH	44113	216-771-8084
Carl D. Rafoth	40 N. Phelps Street	Youngstown	OH	44503	216-744-4137
Joel Hall Rathbone	601 Rockwell Ave., Suite 610	Cleveland	OH	44114	216-623-0000
Henry Buswell Roberts, Jr.	520 Madison Avenue	Toledo	OH	43604	419-255-3036
Marvin A. Sicherman	1100 Ohio Savings Plaza	Cleveland	OH	44114	216-696-6000
Anne Peiro Silagy	P.O. Box 1459	Akron	OH	44309	216-762-1414
David Oscar Simon	600 Standard Bldg.	Cleveland	OH	44114	216-621-6201
Alan Jay Treinish	700 Standard Building	Cleveland	OH	44113	216-566-7022
Elizabeth Ann Vaughan	243 N. Huran, #601	Toledo	OH	43604	419-241-1969
Richard Alva Wilson	P.O. Box 3307	Kent	OH	44240-3307	216-678-2850
Waldemar J. Wojcik	601 Rockwell Ave., #610	Cleveland	OH	44114	216-241-2628
Louis J. Yoppolo	711 Adams Street	Toledo	OH	43624	419-243-6281
Richard Glenn Zellers	309 Legal Arts Centre	Youngstown	OH	44503	216-744-5103

Ohio - Southern

Name	Address	City	State	Zip	Telephone
Ernest Hanlin Bavely	432 Walnut Street, 604 Tri-State Bldg.	Cincinnati	OH	45202	513-621-0550
John R. Butz	125 E. McCreight Ave.	Springfield	OH	45504	513-324-1000
James C. Cissell	602 Main St., 320 Gynne Bldg.	Cincinnati	OH	45202	513-421-1000
Thomas W. Coffey	441 Vine Street, 1200 Carew Tower	Cincinnati	OH	45202	513-852-8215
William Michael Conway, II	130 W. Second St., Suite 800	Dayton	OH	45402-1601	513-223-6003
Sara Jane Daneman	3300 Mann Road	Blacklich	OH	43001	614-855-0833
David William Davis	3800 Jefferson Street, Suite 101	Bellaire	OH	43906	614-676-2034

Name	Address	City	State	Zip	Telephone
Elizabeth H. Doucet	533 South 5th Street	Columbus	OH	43206	614-224-7677
Eileen Kay Field	441 Vine St., 2212 Carew Tower	Cincinnati	OH	45202	513-621-2666
Todd G. Finneran	380 S. Fifth Street, Suite 3	Columbus	OH	43215	614-464-0776
Townsend Foster, Jr.	210 West Main Street	Troy	OH	45373	513-339-0511
Thomas James Geygan	8050 Hoobrook Rd., Suite 107	Cincinnati	OH	45236	513-791-1673
Paul D. Gilbert	503 Hulman Building	Dayton	OH	45402	513-224-7311
Mark Alan Greenberger	105 E. 4th Street, 9th Floor	Cincinnati	OH	45202	513-721-5151
Michael T. Gunner	3455 Mill Run Drive	Hilliard	OH	43206	614-777-1204
Donald F. Harker, III	130 W. 2nd St., Suite 1600	Dayton	OH	45402	513-461-8800
Thomas Mck. Hazlett	185 West Main Street	St. Clairsville	OH	43950	614-695-9202
Harold Jarnicki	27 N. East Street	Lebanon	OH	45036	513-932-5792
Carl E. Juergens	1504 North Limestone Street	Springfield	OH	45502	513-399-8180
Eric Henderson Kearney	2100 PNC Center	Cincinnati	OH	45202	513-621-2120
David Willard Kuhn	612 6th Ave, Suite A, Courthouse Annex	Portsmouth	OH	45662	614-354-1454
William Boyd Logan, Jr.	50 W. Broad Street, Suite 1200	Columbus	OH	43215-3374	614-229-4449
Frederick Morris Luper	50 W. Broad St., #1200	Columbus	OH	43215	614-229-4409
Roger E. Luring	314 West Main Street	Troy	OH	45373	513-339-2627
Larry J. McClatchey	65 East State Street, Ste. 1800	Columbus	OH	43215	614-462-5400
Henry Edward Menninger, Jr.	600 Vine St., 2500 Cincinnati Commerce	Cincinnati	OH	45202	513-852-6033
Richard D. Nelson	525 Vine Street, 16th Floor	Cincinnati	OH	45202	513-421-4020
Thomas R. Noland	900 Talbott Tower-131 1st Street	Dayton	OH	45402	513-223-1201
Elliott Polaniecki	105 E. Fourth St., Suite 700	Cincinnati	OH	45202	513-381-3818
Frederick L. Ransier, III	66 Thurman Avenue	Columbus	OH	43206	614-443-7429
John Paul Rieser	130 W. 2nd Street, Suite 2050	Dayton	OH	45402	513-224-4128
Arthur J. Schuh	2662 Madison Road, Suite 300	Cincinnati	OH	45208	513-321-2662
Thomas C. Scott	10 W. Broad Street, Suite 700	Columbus	OH	43215	614-469-3200
Ruth Ann Slone-Stiver	1020 Woodman Dr., Suite 360	Dayton	OH	45432	513-253-9687
Norman L. Slutsky	602 Main Street, Suite 206	Cincinnati	OH	45202	513-421-0042
Larry Eugene Staats	50 W. Broad Street, Suite 1100	Columbus	OH	43215	614-461-1516
Dennis E. Stegner	111 East Cecil Street	Springfield	OH	45504	513-322-2161
Myron N. Terlecky	575 South Third Street	Columbus	OH	43215	614-228-6345
James R. Warren	4 W. Main St., Suite 216	Springfield	OH	45501	513-323-1131
Arnold S. White	844 South Front Street	Columbus	OH	43206	614-443-0310
David M. Whittaker	50 West Broad St., Suite 1200	Columbus	OH	43215	614-229-4454

REGION 10

Illinois - Central

Name	Address	City	State	Zip	Telephone
Richard E. Barber	318 Hill Arcade Building	Galesburg	IL	61401	309-342-4139
Glen R. Barmann	189 E. Court Street, Suite 500	Kankakee	IL	60901	815-939-1133
William H. Christison, III	101 S.W. Adams, Suite 800	Peoria	IL	61602-1335	309-637-4900
Charles E. Covey	525 Peoria Savings Plaza	Peoria	IL	61602	309-673-3807
Arthur Clay Cox	P.O. Box 3067	Bloomington	IL	61702-3067	309-828-7331
Mark Thomas Dunn	P.O. Box 3488	Bloomington	IL	61702-3488	309-828-6241
James R. Geekie	209 North Central Avenue	Paris	IL	61944	217-465-7681
Vernon H. Houchen	516 Millikin Court	Decatur	IL	62525	217-422-8874
John E. Maloney	135 West Main Street	Urbana	IL	61801	217-384-7111
P. Stephen Miller	11 East North Street	Danville	IL	61832	217-442-0350
William F. Nissen	522 Vermont Street, Suite 2	Quincy	IL	62301	217-222-1569
Mariann Pogge	5240 S. Sixth Street Road	Springfield	IL	62705	217-786-2531
John Lee Swartz	P.O. Box 2117	Springfield	IL	62705	217-525-1571
Jeffrey Cuin Taylor	420 Millikin Court	Decatur	IL	62523	217-428-2100

Illinois - Southern

Name	Address	City	State	Zip	Telephone
Laura K. Grandy	720 West Main, Suite 100	Belleville	IL	62220	618-234-9800
Donald E. Hoagland	209 South Franklin Street	Robinson	IL	62454	618-546-5441
Steven Neil Mottaz	307 Henry Street	Alton	IL	62002	618-462-9201
Donald M. Samson	120 West Main Street	Belleville	IL	62220	618-235-2226
Michelle Leigh Vieira	103 Airway Drive, Suite II	Marion	IL	62959	618-997-6878
Tamalou M. Williams	P.O. Box 518	Benton	IL	62812	618-435-4494

Name	Address	City	State	Zip	Telephone

Indiana - Northern

Name	Address	City	State	Zip	Telephone
Ray D. Boyer	300 Metro Building	Fort Wayne	IN	46802	219-422-7422
Gary D. Boyn	121 W. Franklin St., Suite 400	Elkhart	IN	46516	219-294-7491
Joseph D. Bradley	105 E. Jefferson Blvd., Suite 512	South Bend	IN	46601	219-234-5091
Edward Chosnek	P.O. Box 708	Lafayette	IN	47902	317-742-9081
David R. DuBois	2545 Portage Mall	Portage	IN	46368	219-762-5574
Daniel L. Freeland	2617 45th Avenue	Highland	IN	46322	219-924-9820
Gordon E. Gouveia	521 East 86th Avenue, Suite E	Merrillville	IN	46410	219-736-6020
Calvin D. Hawkins	P.O. Box M859	Gary	IN	46401	219-887-2626
Kenneth A. Manning	200 Monticello Drive	Dyer	IN	46311	219-865-8376
Frank O. McLane	569 W. Shore Drive	Culver	IN	46511	219-842-3954
Lynn M. Miller	112 North Second Street	Elkhart	IN	46516	219-293-2554
J. Richard Ransel	310 W. McKinley Avenue	Mishawaka	IN	46545	219-256-5660
Margret Ann Robb	710 Brown Street	Lafayette	IN	47902	317-423-2688
Mark Allen Warsco	927 S. Harrison, Suite 200	Fort Wayne	IN	46802	219-423-2537

Indiana - Southern

Name	Address	City	State	Zip	Telephone
Philip F. Boberschmidt	111 Monument Circle, Suite 302	Indianapolis	IN	46204	317-632-5892
Richard Eugene Boston	Bank One Building, Ste. 400	Richmond	IN	47374	317-962-7527
Richard L. Darst	8888 Keystone Blvd., #800	Indianapolis	IN	46240	317-573-8888
Edward P. Dechert	127 West Mulberry Street	Kokomo	IN	46901	317-459-0764
Dennis J. Dewey	107 State Street	Newburgh	IN	47630	812-853-3357
Gregory S. Fehribach	50 S. Meridian St., #700	Indianapolis	IN	46204	317-638-2400
Charles G. Fifer	420 Wall St., P.O. Box 1446	Jeffersonville	IN	47131	812-284-1446
Paul D. Gresk	1800 Indiana Nat'l Bank Tower	Indianapolis	IN	46204	317-634-9277
Joseph W. Hammes	One Indiana Square, Suite 2150	Indianapolis	IN	46204	317-634-1317
Donald G. Henderson	303 Citizens National Bank	Bedford	IN	47421	812-279-9654
Rex Morris Joseph, Jr.	6125 U.S. Hwy 31 South	Indianapolis	IN	46227	317-788-4000
Thomas A. Krudy	236 E. 15th St.	Indianapolis	IN	46202	317-635-2502
Robert Stephen LaPlante	1402 Old National Bank Bldg.	Evansville	IN	47733	812-424-5558
Wayne Jay Lennington	105 E. Washington St.	Muncie	IN	47305	317-289-2167
Elliott D. Levin	342 Massachusetts Ave., 500	Indianapolis	IN	46204	317-634-0300
Richard W. Lorenz	P.O. Box 46	Spencer	IN	47460-0046	812-829-2221
Malcolm G. Montgomery	2811 First Avenue	Evansville	IN	47710	812-424-8248
Merrill Moores	244 North College Avenue	Indianapolis	IN	46202	317-639-3315
John James Petr	20 North Meridian Street	Indianapolis	IN	46204	317-634-6328
Neil E. Shook	342 Mass. Ave., 500 Marott Ctr.	Indianapolis	IN	46204-2161	317-634-0300
Gregory Kent Silver	342 Massachusetts Ave. #400	Indianapolis	IN	46204	317-263-9417
William J. Tabor	P.O. Box 328	Terre Haute	IN	47808	812-877-3750
David J. Theising	P.O. Box 2850	Indianapolis	IN	46206	317-635-9000
William Jake Tucker	50 S. Meridian St. #400	Indianapolis	IN	46204	317-264-4040
Michael J. Walro	426 East Main Street	Madison	IN	47250	812-265-3616
Randall Lee Woodruff	200 E. 11th St., Suite 103	Anderson	IN	46016	317-644-6464

REGION 11

Illinois - Northern

Name	Address	City	State	Zip	Telephone
Joseph A. Baldi	55 E. Monroe Street, Ste. 4620	Chicago	IL	60603	312-236-5622
Stephen G. Balsley	102 S. Madison Street	Rockford	IL	61101	815-962-6611
Michael G. Berland	140 S. Dearborn St., Ste. 1606	Chicago	IL	60603	312-855-1272
William A. Brandt, Jr.	70 West Madison St., Ste. 2300	Chicago	IL	60602-4205	312-263-4141
David R. Brown	1024 North Boulevard, Suite 201	Oak Park	IL	60301	708-848-0400
James E. Carmel	180 North LaSalle St., Suite 2630	Chicago	IL	60601	312-201-8080
Joseph E. Cohen	2 North LaSalle St., Suite 1776	Chicago	IL	60602	312-368-0300
Eugene Crane	135 South LaSalle Street, #1540	Chicago	IL	60603	312-641-6777
Joseph L. D'Amico	203 North LaSalle St., 25th Fl.	Chicago	IL	60601	312-701-5650
Allan J. DeMars	100 West Monroe St., Ste. 1701	Chicago	IL	60603	312-726-3377
Daniel M. Donahue	850 North Church Street	Rockford	IL	61105	815-963-8451
Deborah K. Ebner	11 East Adams St., Suite 800	Chicago	IL	60603	312-922-3030

Name	Address	City	State	Zip	Telephone
Lawrence Fisher	321 North Clark St., Suite 3200	Chicago	IL	60610	312-245-8780
Richard M. Fogel	3 First Nat'l Plaza, Ste. 4300	Chicago	IL	60602	312-558-4289
John E. Gierum, Jr.	1300 W. Higgins Road	Park Ridge	IL	60068	708-698-9600
Ilene F. Goldstein	55 East Monroe St., Suite 4620	Chicago	IL	60603	312-236-5622
Karen R. Goodman	222 North LaSalle St., Suite 300	Chicago	IL	60601	312-704-3386
William H. Grabscheid	200 West Madison St., Suite 2250	Chicago	IL	60605	312-407-6440
David E. Grochocinski	7804 College Drive	Palos Hills	IL	60463	708-923-3000
Leonard M. Groupe	175 W. Jackson Blvd., Suite A-1710	Chicago	IL	60604	312-663-1300
Brenda P. Helms	27 East Monroe St., Suite 1000	Chicago	IL	60603	312-606-0808
David R. Herzog	303 W. Madison Street, Ste. 1600	Chicago	IL	60606	312-977-1600
Glenn R. Heyman	135 S. LaSalle Street, #1540	Chicago	IL	60603	312-641-6777
Pamela S. Hollis	One Quincy Court, Suite 1204	Chicago	IL	60604	312-427-0702
Daniel Hoseman	77 West Washington St., Suite 1220	Chicago	IL	60602	312-372-5139
Leroy G. Inskeep	203 N. LaSalle Street, #1800	Chicago	IL	60601	312-368-4067
Donald E. Johnson	One Quincy Court, Ste. 1204	Chicago	IL	60604	312-427-0700
Emmanuel M. Katten	33 West Monroe St., Rm. 915	Chicago	IL	60603	312-507-6713
Robert B. Katz	135 South LaSalle St., Suite 3805	Chicago	IL	60603	312-332-0510
Alexander S. Knopfler	10 S. Wacker Dr., Ste. 3900	Chicago	IL	60606	312-715-4980
Gina B. Krol	2 N. LaSalle St., Suite 1776	Chicago	IL	60602	312-368-0300
David P. Leibowitz	311 S. Wacker Drive, Suite 3000	Chicago	IL	60606	312-360-6000
Thomas J. Lester	220 East State Street	Rockford	IL	61105	815-963-8488
Phillip D. Levey	135 S. LaSalle St., Ste. 1527	Chicago	IL	60603	312-726-4475
Louis W. Levit	150 North Michigan Ave., Suite 2500	Chicago	IL	60601	312-558-1000
Philip V. Martino	203 North LaSalle St., Suite 1800	Chicago	IL	60601	312-368-2165
Richard J. Mason	150 North Michigan St., Suite 2500	Chicago	IL	60601	312-558-1000
Andrew J. Maxwell	135 South LaSalle St., Suite 3805	Chicago	IL	60603	312-368-1138
Robert B. Millner	8000 Sear Tower	Chicago	IL	60606	312-876-7994
Alex D. Moglia	911 N. Plum Grove, Suite H	Schaumburg	IL	60173	708-995-9010
Charles J. Myler	111 West Downer Place	Aurora	IL	60506	708-897-8475
Bernard J. Natale	308 West State Street, Suite 470	Rockford	IL	61101	815-964-4700
Norman B. Newman	200 N. LaSalle St., Ste. 2100	Chicago	IL	60601	312-346-3100
Joseph D. Olsen	1318 East State Street	Rockford	IL	61104-2228	815-965-8635
Gus A. Paloian	55 East Monroe Street, 42nd Floor	Chicago	IL	60603	312-346-8000
Ronald R. Peterson	One IBM Plaza, 38th Floor	Chicago	IL	60611	312-222-9350
Thomas E. Raleigh	27 East Monroe, Suite 1000	Chicago	IL	60603	312-606-0808
N. Neville Reid	190 S. LaSalle Street	Chicago	IL	60603	312-701-7934
Ray O. Rodriguez	3 First National Plaza, Ste. 1200	Chicago	IL	60602	312-372-3500
Roy A. Safanda	102 East Main Street	St. Charles	IL	60174	708-584-5566
Joel Schechter	53 West Jackson Blvd., #915	Chicago	IL	60604	312-332-0267
Sheldon L. Solow	30 S. Wacker Dr., #2900	Chicago	IL	60606	312-207-6545
Catherine L. Steege	One IBM Plaza, 38th Floor	Chicago	IL	60611	312-222-9350
Joseph Stein	30 S. Wacker Drive, Suite 2900	Chicago	IL	60606	312-207-1000
Jay A. Steinberg	Three First National Plaza, #4300	Chicago	IL	60602	312-558-5186
James E. Stevens	One Madison Street	Rockford	IL	61104	815-962-6611
Thomas B. Sullivan	7804 College Drive, Suite 2NE	Palas Hts.	IL	60463	708-923-3000
Joseph R. Voiland	346 North Lake Street	Aurora	IL	60506	708-844-1644
Bradley J. Waller	216 W. State Street, Suite A	Sycamore	IL	60178	815-756-6328
Nathan Yorke	53 West Jackson Blvd., #1524	Chicago	IL	60604	312-461-9485
Bruce E. de'Medici	208 S. LaSalle, Suite 650	Chicago	IL	60604	312-346-4740

Wisconsin - Eastern

Name	Address	City	State	Zip	Telephone
Faith Lleva Anderson	1120 Elm Grove Street, P.O. Box 154	Elm Grove	WI	53122-0154	414-797-2021
Michael F. Dubis	208 East Main Street	Waterford	WI	53185	414-534-6950
Todd C. Esser	2300 North Mayfair Rd., Suite 1165	Wauwatosa	WI	53226	414-258-0186
Bruce A. Lanser	525 East Wells St., Suite 216	Milwaukee	WI	53202	414-272-5700
Helen Margaret Ludwig	10150 W. National Avenue, Suite 390	West Allis	WI	53227	414-321-0078
Douglas F. Mann	740 North Plankinton Avenue	Milwaukee	WI	53203	414-276-5355
Neil R. McKloskey	128 North Madison, P.O. Box 1863	Green Bay	WI	54305-1863	414-432-8677
Lawrence M. Phillips	Arbor Terrace II, 205 Bishops Way #224	Brookfield	WI	53005	414-789-1208
Karma Sarah Rodgers-Butler	1110 N. Old World 3rd Street, Suite 670	Milwaukee	WI	53203	414-271-8850
John M. Scaffidi	P.O. Box 11975	Milwaukee	WI	53211	414-963-9303

Name	Address	City	State	Zip	Telephone
Paul G. Swanson	P.O. Box 617	Oshkosh	WI	54902-0617	414-235-6690
John F. Waldschmidt	238 West Wisconsin, Suite 800	Milwaukee	WI	53203	414-289-0800
Robert M. Waud	152 West Wisconsin, Suite 414	Milwaukee	WI	53203	414-271-3728

Wisconsin - Western

Name	Address	City	State	Zip	Telephone
Arthur L. Eberlein	606 Jackson Street	Wausau	WI	54401	715-842-4340
Peter M. Gennrich	16 North Carroll St., Ste. 900	Madison	WI	53703	608-257-9281
Peter F. Herrell	1280 W. Clairemont Avenue	Eau Claire	WI	54702	715-834-8101
Melvyn L. Hoffman	312 South Third St., Suite A	La Crosse	WI	54602-1503	608-782-8098
Michael E. Kepler	353 West Mifflin Street	Madison	WI	53703	608-257-5424
Martha M. Markusen	302 West Superior Street, Suite 700	Duluth	MN	55802-1863	218-722-0861
James W. McNeilly, Jr.	P.O. Box 966	La Crosse	WI	54602-0966	608-782-1469
Randi L. Osberg	402 Graham Avenue	Eau Claire	WI	54702	715-834-3425
William J. Rameker	2 East Mifflin St.	Madison	WI	53701	608-257-7181
Scott F. Shadel	100 South Main Street	Janesville	WI	53547	608-755-8100
Edward F. Zappen	223 South Central Avenue	Marshfield	WI	54449-0009	715-387-1231

REGION 12

Iowa - Northern

Name	Address	City	State	Zip	Telephone
Larry S. Eide	800 Brick & Tile Bldg., PO Box 1588	Mason City	IA	50401	515-423-4264
Wil L. Forker	232 Davidson Bldg., 505 6th Street	Sioux City	IA	51101-1242	712-255-0189
Donald H. Molstad	224 Davidson Building	Sioux City	IA	51101	712-255-8036

Iowa - Northern & Southern

Name	Address	City	State	Zip	Telephone
Michael C. Dunbar	Chicago Centeral Bldg., Ste. 738	Waterloo	IA	50704	319-233-6327
Paul J. Fitzsimmons	790 Town Clock Plaza	Dubuque	IA	52001	319-588-4088
Habbo Gerd Fokkena	109 North Main Street	Clarksville	IA	50619	319-278-4766
Eric W. Lam	2720 First Avenue N.E., P.O. Box 1943	Cedar Rapids	IA	52402	319-366-7331
Thomas G. McCuskey	401 Old Marion Road NE, P.O. Box 10020	Cedar Rapids	IA	52402	319-395-7400
Donald F. Neiman	801 Grand Ave., Suite 3700	Des Moines	IA	50308	515-243-4191
Deborah Louise Petersen	215 South Main St., P.O. Box 1016	Council Bluffs	IA	51502	712-328-1575
David A. Sergeant	1728 Central Ave., P.O. Box 1315	Fort Dodge	IA	50501	515-576-0333
Harry R. Terpstra	830 Higley Building	Cedar Rapids	IA	52401	319-364-2467

Iowa - Southern

Name	Address	City	State	Zip	Telephone
A. Fred Berger	326 West Third Street	Davenport	IA	52801	319-326-1000
Burton H. Fagan	206 Commerce Exchange Bldg. 2535 Tech Dr.	Bettendorf	IA	52722	319-332-6549
Thomas L. Flynn	2000 Financial Center	Des Moines	IA	50309	515-243-7100
Anita L. Shodeen	321 East Walnut	Des Moines	IA	50309	515-288-6572
Charles L. Smith	25 Main Place, Suite 200	Council Bluffs	IA	51503	712-325-9000

Minnesota

Name	Address	City	State	Zip	Telephone
Edward W. Bergquist	600 Title Insurance Bldg., 400 2nd Ave. S	Minneapolis	MN	55401	612-339-5581
Sheridan J. Buckley	101 East Fifth Street, Ste. 1614	St. Paul	MN	55101	612-224-3361
Julia A. Christians	120 South Sixth St., Suite 1800	Minneapolis	MN	55402	612-338-5815
Michael S. Dietz	505 Marquette Bank Bldg., P.O. Box 549	Rochester	MN	55903	507-288-9111
Michael J. Farrell	Box 519	Barnesville	MN	56514	218-354-7356
Greg C. Gilbert	811 Norwest Ctr., 230 W. Superior St.	Duluth	MN	55802	218-722-6331
Mark C. Halverson	P.O. Box 3544	Mankato	MN	56002	507-345-1535
John A. Hedback	2489 Rice Street, Suite 209	Roseville	MN	55113	612-482-1451
Michael J. Iannacone	101 East Fifth St., Suite 1614	St. Paul	MN	55101	612-224-3361
Brian F. Kidwell	800 Norwest Center	St. Paul	MN	55101	612-227-9505
Dorraine A. Larison	1010 West St. Germain	St. Cloud	MN	56301	612-252-4414
Brian F. Leonard	800 Norwest Center, 55 East 5th St.	St. Paul	MN	55101	612-227-9505
Dwight R.J. Lindquist	1510 Rand Tower, 527 Marquette Ave.	Minneapolis	MN	55402	612-332-8871

Name	Address	City	State	Zip	Telephone
Thomas F. Miller	330 Second Ave. South	Minneapolis	MN	55401	612-332-5933
Timothy D. Moratzka	1600 TCF Tower, 121 S. Eight Street	Minneapolis	MN	55402	612-333-1341
James E. Ramette	P.O. Box 940	Chanhassen	MN	55317	612-937-8984
Charles W. Ries	P.O. Box 908	Mankato	MN	56002-0908	507-387-3002
Paul J. Sandelin	308 First Street, Box 298	Pequot Lakes	MN	56472	218-568-8481
Molly T. Shields	3500 Fifth St. Towers, 150 S. Fifth St.	Minneapolis	MN	55402-4235	612-340-5555
John R. Stoebner	1800 One Financial Plaza, 120 S. 6th St.	Minneapolis	MN	55402	612-338-5815

North Dakota

Name	Address	City	State	Zip	Telephone
Phillip D. Armstrong	12 South Main Street, Suite 202	Minot	ND	58701	701-838-9422
Wayne E. Drewes	P.O. Box 1021	Fargo	ND	58107	701-237-6650
Reed Alan Soderstrom	20 SW 1st Street, P.O. Box 1000	Minot	ND	58702	701-852-0381
Michael Leonard Wagner	220 N. Fourth Street, Box 2056	Bismarck	ND	58501	701-223-5300

North Dakota & Minnesota

Name	Address	City	State	Zip	Telephone
Kip M. Kaler	808 3rd Avenue S., Ste 400	Fargo	ND	58103	701-232-8757

South Dakota

Name	Address	City	State	Zip	Telephone
John S. Lovald	117 East Capitol, P.O. Box 66	Pierre	SD	57501	605-224-8851
William J. Pfeiffer	P.O. Box 1585	Aberdeen	SD	57402-1585	605-229-1144
A. Thomas Pokela	406 South Second Ave., P.O. Box 1102	Sioux Falls	SD	57101	605-338-6151
Dennis C. Whetzal	P.O. Box 8285	Rapid City	SD	57709	605-343-9671
Rick A. Yarnall	300 North Dakota Ave., Ste. 609	Sioux Falls	SD	57101-1925	605-336-0748

REGION 13

Arkansas - Eastern

Name	Address	City	State	Zip	Telephone
Richard L. Cox	835 Central, Suite 509	Hot Springs	AR	71901	501-623-1759
Walter M. Dickinson	3101 Hinson Road	Little Rock	AR	72212	501-221-2020
James F. Dowden	P.O. Box 70	Little Rock	AR	72203	501-376-1171
Warren Eugene Dupwe	300 West Jefferson	Jonesboro	AR	72401	501-935-5845
James C. Luker	P.O. Box 216, 218 N. Terry	Wynne	AR	72396	501-238-8588
Richard L. Ramsay	P.O. Box 70	Little Rock	AR	72203	501-376-1171
Mark Randy Rice	523 S. Louisiana, Suite 300	Little Rock	AR	72201	501-374-1019
Daniel Kent Schieffler	P.O. Box 2309	West Helena	AR	72390	501-572-2161
A. Jan Thomas, Jr.	306 West Bond Street	West Memphis	AR	72301-3996	501-735-7700

Arkansas - Western

Name	Address	City	State	Zip	Telephone
Ben T. Barry	P.O. Drawer 848	Ft. Smith	AR	72902	501-782-8813
Jill R. Jacoway	P.O. Drawer 3456	Fayetteville	AR	72702	501-521-2621
Claude R. Jones	P.O. Box 1577	Harrison	AR	72602	501-741-4100
John T. Lee	P.O. Box 1348	Siloam Springs	AR	72761	501-524-2337
William S. Meeks	300 E. Adams, P.O. Box 71	Hamburg	AR	71646	501-853-5461
Jan K. Nielsen	3103 Alma Hwy, P.O. Drawer M	Van Buren	AR	72956	501-471-1533
Thomas E. Robertson, Jr.	P.O. Box 23	Fort Smith	AR	72902	501-782-7911
Frederick S. Wetzel, III	2100 Riverfront Drive, Suite 240	Little Rock	AR	72202-1793	501-663-0535

Missouri - Eastern

Name	Address	City	State	Zip	Telephone
Robert J. Blackwell	1010 Market Street, Ste 1440	St. Louis	MO	63101	314-621-3535
Rice P. Burns, Jr.	733 N. Main, P.O. Box 67	Sikeston	MO	63801	314-472-0290
Ella Rebecca Case	7733 Forsyth, Ste. 500	St. Louis	MO	63105	314-721-7011
Fredrich J. Cruse	716 Broadway P.O. Box 914	Hannibal	MO	63401	314-221-2150
Leslie A. Davis	120 S. Central, Ste. 1700	Clayton	MO	63105	314-725-7600
A. Thomas DeWoskin	10 South Broadway, 18th Floor	St. Louis	MO	63102	314-241-9090
William Henry Frye	1021 N. Kingsway, Suite 10	Cape Girardeau	MO	63701	314-335-2573
John V. LaBarge, Jr.	1401 S. Brentwood #650	St. Louis	MO	63144	314-963-0000
Thomas K. O'Loughlin, II	1736 N. Kings Highway	Cape Girardeau	MO	63701	314-334-9104
Stuart Jay Radloff	7700 Bonhomme Ave., Ste. 400	Clayton	MO	63105	314-725-9400

Name	Address	City	State	Zip	Telephone
Charles W. Riske	7700 Bonhomme Ave., Ste. 400	Clayton	MO	63105	314-725-9400
David A. Sosne	8909 Ladue Road	St. Louis	MO	63124	314-991-4999

Missouri - Western

Name	Address	City	State	Zip	Telephone
Gary Don Barnes	P.O. Box 26006	Kansas City	MO	64196	816-421-4800
Steven C. Block	4505 Madison	Kansas City	MO	64111-3500	861-531-0509
Jack Edward Brown	P.O. Box 7628	Columbia	MO	65205	314-442-4011
Thomas J. Carlson	P.O. Box 50280	Springfield	MO	65805	417-864-5956
James Kevin Checkett	517 S. Main P.O. Box 409	Carthage	MO	64836	417-358-4049
Max Jevinsky	1006 Grand, Suite 1600	Kansas City	MO	64106	816-471-5900
Erlene Krigel	1111 Main #900	Kansas City	MO	64105	816-474-7800
John Lewis, Jr.	4435 Main, Suite 1100	Kansas City	MO	64111	816-531-1700
Jere L. Loyd	507 Francis Street	St. Joseph	MO	64501	816-364-3020
Fred Charles Moon	1705 North Jefferson	Springfield	MO	65803	417-862-3704
Danny Ray Nelson	214 Woodruff Building, P.O. Box 50575	Springfield	MO	65805	417-831-3140
Thomas J. O'Neal	901 St. Louis Street, #1200	Springfield	MO	65806	417-865-1200
Robert A. Pummill	922 Walnut Ave., Suite 1200	Kansas City	MO	64106	816-471-1800
John Charles Reed	325 Jefferson Street	Jefferson City	MO	65102	314-635-8500
Norman E. Rouse	3010 McClelland Blvd., P.O. Box 1846	Joplin	MO	64802	417-782-2222
David C. Stover	3000 Brooktree Lane, Suite 100	Kansas City	MO	64119-1850	816-454-5600
Bruce E. Strauss	1044 Main Street, 7th Fl.	Kansas City	MO	64105	816-221-8855

Nebraska

Name	Address	City	State	Zip	Telephone
Joseph H. Badami	206 South 13th Street	Lincoln	NE	68508	402-474-0321
Richard J. Butler	811 South 13th Street	Lincoln	NE	68508	402-475-0811
Philip M. Kelly	105 East 16th Street	Scottsbluff	NE	69363	308-632-7191
Richard D. Myers	11404 West Dodge Rd., Suite 700	Omaha	NE	68154	402-493-7700
Ronald L. Sanchez	121 West 2nd St., P.O. Box 1005	North Platte	NE	69103	308-532-0551
Thomas D. Stalnaker	P.O. Box 24268	Omaha	NE	68124	402-393-5421
James J. Stumpf	10050 Regency Circle, Suite 101	Omaha	NE	68114	402-397-1200
John A. Wolf	Norwest Bank Bldg., Suite 201	Grand Island	NE	68802	308-384-1635

REGION 14

Arizona

Name	Address	City	State	Zip	Telephone
Robert P. Abele	P.O. Box 5478	Mesa	AZ	85274	602-844-1624
Ronald L. Ancell	2573 N. 1st Avenue, Suite A	Tucson	AZ	85719	602-791-9274
John D. Barkley	2666 N. First Ave., Suite A4	Tucson	AZ	85719	602-791-9194
Raymond Bernal	4730 N. Oracle, #218	Tucson	AZ	85705	602-293-4126
David Allen Birdsell	216 N. Center	Mesa	AZ	85201	602-644-1080
Roger W. Brown	2211 E. Highland Avenue, #240	Phoenix	AZ	85064-2967	602-956-2218
Robert Francis Coleman	3101 N. Central Avenue, Suite 1100	Phoenix	AZ	85012	602-241-1200
Robert J. Davis	P.O. Box 55120	Phoenix	AZ	85078-5120	602-993-4245
Stanley W. Fogler	P.O. Box 47218	Phoenix	AZ	85068	602-993-3040
James Daniel Fox	P.O. Box 599	Scottsdale	AZ	85252	602-946-1412
Maureen R. Gaughan	2095 N. Alma School Rd., Suite 12-124	Chandler	AZ	85224	602-899-2036
Lothar H. Goernitz	P.O. Box 32931	Phoenix	AZ	85064	602-956-2269
Joseph James Janas	14435 North 7th St., #202	Phoenix	AZ	85022	602-993-3850
Alvin E. Kackley	P.O. Box 12461	Tucson	AZ	85732	602-722-3311
Linda Diane Mann	10537 N. 119th Street	Scottsdale	AZ	85259	602-661-7876
Louis Allan Movitz	P.O. Box 3137	Carefree	AZ	85201	602-482-3733
Charles L. Riley, Jr.	P.O. Box 25619	Tempe	AZ	85285-5619	602-839-4224
Jim D. Smith	221 S. Second Avenue	Yuma	AZ	85364	602-783-7809
Alan Richard Solot	459 N. Granada Avenue	Tucson	AZ	85701	602-622-4622
Walter T. Thompson	P.O. Box 4640	Scottsdale	AZ	85261-4640	602-991-5242
Dale Ulrich	1025 E. Bell Road, #316	Phoenix	AZ	85022	602-264-4124
Absalom M. Valenzuela, Sr.	P.O. Box 7897	Tucson	AZ	85725	602-629-0051
Robert G. Vucurevich	P.O. Box 42327	Phoenix	AZ	85080	602-955-1682
Lawrence Joseph Warfield	7835 E. Redfield Road #200	Scottsdale	AZ	85260	602-948-1711
John Albert Weil	P.O. Box 1977	Yuma	AZ	85364	602-783-2161

Name	Address	City	State	Zip	Telephone

REGION 15

California - Southern

Name	Address	City	State	Zip	Telephone
Gregory A. Akers	350 West Ash St., #600	San Diego	CA	92101	619-233-4882
Ralph O. Boldt	12265 World Trade Dr., Ste. A	San Diego	CA	92128	619-487-3779
Gerald Holt Davis	110 West "C" St., Suite 1611	San Diego	CA	92101	619-233-0266
James L. Kennedy	P.O. Box 28459	San Diego	CA	92128	619-451-8859
Richard M. Kipperman	P.O. Box 3939	La Mesa	CA	91944-3939	619-668-4501
Michael Leroy Rood	444 S. 8th Street	El Centro	CA	92243	619-352-7777
Harold S. Taxel	P.O. Box 2026	La Jolla	CA	92038	619-295-0334

Guam

Name	Address	City	State	Zip	Telephone
Loring E. Jahnke	275-G Farenholt Ave, Suite 247	Tamuning	GU	96911	671-649-0852

Hawaii

Name	Address	City	State	Zip	Telephone
James Burton Nicholson	735 Bishop Street, Suite 320	Honolulu	HI	96813	808-923-5477
Paul S. Sakuda	2170 Kuhio Avenue	Honolulu	HI	96815	808-921-0332
Mary Louise Woo	150 Hamakua Drive, #411	Kailua	HI	96734	808-261-0475

REGION 16

California - Central

Name	Address	City	State	Zip	Telephone
Theodor C. Albert	660 Newport Center Dr., Suite 1400	Newport Beach	CA	92660	714-759-6238
Peter C. Anderson	6055 East Washington Blvd., Suite 430	Los Angeles	CA	90040-2466	213-724-3200
Karl T. Anderson	477 S. Palm Canyon Dr., Suite 8	Palm Springs	CA	92262	619-320-2424
Sandra L. Bendon	73-710 Fred Waring Drive	Palm Desert	CA	92260	619-776-6560
Thomas H. Casey	2700 N. Main St., Suite 600	Santa Ana	CA	92701	714-541-0301
Arturo M. Cisneros	290 N. "D" Street, Suite 723	San Bernardino	CA	92401	909-884-6882
Charles W. Daff	2700 North Main Street, Suite 600	Santa Ana	CA	92701	714-541-0301
Lawrence A. Diamant	1888 Century Park East, #1500	Los Angeles	CA	90067	310-277-7400
Richard Kenneth Diamond	1800 Century Park East, 7th Fl.	Los Angeles	CA	90067	310-277-0077
Ronald L. Durkin	101 North Westlake Blvd.	Westlake Village	CA	91362	805-371-1113
Marc Howard Ehrenberg	300 South Grand Avenue, 14th Floor	Los Angeles	CA	90071	213-626-2311
David Y. Farmer	1254 Marsh Street	San Luis Obispo	CA	93401	805-541-1626
Helen R. Frazer	13304 E. Alondra Boulevard	Cerritos	CA	90701	310-404-4444
David A. Gill	1800 Century Park East, 7th Fl.	Los Angeles	CA	90067	310-277-0077
David R. Haberbush	6055 E. Washington Blvd., #430	Los Angeles	CA	90040-2466	213-724-3200
Richard A. Halderman, Jr.	2424 S.E. Bristol Street, Suite 350	Newport Beach	CA	92660	714-474-0600
Norman L. Hanover	665 North Arrowhead Avenue	San Bernardino	CA	92401	909-884-7215
Donald W. Henry	5525 Oakdale Ave., #165	Woodland Hills	CA	91364	818-348-1244
John Wallace Hyde	1888 Central Park East, Suite 1777	Los Angeles	CA	90067	310-282-0871
James J. Joseph	1800 Century Park East, 7th Fl.	Los Angeles	CA	90067	310-277-0077
Nancy Knupfer	445 S. Figueroa Street, Suite 2400	Los Angeles	CA	90071	213-895-4500
Michael S. Kogan	700 S. Flower St., 30th Floor	Los Angeles	CA	90017	213-629-9375
Weneta M. A. Kosmala	Griffin Towers, #900, 6 Hutton Ctr Drive	Santa Ana	CA	92707	714-540-3600
Arnold Kupetz	300 S. Grand Ave., 14th Floor	Los Angeles	CA	90071	213-626-2311
Heide C. Kurtz	10900 Wilshire Boulevard, 3rd Floor	Los Angeles	CA	90024	310-824-5700
Denise Lamaute	8383 Wilshire Blvd., Suite 840	Beverly Hills	CA	90211	213-655-1560
Heidi K. Leanders	P.O. Box 18972	Irvine	CA	92713	714-833-0318
Richard A. Marshack	Six Hutton Centre Dr., Suite 900	Santa Ana	CA	92707	714-540-5400
Byron Z. Moldo	10960 Wilshire Blvd., 10th Floor	Los Angeles	CA	90024	310-444-6400
Raymond Todd Neilson	2029 Century Park East, Suite 900	Los Angeles	CA	90067	310-282-9911
Archie C. Purvis	2040 Avenue of the Stars - 4th Floor	Los Angeles	CA	90067	310-557-3600
David L. Ray	10960 Wilshire Blvd., 10th Fl.	Los Angeles	CA	90024	310-473-8405
Duke C. Salisbury	11150 Olympic Blvd., #940	Los Angeles	CA	90064	310-445-3101
David Seror	1875 Century Park East, #500	Los Angeles	CA	90067	310-556-8861
Alfred H. Siegel	15233 Ventura Blvd., 9th Floor	Sherman Oaks	CA	91403	818-379-2414
Steven E. Smith	650 S. Grand Ave., #500	Los Angeles	CA	90017	213-622-9012
Robert G. Uriarte	800 E. Colorado Blvd., #850.	Pasadena	CA	91101	818-585-6900
Gilbert R. Vasquez	510 W. Sixth St., Suite 400	Los Angeles	CA	90014	213-629-9094

Name	Address	City	State	Zip	Telephone
Robert S. Whitmore	715 N. Arrowhead Ave., #2025	San Bernardino	CA	92401	909-885-6668
John M. Wolfe	520 S. Grand Ave., #360	Los Angeles	CA	90071	213-624-0994
Edward M. Wolkowitz	1888 Century Park E., #1500	Los Angeles	CA	90067	310-277-7400
Patricia J. Zimmermann	670 N. Arrowhead Ave., Suite C	San Bernardino	CA	92401	909-383-1644

REGION 17

California - Central

Robert Dennis Pryce	333 S. Grand Avenue, Suite 2000	Los Angeles	CA	90071	213-626-0999

California - Eastern

Martha Bowman	P.O. Box 2408	Fair Oaks	CA	95623	916-965-9113
Ellen Cole Briones	P.O. Box 14149	Pinedale	CA	93650-4149	209-227-0740
Gary R. Farrar	1801 H Street, B5-335	Modesto	CA	95354	209-551-1110
Kenny W. Flinn	P.O. Box 799	El Dorado	CA	95623	916-672-3160
Robert A. Hawkins	1849 N. Helm, Suite 110	Fresno	CA	93727	209-255-0555
J. Calvin Hermansen	P.O. Box 254511	Sacramento	CA	95865-4511	916-484-4363
Patrick Kavanagh	1331 "L" Street	Bakersfield	CA	93301	805-322-5553
Michael D. McGranahan	P.O. Box 5018	Modesto	CA	95352	209-524-1782
Lia Fischer Neal	5050 Laguna Blvd., Suite 112-479	Elk Grove	CA	95758	916-684-8912
Randell Parker	3820 Herring Road	Arvin	CA	93323	805-325-1614
Kenneth R. Sanders	P.O. Box 214205	Sacramento	CA	95821	916-971-2760
Henry M. Spacone	P.O. Box 255264	Sacramento	CA	95865	916-485-5530
Larry James Taylor	P.O. Box 22268	Sacramento	CA	95822-0268	916-453-0540

California - Eastern & Northern

Jerome E. Robertson	129 Fremont Avenue	Los Altos	CA	94022	415-949-9266
Linda Schuette	P.O. Box 743	Palo Cadra	CA	96073	916-222-3888

California - Northern

William H. Broach	P.O. Box 9	Lafayette	CA	94549	510-946-1982
Raymond A. Carey	1152 State Farm Drive	Santa Rosa	CA	95403	707-578-4125
Robert M. Damir	One Post Street, #575	San Francisco	CA	94104	415-433-9400
Suzanne L. Decker	1032 East 14th Street	San Leandro	CA	94577	510-562-9410
John T. Kendall	180 Grand Ave., Suite 950	Oakland	CA	94612	510-523-9821
Jeffry G. Locke	810 College Avenue, Suite 9	Kentfield	CA	94904	415-258-8111
Mohamed Poonja	167 S. San Antonio Road, Ste. 17	Los Altos	CA	94022	415-941-3400
John W. Richardson	2901 Park Ave., C-2	Soquel	CA	95073-2831	408-475-2202
Charles E. Sims	37 Old Courthouse Sq., Suite 208	Santa Rosa	CA	95402	707-526-4265
Richard J. Spear	405 14th Street, Suite 1000	Oakland	CA	94612	510-465-4448
Tevis T. Thompson, Jr.	2307 South Crest Avenue	Martinez	CA	94553	510-228-0120
Edward M. Walsh	1255 Post Street, #948	San Francisco	CA	94109	415-776-2626

Nevada

Larry Lee Bertsch	Box 448, 5025 S. Eastern Ave., #16	Las Vegas	NV	89119	702-456-9512
Angelique L.M. Clark	P.O. Box 1521	Sparks	NV	89432	702-356-8099
Robert R. Cochrane	P.O. Box 27655	Las Vegas	NV	89126	702-871-8408
Jeri Ann Coppa-Knudson	145 Mt. Rose Street	Reno	NV	89509	702-329-1528
Richard A. Davis	2140-A West Charleston	Las Vegas	NV	89102	702-382-4700
Jack Fidelman	3170 West Sahara Ave., Suite D-21	Las Vegas	NV	89102	702-368-0664
Tom R. Grimmett	1455 E. Tropicana, Suite 490	Las Vegas	NV	89119	702-795-2311
Ione Jackman	P.O. Box 665	Ely	NV	89301	702-289-4651
James S. Proctor	50 W. Liberty, Suite 905	Reno	NV	89502	702-323-2577
Barry L. Solomon	1000 Bible Way, Suite 34	Reno	NV	89502	702-324-0922

REGION 18

Alaska

William M. Barstow, III	P.O. Box 240261	Anchorage	AK	99524	907-274-9253

Name	Address	City	State	Zip	Telephone
Kenneth Battley	629 "L" Street, Suite 201	Anchorage	AK	99501	907-274-6683
Larry D. Compton	400 D Street, Suite 210	Anchorage	AK	99501	907-276-6660

Idaho

Name	Address	City	State	Zip	Telephone
John Ford Elsaesser, Jr.	P.O. Box 2220	Sandpoint	ID	83864	208-263-8871
L. D. Fitzgerald	845 W. Center Door E.	Pocatello	ID	83205	208-233-0593
John H. Krommenhoek	P.O. Box 8358	Boise	ID	83707	208-375-1288
Bernie R. Rakozy	P.O. Box 1738	Boise	ID	83701	208-343-4474
S. David Swayne	P.O. Box 9104	Moscow	ID	83843	208-883-8823
C. Barry Zimmerman	P.O. Box 70	Meridian	ID	83680-0070	208-888-5984

Montana

Name	Address	City	State	Zip	Telephone
Gary S. Deschenes	Strain Bldg., Suite 508, P.O. Box 3502	Great Falls	MT	59403	406-761-6112
William M. Kebe, Jr.	One Norwest Bank Bldg.	Butte	MT	59701	406-723-5411
Craig D. Martinson	303 N. Broadway, Suite 830	Billings	MT	59101	406-248-9346
Ross P. Richardson	116 West Granite, P.O. Box 399	Butte	MT	59703	406-723-3219
Richard J. Samson	P.O. Box 8479	Missoula	MT	59807	406-721-7772
Donald W. Torgenrud, Jr.	P.O. Box 490	St. Ignatius	MT	59865	406-745-2711
Joseph V. Womack	Suite 805, 1st Bank Bldg., 303 N. Broadway	Billings	MT	59101	406-252-7200

Oregon

Name	Address	City	State	Zip	Telephone
Michael B. Batlan	P.O. Box 3729	Salem	OR	97302	503-588-9192
Kenneth S. Eiler	P.O. Box 53	Seaside	OR	97138	503-738-3314
Michael A. Grassmueck, Inc.	P.O. Box 1783	Medford	OR	97501-0140	503-773-8108
Donald H. Hartvig	P.O. Box 518	Beaverton	OR	97075-0518	503-646-0566
Edward C. Hostmann	P.O. Box 189	Portland	OR	97207	503-228-6542
Thomas A. Huntsberger	870 W. Centennial	Springfield	OR	97477	503-746-6573
John Harvey Mitchell	1030 NE Couch Street	Portland	OR	97232	503-230-1230
Robert K. Morrow	P.O. Box 1328	Portland	OR	97207	503-227-5120
Robert E. Ridgway	P.O. Box 993	Pendleton	OR	97801	503-276-0124
Eric R.T. Roost	1280 Pearl Street	Eugene	OR	97401	503-485-8565
Jerome B. Shank	1000 SW Broadway, Suite 1400	Portland	OR	97205-3066	503-227-1111
Ronald R. Sticka	401 E. 10th Street, Suite 370	Eugene	OR	97401	503-344-0695
Boyd C. Yaden	701 Pacific Terrace	Klamath Falls	OR	97601	503-883-2000

Washington - Eastern

Name	Address	City	State	Zip	Telephone
Gregory A. Beeler	P.O. Box E	Tri-Cities	WA	99302-2020	509-547-5000
Bruce R. Boyden	621 W. Mallon, Suite 509, Flour Mill	Spokane	WA	99201	509-327-3457
J. Kirk Bromiley	P.O. Box 1688	Wenatchee	WA	98807	509-662-3685
Vannoy Culpepper	601 N. 1st, Suite A	Yakima	WA	98901	509-457-0290
Jeffrey B. Earl	1334 South Pioneer Way	Moses Lake	WA	98837	509-765-1705
Joseph A. Esposito	960 Paulsen Bldg.	Spokane	WA	99201	509-624-9219
Anthony E. Grabicki	1500 Seafirst Financial Center	Spokane	WA	99201	509-747-2052
Terry R. Nealey	P.O. Box 7	Dayton	WA	99328	509-382-2541
Dan P. O'Rourke	960 Paulsen Bldg.	Spokane	WA	99201	509-624-0159
Jack R. Reeves	1728 Northwest Blvd.	Spokane	WA	99205	509-326-1700

Washington - Western

Name	Address	City	State	Zip	Telephone
Peter H. Arkison	103 E. Holly Street, Suite 502	Bellingham	WA	98225	206-671-0300
William L. Beecher	615 Commerce, Suite 150	Tacoma	WA	98402	206-627-0132
Ronald G. Brown	4040 First Interstate Ctr., 999 3rd Ave.	Seattle	WA	98014	206-583-2714
Brian Lowell Budsberg	P.O. Box 187	Olympia	WA	98507	206-943-8320
Dennis L. Burman	P.O. Box 1620	Marysville	WA	98270	360-653-6902
Jay Carey	P.O. Box 190	Arlington	WA	98223	206-435-5707
Daniel E. Forsch	One Union Square, Suite 2505	Seattle	WA	98101	206-622-7434
Geoffrey Groshong	3600 Columbia Center, 701 Fifth Avenue	Seattle	WA	98104-7081	206-292-4900
Michael D. Hitt	P.O. Box 1157	Tacoma	WA	98401	206-572-5050
Nancy L. James	15008 63rd Drive, S.E.	Snohomish	WA	98290	206-485-5541
Scott M. Kilpatrick	1000 Twelfth Avenue, Suite 2	Longview	WA	98632	206-423-5220

Name	Address	City	State	Zip	Telephone
Bruce P. Kriegman	One Union Square, Suite 3000	Seattle	WA	98101	206-340-1855
Michael B. McCarty	One Union Square, Suite 2505	Seattle	WA	98101	206-622-7434
Jeffrey A. Meehan	915 Broadway, Suite 400	Vancouver	WA	98666	206-696-3312
John S. Peterson	P.O. Box 829	Kingston	WA	98346	206-297-3194
James F. Rigby	826 United Airlines Bldg., 2033 6th Ave.	Seattle	WA	98121	206-441-0826
Paul B. Snyder	1102 Broadway, Suite 500	Tacoma	WA	98401	206-627-1181
Robert D. Steinberg	11101 N.E. 8th Street, Suite 206	Bellevue	WA	98004	206-455-5045
Mark D. Waldron	6711 Regents Blvd. West	Tacoma	WA	98466	206-565-5800
Robert E. Wiswall	P.O. Box 59	Vancouver	WA	98666	206-694-7585
Edmund J. Wood	1601 5th Avenue, Suite 710	Seattle	WA	98101	206-623-4382

REGION 19

Colorado

Name	Address	City	State	Zip	Telephone
Glen R. Anstine	4704 Harlan St., Suite 610	Denver	CO	80212	303-455-6600
James R. Chadderdon	2125 N. Academy Blvd.	Colorado Springs	CO	80909	719-597-4400
John A. Cimino	1900 Grant, #1100	Denver	CO	80203	303-830-7274
Thomas H. Connolly	1121 Broadway, #202	Boulder	CO	80302	303-945-4468
Clifford E. Eley	1133 Pennsylvania Avenue	Denver	CO	80203	303-863-7500
John E. Fitzgibbons	936 East 18th Avenue	Denver	CO	80218	303-861-7717
Robert C. Freeman	280 Union Street, 132 W.B. Street	Pueblo	CO	81003	719-542-1263
Paul T. Gefreh	2125 N. Academy Blvd.	Colorado Springs	CO	80909	719-596-9010
Jeffrey Lee Hill	2280 South Xanadu Way, #305	Aurora	CO	80014	303-745-4830
Albert Hoffman	210 University Blvd., Suite 740	Denver	CO	80206	303-333-5488
Jeanne Y. Jagow	4 West Dry Creek Circle, #240	Littleton	CO	80120	303-794-8034
Dennis W. King	P.O. Box 460668	Aurora	CO	80046-0668	303-751-3303
Douglas E. Larson	Central Bank Bldg., 3rd Fl., 422 White Ave	Grand Junction	CO	81501	303-245-8021
David E. Lewis	1400 Main St., Suite 200	Louisville	CO	80027	303-666-4557
Jon S. Nicholls	1801 Broadway, Suite 1100	Denver	CO	80202	303-292-0110
Dean T. Ogawa	115 S. Weber St., Suite 100	Colorado Springs	CO	80903	719-632-3450
David A. Palmer	701 Valley Fed. Bldg., P.O. Box 4244	Grand Junction	CO	81502-4244	303-241-1924
M. Stephen Peters	4501 Wadsworth Blvd., Suite 301	Wheatridge	CO	80033	303-422-8502
Harvey Sender	1999 Broadway, Suite 2305	Denver	CO	80202	303-296-1999
Cynthia V. Skeen	1700 Lincoln #3050	Denver	CO	80203	303-798-8446
Janice A. Steinle	4 West Dry Creek Circle, #240	Littleton	CO	80120	303-794-8034
C. Edward Stirman	P.O. Box 9676	Ft. Collins	CO	80525-9676	303-221-4398
Gene Timmermans	1st Nat'l Tower Bldg., Suite 600	Ft. Collins	CO	80521	303-221-1144
Ross J. Wabeke	325 East 7th Street	Loveland	CO	80537	303-667-2131
Jeffrey A. Weinman	1600 Stout St., #1300	Denver	CO	80202	303-572-1010

Utah

Name	Address	City	State	Zip	Telephone
Steven R. Bailey	2454 Washington Blvd.	Ogden	UT	84401	801-621-4430
J. Kevin Bird	2230 N. University Pkwy., #9A	Provo	UT	84604	801-377-7190
Duane H. Gillman	50 West Broadway, 12th Fl.	Salt Lake City	UT	84101	801-359-3500
David L. Gladwell	P.O. Box 12069	Ogden	UT	84412	801-626-2408
R. Kimball Mosier	600 Kennecott Bldg.	Salt Lake City	UT	84133	801-521-4135
Stephen W. Rupp	600 Kennecott Bldg.	Salt Lake City	UT	84133	801-521-4135
Kenneth A. Rushton	P.O. Box 212	Lehi	UT	84043	801-768-8416
Roger G. Segal	525 E. 100 So., 5th Fl.	Salt Lake City	UT	84102	801-532-2666
Harriet E. Styler	50 W. Broadway, Suite 800	Salt Lake City	UT	84101	801-531-7090

Wyoming

Name	Address	City	State	Zip	Telephone
Gary A. Barney	267 Main Street	Lander	WY	82520	307-332-4848
Timothy C. Kingston	2850 LaGrange Circle	Boulder	CO	80303	303-291-4719
Randy L. Royal	P.O. Box 551	Greybull	WY	82426	307-765-4433

REGION 20

Kansas

Name	Address	City	State	Zip	Telephone
Lynn D. Allison	301 West Central	Wichita	KS	67202	316-265-2992

Name	Address	City	State	Zip	Telephone
Robert L. Baer	534 Kansas Ave., Ste. 1100	Topeka	KS	66603	913-235-9511
D. Michael Case	212 N. Market, Suite 102	Wichita	KS	67202-2014	316-265-0797
Carl R. Clark	9260 Glenwood, P.O. Box 12167	Overland Park	KS	66282-2167	913-648-0600
J. Michael Morris	301 N. Main, Suite 1600	Wichita	KS	67202	316-267-0331
Edward J. Nazar	200 W. Douglas, 9th Floor	Wichita	KS	67202-3089	316-262-8361
Eric C. Rajala	11900 College Blvd., Suite 341	Overland Park	KS	66210	913-339-9806
Steven R. Rebein	600 Security Bank Bldg.	Kansas City	KS	66101	913-621-5400
Christopher J. Redmond	200 W. Douglas, 9th Floor	Wichita	KS	67202-3089	316-262-8361
Timothy J. Sear	7300 College Blvd., Ste. 300	Overland Park	KS	66210	913-451-8788
David C. Seitter	6310 Lamar Ave., Suite 220	Overland Park	KS	66202	913-642-5100
William B. Sorensen, Jr.	200 West Douglas, 4th Floor	Wichita	KS	67202-3084	316-262-2671
Darcy D. Williamson	700 Jackson, Suite 404	Topeka	KS	66603	913-233-9908
Joseph I. Wittman	435 S. Kansas Avenue, 2nd Fl.	Topeka	KS	66603	913-234-3663

New Mexico

Name	Address	City	State	Zip	Telephone
James E. Burke	320 Gold Ave SW #800, P.O. Box 2266	Albuquerque	NM	87103	505-242-9350
Michael J. Caplan	827 East Santa Fe	Grants	NM	87020	505-287-8891
Robert L. Finch	555 E. Main Street	Farmington	NM	87401	505-325-2028
Oralia B. Franco	P.O. Box 15038	Las Cruces	NM	88004	505-524-6811
Yvette Jo Gonzales	320 Gold Ave., SW, #800	Albuquerque	NM	87103	505-242-9350
Steve H. Mazer	122 10th Street, N.W.	Albuquerque	NM	87102	505-247-9765
Billy Joe Sholer	5353 Wyoming Blvd., NE., #1	Albuquerque	NM	87102	505-821-3343

Oklahoma - Eastern

Name	Address	City	State	Zip	Telephone
Kenneth G.M. Mather	4100 BOK Tower	Tulsa	OK	74172	918-581-8200

Oklahoma - Northern

Name	Address	City	State	Zip	Telephone
Robert J. Getchell	100 West 5th St., Suite 610	Tulsa	OK	74103	918-587-9191
Scott P. Kirtley	P.O. Box 1046	Tulsa	OK	74101	918-583-1232
Patrick Joseph Malloy III	1924 South Utica, Suite 810	Tulsa	OK	74104	918-747-3491
Steven W. Soule	4100 Bank of Oklahoma Tower	Tulsa	OK	74172	918-588-2740

Oklahoma - Northern & Eastern

Name	Address	City	State	Zip	Telephone
Joseph Q. Adams	650 S. Cherokee	Catoosa	OK	74015	918-266-2232
Gerald R. Miller	627 W. Broadway, P.O. Box 2011	Muskogee	OK	74402-2011	918-687-1347

Oklahoma - Western

Name	Address	City	State	Zip	Telephone
Robert Dale Garrett	4334 Northwest Expressway, Suite 297	Oklahoma City	OK	73116	405-842-0230
Gary D. Hammond	101 N. Broadway	Oklahoma City	OK	73102	405-239-6444
Lester W. Holbrook, Jr.	120 N. Robinson	Oklahoma City	OK	73102	405-232-8131
Janice D. Loyd	1100 Colcord Bldg., 15 N. Robinson	Oklahoma City	OK	73102	405-235-9371
Susan J. Manchester	625 Northwest 13th Street	Oklahoma City	OK	73103	405-525-2232
Michael Mitchelson	301 N.W. 63 Street, Suite 600	Oklahoma City	OK	73116	405-840-2731
Lyle R. Nelson	St. 2100 City Pl., 204 N. Robinson	Oklahoma City	OK	73102	405-232-4021
Kenneth Lee Spears	P.O. Box 687	Oklahoma City	OK	73101	405-236-1503

REGION 21

Florida - Middle

Name	Address	City	State	Zip	Telephone
Eugene V. Allen	12569 Ulmerton Road	Largo	FL	34644	813-595-2944
Victor J. Brook, Jr.	3214 Ninth Street, North	St. Petersburg	FL	33731	813-821-5010
Stephany Sturges Carr	501 Goodlette Road, #B-300	Naples	FL	33940	813-263-1991
Gene T. Chambers	800 N. Magnolia Ave., #1650	Orlando	FL	32853	407-872-7447
Lynnea S. Concannon	800 N. Magnolia Ave., #1650	Orlando	FL	32853	407-872-7447
Gregory K. Crews	206 Marine Bank Bldg.	Jacksonville	FL	32202	904-354-1750
Charles W. Grant	112 West Adams St., Suite 1802	Jacksonville	FL	32202-3839	904-353-5962
Ralph Jay Harpley	1602 W. Sligh Avenue	Tampa	FL	33604	813-931-1700
Larry S. Hyman	P.O. Box 18614	Tampa	FL	33679	813-251-5885
Diane L. Jensen	P.O. Drawer 1507	Fort Myers	FL	33902	813-334-2195

Name	Address	City	State	Zip	Telephone
Lauren P. Johnson-Greene	7190 Seminole Blvd.	Seminole	FL	34642	813-393-0384
Gordon P. Jones	P.O. Box 2059	Ponte Vedra Beach	FL	32004	904-273-9017
Gordon L. Kiester, Jr.	115 North MacDill Avenue	Tampa	FL	33609	813-933-3707
Valerie Hall Manuel	P.O. Box 1258	Jacksonville	FL	32201	904-355-9441
Leigh R. Meininger	135 W. Central Blvd., Suite 1230	Orlando	FL	32801	407-246-1585
Stephen L. Meininger	4919 Memorial Hwy., Suite 205	Tampa	FL	33634	813-884-6575
Douglas N. Menchise	300 Turner Street	Clearwater	FL	34616	813-442-2186
George E. Mills, Jr.	9334 Bay Vista Estates Blvd.	Orlando	FL	32836	407-352-0405
James Craig Orr	1551 Garden Street	Titusville	FL	32796	407-268-8810
Jerald I. Rosen	P.O. Box 915107	Longwood	FL	32791-5107	407-682-2290
Bethann Scharrer	P.O. Box 1368	Clearwater	FL	34617-1368	813-461-2535
Alexander Gilbert Smith	2601 University Blvd., West	Jacksonville	FL	32217-2212	904-733-2000
Traci K. Strickland	P.O. Box 41144	St. Petersburg	FL	33743	813-345-8090
Laurie K. Weatherford	P.O. Box 633	Orlando	FL	32802	407-843-4421
Charles Louis Weissing	4230 S. MacDill Ave., Suite C	Tampa	FL	33611	813-831-9944
Susan K. Woodard	P.O. Box 7828	St. Petersburg	FL	33734-7828	813-521-3355

Florida - Northern

Name	Address	City	State	Zip	Telephone
Mark Freund	P.O. Box 10171	Tallahassee	FL	32302	904-681-0066
William J. Miller, Jr.	P.O. Box 1109, 1157 E. Tennessee St.	Tallahassee	FL	32302	904-222-9511
Sharon T. Sperling	500 E. University Ave., Ste. C	Gainesville	FL	32601	904-375-5602
John Edward Venn, Jr.	P.O. Box 1133	Gulf Breeze	FL	32562	904-932-1709

Florida - Southern

Name	Address	City	State	Zip	Telephone
Daniel L. Bakst	P.O. Drawer 3948	West Palm Beach	FL	33402-3948	407-640-8000
John P. Barbee	2626 E. Oakland Park Blvd., Suite 400	Fort Lauderdale	FL	33306	305-564-4228
Jeffrey H. Beck	200 East Broward Blvd., Ste. 1500	Fort Lauderdale	FL	33301	305-527-2446
Donna A. Bumgardner	7967 West McNab Road	Tamarac	FL	33321	305-724-4366
Lucy DiBraccio	2211 Hollywood Blvd.	Hollywood	FL	33020	305-925-5279
Marcia T. Dunn	P.O. Box 4240	Hialeah	FL	33014-0240	305-826-4241
Patricia Dzikowski	4300 N. University Dr., Suite B103	Lauderhill	FL	33351	305-748-4377
James S. Feltman	One Biscayne Tower, Suite 2100	Miami	FL	33131-1801	305-789-2492
Robert C. Furr	1499 W. Palmetto Park Rd., #412	Boca Raton	FL	33486	407-395-0500
Irving E. Gennet	6461 N.W. 2nd Avenue	Boca Raton	FL	33487	407-994-1468
Soneet R. Kapila	P.O. Box 14213	West Palm Beach	FL	33302	305-761-8707
Elena Maria Magolnick	150 West Flagler Street, Suite 2100	Miami	FL	33130	305-379-8300
Joel L. Tabas	919 Ingraham Bldg., 25 SE 2nd Ave.	Miami	FL	33131	305-358-4989
Marika Tolz	2344 North Federal Highway	Hollywood	FL	33021	305-923-6536
Kenneth A. Welt	3005 Greene Street	Hollywood	FL	33020	305-931-8300

Georgia - Middle

Name	Address	City	State	Zip	Telephone
Michael Patrick Cielinski	900 Second Avenue	Columbus	GA	31902	706-323-4357
William M. Flatau	355 Cotton Avenue	Macon	GA	31201	912-742-6481
Ernest V. Harris	P.O. Box 1586	Athens	GA	30603	706-613-1953
Walter W. Kelley	504 N. Jefferson Street	Albany	GA	31702	912-888-9128
Ernest Kirk, III	318 11th Street	Columbus	GA	31994	706-324-3711
John C. Tidwell	341 Third Street	Macon	GA	31201	912-743-9318

Georgia - Northern

Name	Address	City	State	Zip	Telephone
L. Lou Allen	1360 Peachtree St., N.E., Suite 1100	Atlanta	GA	30309	404-870-1800
Paul Henry Anderson	600 W. Peachtree St., NW, Ste. 1460	Atlanta	GA	30308	404-892-4144
Herbert C. Broadfoot, II	Suite 1050, North Terraces	Atlanta	GA	30346	404-392-4800
Gary W. Brown	12 Jackson Street	Newnan	GA	30263	404-251-1567
Paul T. Carroll, III	P.O. Box 1804, 111 Bridgepoint Plaza #110	Rome	GA	30162-1804	404-295-3400
Lyonnette Maynor Davis	1355 Peachtree St., N.E. Suite 300	Atlanta	GA	30309-3238	404-888-6181
Richard D. Ellenberg	170 Mitchell Street, SW	Atlanta	GA	30303	404-525-4000
Ira D. Gingold	10 Piedmont Ctr., 3495 Piedmont Rd., NE	Atlanta	GA	30305	404-233-3040
John J. Goger	75 14th Street, Suite 2600	Atlanta	GA	30309	404-873-8000
Dale R.F. Goodman	Seven Piedmont Center, Suite 615	Atlanta	GA	30305	404-237-0800

Name	Address	City	State	Zip	Telephone
Neil Clark Gordon	133 Carnegie Way, Ste. 700	Atlanta	GA	30303	404-393-8221
Dennis M. Hall	880 West Peachtree Street	Atlanta	GA	30357	404-885-1400
Michael Harrison	3060 Mercer University Drive, Ste. 300	Atlanta	GA	30341	404-455-4361
Griffin E. Howell III	P.O. Box 551	Griffin	GA	30224	404-227-0110
Bradley M. Hoyt	3005 Chamblee Tucker Rd., Suite 500	Atlanta	GA	30341	404-457-1850
Howard W. Jones	P.O. Box 1147	Calhoun	GA	30701	404-625-2233
Richard J. MacLeod	P.O. Box 5751	Rome	GA	30162-5751	404-234-5678
Theo Davis Mann	28 Jackson Street	Newnan	GA	30264	404-253-2222
James R. Marshall	Suite 1750, 999 Peachtree St., NE	Atlanta	GA	30303	404-872-0000
Martha A. Miller	141 Walton Street	Atlanta	GA	30303	404-522-3000
Roger W. Moister, Jr.	3400 Peachtree Rd., NE #1515	Atlanta	GA	30326	404-266-3950
C. Ray Mullins	1100 Peachtree Street, Suite 2800	Atlanta	GA	30309	404-815-6500
Albert F. Nasuti	4845 Jimmy Carter Blvd.	Norcross	GA	30093	404-925-0111
Harry W. Pettigrew	P.O. Box 56964	Atlanta	GA	30343	404-577-5244
John W. Ragsdale, Jr.	229 Peachtree Street, N.E., Suite 2400	Atlanta	GA	30303-1629	404-588-0500
David S. Rogers	1718 Peachtree Street, Suite 1080	Atlanta	GA	30309	404-876-6647
Robert B. Silliman	211 Roswell Street	Atlanta	GA	30061	404-424-8000
Barbara B. Stalzer	Suite 995, 50 Hurt Plaza	Atlanta	GA	30303	404-521-3100
C. Brooks Thurmond III	6 North Parkway Square	Atlanta	GA	30327	404-261-0033
Robert Trauner	38 Old Ivy Road, N.E.	Atlanta	GA	30342	404-233-1900
William H. Willson, Jr.	3343 Peachtree Road, NE, Suite 550	Atlanta	GA	30326	404-262-7373

Georgia - Southern

Name	Address	City	State	Zip	Telephone
Lisa L. Clarke	1500 1st Union Bank Bldg.	Augusta	GA	30910	706-722-7542
Edward J. Coleman III	901 Trust Company Bank Bldg.	Augusta	GA	30901	706-722-3301
James L. Drake, Jr.	P.O. Box 9149	Savannah	GA	31412	912-238-2750
Stephen L. Jackson	P.O. Drawer 1589	Waycross	GA	31501	912-283-3858
Anne R. Moore	32 Courtland Street	Statesboro	GA	30458	912-764-6384
Karen Jenkins Rice	210 East Gaines Street	Dublin	GA	31040	912-275-9575
Arthur Stephenson Wallace	462 Telfair Street	Augusta	GA	30901	404-722-7574
Wiley A. Wasden III	P.O. Box 8047	Savannah	GA	31412	912-232-6700

Puerto Rico

Name	Address	City	State	Zip	Telephone
Vincent Aponte	Condominio Darlington, Apartment #1206	Rio Piedras	PR	00925	809-764-8900
Maria Luisa Contreras	P.O. Box 2124	San Juan	PR	00903	809-759-7450
Diego Andres Ferrer	1428 Aleli Street, Round Hills	Trujillo Alto	PR	00976	809-761-2163
Antonio N. Fiol-Matta	461 Banco Papular Bldg.	San Juan	PR	00901	809-723-5916
Richard A. Lee	GPO Box 363068	San Juan	PR	00936	809-722-3755
Hans Lopez-Stubbe	HC-01 Box 29030, PMB418	Caquas	PR	00725	809-732-1863
Reynaldo Quinonies Marquez	Padre Las Casas 114, El Vedado	Hato Rey	PR		809-754-9204
Frank Pola, Jr.	El Centro II, Suite 260	Hato Rey	PR	00918	809-250-0610
Reynaldo M. Quinones	Padre Las Casas 114, El Vedado	Hato Rey	PR	00731	809-754-9204
Julio Rivera	San Jacinto 1396 Altamesa	San Juan	PR	00921	809-781-2784
Nelson Diaz Robles	Lower Mall, Cobian's Plaza Bdg.	San Juan	PR	00915	809-722-8666
Carlos E. Rodriguez-Quesada	232 Ponce De Leo Avenue	Hato Rey	PR	00917	809-751-1930
Roberto Velez-Colon	1st F-10 Parue Montebello	Trujillo	PR	00976	809-755-6871
John Addison Zerbe, Jr.	165 Ave. De Diego	Rio Piedras	PR	00927	809-765-8877

Virgin Islands

Name	Address	City	State	Zip	Telephone
James Sandy Alston	P.O. Box 7115	St. Thomas	VI	00801	809-775-4103
Ronald W. Belfon	#19 Norre Gade	St. Thomas	VI	00804	809-774-6490
Erik Bonde-Henriksen	P.O. Box 783	St. Thomas	VI	00804	809-775-1765
Alan Joel Bronstein	1B King Street	Christiansted, St. Croix	VI	00820	809-773-0096
Kevin F. D'Amour	Upper Level Drakes Passage	St. Thomas	VI	00802	809-774-6011
John Ellis	P.O. Box 24492	Christiansted, St. Croix	VI	00824-0492	809-773-9643

Name	Address	City	State	Zip	Telephone
Kevin A. Rames	2111 Company Street, Suite 3	Christianted, St. Croix	VI	00820	809-773-7284
Maryleen Thomas	P.O. Box 1030 24-25 Kongensgade	St. Thomas	VI	00804	809-774-1320

Chapter 13 Standing Trustees

Name	Address	City	State	Zip	Telephone
REGION 1					
Boyajian, John	182 Waterman Street	Providence	RI	02906	401-273-9600
Calabrese, Cecilia	P.O. Box 252	Feeding Hills	MA	01030	413-786-1313
Fessenden, Peter C.	20 Federal Street	Brunswick	ME	04011	207-729-4114
Sumski, Lawrence P.	12 Liberty Park	Amherst	NH	03031	603-672-1500
REGION 2					
DeRosa, Marianne	330 Old Country Rd., Ste. 204	Mineola	NY	11501	516-739-2233
Gelberg, Stuart P.	600 Old Country Road, Ste. 410	Garden City	NY	11530	516-228-4280
Littlefield, Jr., Robert	350 Northern Blvd.	Albany	NY	12204	518-449-2043
Macco, Michael J.	164 Main Street	Huntington	NY	11743	516-549-7900
Mogavero, Albert J.	110 Pearl St., 6th Floor	Buffalo	NY	14202	716-854-5636
Reiber, George M.	3136 S. Winton Rd., Suite 260	Rochester	NY	14623	716-427-7225
Rosenbaum, Gilbert L.	50 Columbus Blvd.	Hartford	CT	06106	203-278-9410
Sapir, Jeffrey L.	399 Knollwood Road	White Plains	NY	10603	914-328-7272
Sensenich, Jan Michael	6 Palmer Court	White River Junction	VT		802-649-1213
Swimelar, Mark W.	711 University Bldg.	Syracuse	NY	13202	315-471-1499
Weinberg, Sanford I.	184 Sunrise Highway	Rockville Centre	NY	1157	516-766-1860
REGION 3					
DeHart III, Charles J.	13 East Main Street	Hummelstown	PA	17036	717-232-7661
Gaertner, Gary J.	707 Grant Street, Suite 2900	Pittsburgh	PA	15219	412-471-5566
Joseph, Michael B.	824 Market St., Ste. 904	Wilmington	DE	19899	302-575-1555
Reigle, Frederick L.	3506 Perkiomen Avenue	Reading	PA	19606	215-779-8000
Scura, John J.	1510 Hamburg Turnpike	Wayne	NJ	07470	201-696-7587
Sparkman, Edward	620 Chestnus Street	Philadelphia	PA	19106	215-627-1377
Wood, Robert M.	25 Abe Voorhees Drive	Manasquan	NJ	08736	201-223-8484
REGION 4					
Butler III, John B.	1338 Main Street	Columbia	SC	29201	803-256-3929
Charnock, Jr., John N.	523 Peoples Building	Charleston	WV	25321	304-344-2570
Cosby, Ellen W.	7123 Harford Road	Baltimore	MD	21234	410-254-7090
Hyman, Robert E.	1313 E. Main Street, Ste. 339	Richmond	VA	23219	804-775-0979
Lackey, Thomas L.	4325 Northview Drive	Bowie	MD	20716	301-805-4700
Levin, David R.	355 Crawford Parkway, Ste. 820	Portsmouth	VA	23704	804-399-5545
Levy, R. Geoffrey	1320 Richland Street	Columbia	SC	29202	803-779-5180
Morin, Laurence P.	701 Clay Street	Lynchburg	VA	24505	804-528-0098
Niklas, Cynthia A.	4545 42nd Street, NW, Ste. 211	Washington	DC	20016	202-362-8500
O'Donnell, Gerald M.	211 South Alfred Street	Alexandria	VA	22314	703-836-2226
Parrish, Helen P.	250 West Main Street, Ste. 102	Charlottesville	VA	22902	804-971-9620
Santoro, Frank J.	355 Crawford Parkway, Ste. 700	Portsmouth	VA	23705	804-399-1934
Stephenson, Jr., William	2020 Assembly Street	Columbia	SC	29201	803-254-2981
Strickler, J. Glenwood	P.O. Box 1001	Roanoke	VA	24011	703-342-3774
Widener, Jo S.	54 Piedmont Street	Bristol	VA	24201	703-466-4539
REGION 5					
Barkley, Locke D.	5015 I-55 North	Jackson	MS	39206	601-981-7800

Name	Address	City	State	Zip	Telephone
Barkley, Jr., Harold J.	5015 I-55 North	Jackson	MS	39206	601-981-7800
Beaulieu, Jr., Sterling J.	433 Metairie Road, Ste. 515	Metairie	LA	70005	504-831-1313
Bell, J. C.	1210 West Pine Street	Hattiesburg	MS	39401	601-582-5011
Davidson, Paul H.	6007 Financial Plaza, Ste. 713	Shreveport	LA	71129	318-687-1300
Gallaspy, Annette C.	778 Chevelle	Baton Rouge	LA	70806	504-928-3237
Rodriguez, Keith A.	700 St. John, Suite 201	Lafayette	LA	70502	318-233-4413
Simmons, Donald O.	2213 15th Street	Gulfport	MS	39501	601-863-8071

REGION 6

Name	Address	City	State	Zip	Telephone
Bartholow, Molly W.	600 N. Pearl St., Ste. 500	Dallas	TX	75201	214-979-8515
Gross, Harris M.	P.O. Box 697	Tyler	TX	75710	214-593-7777
O'Cheskey, Walter	3223 South Loop 289, Ste. 315	Lubbock	TX	79423	806-793-0123
Truman, Tim	7001 Grapevine Hwy., Ste. 605	Fort Worth	TX	76118	817-589-0270
Wilson, Robert B.	P.O. Box 10236	Lubbock	TX	79408	806-763-9555

REGION 7

Name	Address	City	State	Zip	Telephone
Boudloche, Cindy	711 N. Caranchhua, Suite 1508	Corpus Christi	TX	78475	512-883-5786
Bracher, Phyllis	P.O. Box 26668	El Paso	TX	79926	915-598-7674
Heitkamp, William E.	9821 Katy Freeway, Ste. 590	Houston	TX	77024	713-722-1200
Hendren, Jr., G. Ray	101 E. 9th Street, Ste. 1200	Austin	TX	78701	512-474-6309
Norwood, Gary W.	P.O. Box 2331	Midland	TX	79702	915-686-9452
O'Connell, Daniel E.	1200 S. Highway 146, Ste. 100	La Porte	TX	77571	713-470-1313
Olson, Jr., Marion A.	1020 N.E. Loop 410, Ste. 800	San Antonio	TX	78209	210-824-1460

REGION 8

Name	Address	City	State	Zip	Telephone
Emerson, Jr., George W.	200 Jefferson Ave., Ste. 1113	Memphis	TN	38103	901-576-1313
Guy, William L.	59 Conrad Drive	Jackson	TN	38302	901-664-1313
Hildebrand III, Henry E.	500 Church Street, 3rd Floor	Nashville	TN	37219	615-244-1101
Kerney, Gwendolyn M.	800 Gay Street	Knoxville	TN	37991	615-524-4995
Lawrence, William W.	200 S. 7th Street, Suite 310	Louisville	KY	40202	502-581-9042
Schulman, Suzanne C.	500 Church Street, 3rd Floor	Nashville	TN	37219	615-244-1101
Stevenson, George W.	200 Jefferson Ave., Suite 1113	Memphis	TN	38103	901-576-1313
Still, C. Kenneth	1010 Market Street, Ste. 204	Chattanooga	TN	37401	615-265-2261
White, Sidney N.	101 E. Vine Street, Ste. 500	Lexington	KY	40595	606-233-1527

REGION 9

Name	Address	City	State	Zip	Telephone
Bekofske, Carl L.	510 West Court Street	Flint	MI	48503	810-238-4675
Bolenbaugh, John L.	4710 W. Saginaw	Lansing	MI	48907	517-321-7681
Burks, Margaret A.	303 Executive Bldg.	Cincinnati	OH	45202	513-621-4490
Chrystler, Joseph A.	906 E. Cork Street	Kalamazoo	MI	49001	616-343-0305
DiSalle, Anthony B.	316 N. Michigan St.	Toledo	OH	43624	419-255-0675
Gallo, Michael A.	20 Federal Plaza West, Ste. 600	Youngstown	OH	44503	216-744-0247
Holub, Jerome L.	916 Society Bldg.	Akron	OH	44308	216-762-6335
Johnson, Raymond B.	1122 Leonard St., NE	Grand Rapids	MI	49503	616-732-9000
Ledford, George W.	9 West National Road	Englewood	OH	45322	513-836-4040
McDonald, Jr., Thomas W.	3126 Davenport Ave.	Saginaw	MI	48608	517-792-6766
Pees, Frank M.	130 E. Wilson Bridge Road, #121	Worthington	OH	43085	614-436-6700
Rodgers, Brett N.	1122 Leonard St., NE	Grand Rapids	MI	49503	616-732-9000
Rosen, Toby L.	121 Cleveland Ave. SW	Canton	OH	44702	216-455-2222
Ruskin, David W.	26555 Evergreen Road	Southfield	MI	48076	810-352-7755
Wasserman, Myron E.	910 Leader Building	Cleveland	OH	44114	216-621-4268

REGION 10

Name	Address	City	State	Zip	Telephone
Aikman, Donald M.	202 W. Wayne Street, Ste. 202	Fort Wayne	IN	46802	219-422-7062
Black, Jr., Joseph M.	115 West Tipton Street	Seymour	IN	47274	812-522-2550
Bowers, Richard A.	1800 3rd Avenue, Ste. 402	Rock Island	IL	61201	309-788-9355
Brothers, Robert A.	151 N. Delaware St., Ste. 1940	Indianapolis	IN	46204	317-636-1062
Chael, Paul R.	1164 N. Main Street	Crown Point	IN	46307	219-662-0949

Name	Address	City	State	Zip	Telephone
Clark, Michael D.	311 Fulton Street, Ste. 536	Peoria	IL	61602	309-674-6137
Decker, Donald L.	674 Ohio Street	Terre Haute	IN	47807	812-234-2600
Geekie, James R.	211 North Central Ave.	Paris	IL	61944	217-465-7681
Germeraad, John H.	113 N. Seventh Street	Petersburg	IL	62704	217-632-4346
Kearney, Bobby Gene	104 W. Main	Benton	IL	62812	618-435-3001
McRoberts, James W.	530 Fullerton Road	Bellville	IL	62223	618-277-0086
Mishler, Tedd E.	1912 East US 20, Suite 10	Michigan City	IN	46360	219-879-8896
Musgrave II, Robert P.	123 NW Forth Street	Evansville	IN	47708	812-428-6679
Rosenthal, David A.	210 North 3rd Street, Ste. 150	Lafayette	IN	47902	317-742-8248

REGION 11

Name	Address	City	State	Zip	Telephone
Chatterton, William A.	324 South Hamilton Street	Madison	WI	53701	608-256-2355
Jones, Louis R.	740 N. Plankinton Ave., Ste. 730	Milwaukee	WI	53203	414-271-3943
King, Thomas J.	504 Algoma Boulevard	Oshkosh	WI	54903	414-231-2150
Kohlhorst, James E.	1521 Windsor Road	Loves Park	IL	61132	815-633-7773
McCullough, Jack	224 S. Michigan Ave., Ste. 310	Chicago	IL	60604	321-431-1300
Phelps, Craig	11 East Adams St., Ste. 1500	Chicago	IL	60603	312-294-5900

REGION 12

Name	Address	City	State	Zip	Telephone
Armstrong, Phillip D.	12 S. Main Street, Ste. 202	Minot	ND	58701	701-838-9422
Drewes, Wayne E.	800 N.P. Avenue, #202	Fargo	ND	58102	701-237-6650
Dunbar, Carol F.	P.O. Box 1377	Waterloo	IA	50704	319-233-6327
Mickelson, J. J.	12 South 6th Street	Minneapolis	MN	55402	612-338-7591
Warford, Albert C.	505 5th Avenue, Ste. 1020	Des Moines	IA	50309	515-283-2713
Yarnall, Rick A.	300 North Dakota Ave., Ste. 609	Sioux Falls	SD	57101	605-336-0748

REGION 13

Name	Address	City	State	Zip	Telephone
Fink, Richard V.	818 Grand #700	Kansas City	MO	64106	816-842-1031
LaBarge, Jr., John V.	1401 S. Brentwood, Ste. 650	St. Louis	MO	63144	314-963-0000
Laughlin, Kathleen A.	13930 Gold Circle #201	Omaha	NE	68137	402-697-0437
Coop, David D.	P.O. Box 5006	North Little Rock	AR	721	501-374-1572

REGION 14

Name	Address	City	State	Zip	Telephone
Itule, Margo	177 N. Church Avenue, Ste. 900	Tucson	AZ	85701	602-624-8002
McDonald, Jr., Ralph M.	4020 N. 20th St., Ste. 306	Phoenix	AZ	85016	602-277-3776
Rau, Albert M.	320 E. McDowell Road, Ste. 100	Phoenix	AZ	85067	602-277-8996
Smith, Jim D.	221 S. Second Avenue	Yuma	AZ	85364	602-783-7809

REGION 15

Name	Address	City	State	Zip	Telephone
Hu, Howard M.S.	90 North King Street #214	Honolulu	HI	95817	808-526-3083
Skelton, David L.	620 "C" Street, Suite 413	San Diego	CA	92112	619-338-4006
Wigfall, Dorris Edward	1514 Shadow Knolls Drive	El Cajon	CA	92020	619-440-0332

REGION 16

Name	Address	City	State	Zip	Telephone
Cohen, Amrane	2323 N. Broadway, Ste. 300	Santa Ana	CA	92706	714-479-0141
Curry, Nancy	606 S. Olive St., Ste. 1850	Los Angeles	CA	90014	213-689-3014
Dowell, Edwina E.	333 S. Grand Ave., Ste. 2910	Los Angeles	CA	90071	213-628-2552
Haney, Shannon J.	2323 N. Broadway, #230	Santa Ana	CA	92706	714-547-6665

REGION 17

Name	Address	City	State	Zip	Telephone
Burchard, Jr., David E.	P.O. Box 8059	Foster City	CA	94404	415-345-7801
Enmark, M. Nelson	3447 W. Shaw Avenue	Fresno	CA	93711	209-277-3995
Kester, Duncan H.	P.O. Box 50013	San Jose	CA	95150	408-879-1313
Loheit, Lawrence J.	10276 Rockingham Dr., Ste. 180	Sacramento	CA	95814	916-856-8000
McDonald, Kathleen A.	302 E. Carson Ave., Ste. 200	Las Vegas	NV	89101	702-386-5968
Meyer, Michael H.	P.O. Box 3051	Modesto	CA	95353	209-576-1954
Savage, Anabelle Glenna	995 Forest Street	Reno	NV	89509	702-786-4479

Name	Address	City	State	Zip	Telephone
REGION 18					
Brunner, Daniel H.	540 Lincoln Bldg.	Spokane	WA	99201	509-747-8481
Compton, Larry D.	1399 W. 34th, Suite 204	Anchorage	AK	99503	907-276-6660
Drummond, Robert G.	P.O. Box 1829	Great Falls	MT	59403	406-454-1384
Fitzgerald, L. D.	P.O. Box 4886	Pocatello	ID	83205	208-233-8339
Howe, David M.	P.O. Box 1255	Seattle	WA	98401	206-572-6603
Krommenhoek, John H.	5019 Emerald	Boise	ID	83706	208-375-1288
Long, Fred	P.O. Box 467	Eugene	OR	97440	503-343-1555
Myers, Robert W.	2701 NW Vaughn, Ste. 840	Portland	OR	97210	503-221-0331
Petta, Virginia L.	P.O. Box 737, 1953 - 7th Ave.	Longview	WA	98632	206-577-4464
Rakozy, Bernie R.	P.O. Box 1738	Boise	ID	83701	208-343-4476
Ridgway, Robert E.	P.O. Box 993	Pendleton	OR	97801	503-276-0124
Satterlee, Jr., Herbert F.	2200 One Union Square	Seattle	WA	98101	206-442-9137
Spurgeon, L.C. "JACK"	202 Anton Avenue, Suite 201	Coeur D'Alene	ID	83814	208-664-0593
Zimmerman, Barry	P.O. Box 70	Meridian	ID	83680	208-888-5984
REGION 19					
Dunivent, Sharon A.	P.O. Box 265	Cheyenne	WY	82003	307-632-1727
Richman, Barbara W.	#8 East Broadway, Suite 513	Salt Lake City	UT	84111	801-532-8844
Toscano, Paul James	265 East 100 South #300	Salt Lake City	UT	84111	801-364-1100
Zeman, Sally J.	1888 Sherman, #750	Denver	CO	80201	303-830-1971
REGION 20					
Bonney, William M.	420 West Broadway	Muskogee	OK	74401	918-683-3840
Eck, Lonnie D.	1508 South Carson Avenue	Tulsa	OK	74119	918-559-9901
Griffin, William H.	P.O. Box 3527	Topeka	KS	66601	913-234-1551
Mazer, Steve H.	122 10th Street, NW	Albuquerque	NM	87102	505-243-7240
Spears, Ann M.	321 Dean A. McGee Avenue	Oklahoma City	OK	73101	405-236-4843
Wallace, Royce E.	328 North Main Street, Ste. 200	Wichita	KS	67202	316-267-1791
REGION 21					
Baxter, Barnee C.	P.O. Box 2127	Augusta	GA	30901	706-722-5511
Bone, James H.	100 Peachtree St., Ste. 1100	Atlanta	GA	30303	404-525-2555
Brown, Sylvia Ford	P.O. Box 10556	Savannah	GA	31412	912-234-5052
Davis, Mamie L.	305 Washington Street	Jacksonville	FL	32203	404-358-9589
Hart, Leigh Annette	1105 N. Duval Street	Tallahassee	FL	32303	904-681-2734
Hope, Camille	577 Walnut Street	Macon	GA	31201	912-742-0085
Johnson, Jan P.	Box 70370	San Juan	PR	00936	809-250-8983
Palmer, Richard A.	P.O. Box 1963	Winterpark	FL	32790	407-629-2767
Roth, Robert L.	P.O. Box 450736	Miami	FL	33245	305-536-2113
Smith, Terry Edwin	P.O. Box Caller 25001	Bradenton	FL	34206	813-747-4644
Smith, Anne Kristin	1101 Front Ave., Suite 202	Columbus	GA	31901	706-323-5288
Thomas, Martha Regina	100 Peachtree St., Ste. 1150	Atlanta	GA	30303	404-525-0221
Weiner, Robin F.	1250 E. Hallandale Beach Blvd.	Hallandale	FL	33009	305-454-5200

U.S. Trustees: Regional Management Officials

Name	Title	Address	City	State	Zip	Telephone	Fax
EXECUTIVE OFFICE							
Joseph Patchan	Director	901 E Street, NW, Suite 700	Washington	DC	20530	202-307-1391	202-307-0672
Vacant	Deputy Director	901 E Street, NW, Suite 700	Washington	DC	20530	202-307-1391	202-307-0672

Glossary

adjustment of debt.   The reorganization of debt that occurs in a Chapter 13 bankruptcy.

adversary proceeding.   A legal action usually initiated by a debtor's creditors to obtain their collateral or to complain about some other aspect of the bankruptcy proceeding.

automatic stay.   An action of the court prohibiting a debtor's creditors from calling or writing a debtor and from repossessing or foreclosing on a debtor's property. It also stops law suits. The automatic stay takes effect as soon as a Chapter 7 or Chapter 13 bankruptcy petition is filed with the court. It is over either when the court lifts the stay or when the debtor receives a discharge of bankruptcy.

Bankruptcy Code.   The federal law that governs the bankruptcy process.

Chapter 7.   A bankruptcy process that wipes out most debt. If you have nonexempt property, the trustee will liquidate it and use it to pay off your creditors. Also called a liquidation bankruptcy.

Chapter 13.   A bankruptcy process that allows a consumer or sole proprietorship to keep assets by reorganizing their debt and making regular payments to creditors over a specified period of time. Also called a reorganization bankruptcy.

collateral.   Property used by a debtor to secure or guarantee a loan.

confirmation.   The approval and implementation of a Chapter 13 bankruptcy plan by the court.

creditor.   A person or business to whom money is owed.

creditors' meeting.   Meeting at which the bankruptcy trustee questions the debtor about his financial affairs. In a Chapter 7 bankruptcy filed by a consumer or a Chapter 13 bankruptcy, the debtor's creditors do not usually attend this meeting despite its name. The creditors' meeting usually takes place 40 to 60 days after a bankruptcy is filed.

debtor. An individual who owes money.

discharge. The elimination of debt through a Chapter 7 or Chapter 13 bankruptcy. Some debts cannot be discharged and will continue to be the financial obligations of the debtor.

exempt property. Property a debtor may keep when filing a Chapter 7 bankruptcy. The federal bankruptcy code specifies certain exemptions. Each state also has its own law which defines additional exemptions. See Appendix C for information regarding the exemptions states offer.

liquidation bankruptcy. See definition of a Chapter 7 bankruptcy.

modification request. The method used by a debtor to change the terms of his Chapter 13 plan in order to accommodate new circumstances in the debtor's life such as a reduction in income or the loss of collateral.

nonexempt property. Property a debtor may lose in a Chapter 7 bankruptcy.

non–purchase-money lien. A lien placed on property owned by a debtor in order to secure a loan.

objection to confirmation of the debtor's plan. A legal document that spells out what a creditor doesn't like or objects to in a debtor's reorganization plan.

perfect a lien. To do what is legally necessary to ensure that a secured creditor's lien attaches to the collateral.

petition. The schedules filed in order to initiate a bankruptcy.

priority debt. One of three categories of debt in a Chapter 7 and a Chapter 13 bankruptcy. This type of debt cannot be wiped out or discharged through bankruptcy. Priority debt must be paid in full over the term of a Chapter 13 reorganization plan.

proof of claim. A document that a creditor must file with the court within a specified period of time during the bankruptcy process in order for the creditor to establish a claim for payment by the debtor.

purchase-money lien. Lien placed on property that is purchased on credit and paid for over time. Examples of property commonly associated with a purchase money lien include cars, homes and furniture.

reaffirmation agreement. An agreement between a creditor and a debtor in a Chapter 7 bankruptcy that allows the debtor to continue to make payments on a debt in order to keep a particular asset or, in some cases, to establish new credit.

redemption of property. In a Chapter 7 bankruptcy, a process by which a debtor can retain exempt property worth less than the amount owed on it by paying the full value of the property.

reorganization bankruptcy. See definition of a Chapter 13 bankruptcy.

reorganization plan. In a Chapter 13 bankruptcy, a plan that spells out how a debtor intends to pay as much as possible on his or her debts over a specified period of time, usually three to five years. The plan must be approved by the court.

secured debt. Debt secured or collateralized with property such as a car, house, boat, etc. If a debtor defaults on a secured debt, the lender can recover what's owed by taking the property.

secured creditor. A creditor whose debt is secured by a lien on the debtor's property.

statement of financial affairs. In a Chapter 7 or Chapter 13 bankruptcy, a series of written questions that a debtor must answer so that the court can be sure that the debtor has been forthcoming about all of his or her assets and has not made any inappropriate financial transactions prior to filing.

trustee. In a Chapter 13 bankruptcy, this person, appointed by the court, reviews a debtor's reorganization plan and recommends approval or changes to it, receives and distributes a debtor's payments to creditors and monitors the success of the reorganization plan. In a Chapter 7 bankruptcy, the trustee takes control of a debtor's nonexempt assets, liquidates them and distributes the proceeds to creditors.

unsecured creditor. A creditor whose debt is not secured by a lien on an asset of the debtor.

unsecured debt. Uncollateralized debt. This type of debt includes credit card debt, doctor and hospital bills, money owed to suppliers, signature loans, etc. When preparing a reorganization plan, unsecured debt is given the lowest priority for payment. Also called uncollateralized debt.

Index